ALL OF THIS MUSIC BELONGS TO THE NATION

ALL OF THIS MUSIC
BELONGS TO THE NATION

The WPA's Federal Music Project and American Society

Kenneth J. Bindas

The University of Tennessee Press • Knoxville

Library of Congress Cataloging-in-Publication Data

Bindas, Kenneth J.
   All of this music belongs to the nation : the WPA's Federal Music
Project and American society / Kenneth J. Bindas.—1st ed.
      p. cm.
   Includes bibliographical references and index.
   ISBN 0-87049-909-2 (cloth : alk. paper)
   1. Federal Music Project (U.S.) 2. State aid to music—United
States. I. Title.
ML62.B56 1995
780'.79'73—dc20   95-4375
                                                      CIP
                                                      MN

CONTENTS

ILLUSTRATIONS

PREFACE

Of the many events America has faced in the twentieth century, none challenged the basic concepts of the nation like the Great Depression. The collapse of the stock market in 1929 signaled more than an economic disaster. It also marked the beginning of an era in which America itself underwent redefinition, as the ideals of the first third of the century came under attack from all sides. When he became president in 1933, Franklin D. Roosevelt's promise of a New Deal was complicated by his determination to prevent radical changes while at the same time addressing the inequitable division of wealth. Thus, FDR had to find ways to meet the desperate need for action, which seemed to call for collective, modern methods of government and social activity, while at the same time reinforcing the capitalistic, individualistic ideals of the American Dream. His New Deal became a pragmatic mixture of the new and the old.

To meet the economic needs of the country, the government had to increase its regulatory powers to better control private industry, but in a way that would not threaten employers or capitalism itself. Meeting the country's spiritual needs called for a redefinition of America and its individualistic dream, yet a redefinition that reaffirmed the ideals of the past. Roosevelt had to recognize the class tension that existed and discover the best way for the government to both uplift the working class and not shift the basic economic balance of power. Rhonda F. Levine's recent analysis of Roosevelt's New Deal accurately places his legislation within this dilemma. Levine argues that in the final analysis Roosevelt and his staff recognized the validity of the class struggle and legislated to protect collective action, promote social reform, and regulate profiteering. At the same time, however, FDR also prevented any real transformation of the basic power structure by protecting the economic, social, and political domain of the country's power elite.[1]

Roosevelt, in other words, had to walk a political tightrope to lead the country during these difficult times. His approach had to somehow legitimize as many voices of the population as possible. Given the national identity of the Democratic Party and its many coalitions, Roosevelt and his programs had to meet the needs of different regions, of conservatives and liberals, of employers and workers, of women and, new to the Democratic umbrella, African Americans. FDR had to address the question of recovery from a democratic-pluralistic view, which favored his pragmatic attitude, yet also insured that some programs would succeed marvelously while others would languish and fail. His election had signaled a desire for change and action, but given the fact that he had to that point enunciated few firm political commitments, hope was all he could initially offer. Then, during the famous First Hundred Days, he asked for and received legislation dealing with agriculture, banking, industry, and labor. In hindsight, much of this legislation appears stopgap, but to a nation in the throes of the worst collapse in its history, these were revolutionary actions. Even though this legislation did not end the depression, the symbolism of the blue eagle of the National Industrial Recovery Act (NRA) and parades, the youthful vigor of the Civilian Conservation Corps (CCC), and the American people's belief that the president was indeed on their side endeared him to their hearts. The restoration of hope, while managing the more complicated issues of government action and free enterprise, formed the core of the New Deal.[2]

One of the first problems facing the new administration concerned the federal government's role in the issuance of relief. Local and state agencies could no longer handle the volume of people in need; they had unsuccessfully asked Hoover for aid, and they now appealed to Roosevelt. It had been traditionally thought that relief should come from local agencies first and then from state agencies. The federal government should not be involved. The problem in early 1933 was desperate, however, and in early May one-half billion dollars was allocated for the new Federal Emergency Relief Administration (FERA), to be administered by the president's friend and the head of FERA, Harry Hopkins. Through FERA, Hopkins distributed federal monies to those in need through local and state agencies—in his first five hours he allocated five million dollars. The pace slowed little over the next months, but, as winter approached, Hopkins concluded that FERA was not enough. In response, the president asked for an emergency relief measure called the Civil Works Administration (CWA) to provide work relief to the nation's needy. The CWA paid the unemployed a minimum wage for services performed, reinforcing the idea that everyone was working together to end the crisis. Matching individual skills with relief jobs further promoted the ideal of unity and removed the social stigma of being identified as a person on relief. After winning congressional approval, the CWA employed over 4,230,000 persons by mid-January 1934, and their paychecks had pumped $2,000,000 into the economy. However, it was only a temporary measure. In the spring of 1934, FERA once again took up the relief burden for the nation.[3]

FERA, in general, had two principal drawbacks as far as the administration and Hopkins were concerned. The first had to do with economics. FERA provided only an average of $6.50 a week for relief compared to CWA's $15.04 per week for work, making employment in the CWA much more a stimulant to both individual self-worth and the national economy. Secondly, and perhaps most important to Hopkins, FERA only accepted those willing to undergo a socially humiliating "means test." Thus, the identification of being on relief had detrimental effects on those it sought to help. For the larger society, FERA seemed to reinforce the hopelessness FDR's administration wanted to erase. This national despair might erode the drive necessary to overcome the social and economic devastation of the depression. FDR understood that America's self-image as a hard-working nation and his administration's success were intrinsically bound together. He had promised the people his aid and now told them that the country's future depended "on the determination of the government to give employment to idle men."[4]

Roosevelt's administration thus changed its outlook in the fall of 1934. With several of his programs under attack, and congressional elections giving the New Deal Democrats control in both the House and Senate, FDR sought to expand the role of government into what has been called the welfare state. Both the political left and right attacked his new thrust, which encouraged the growth and empowerment of the middle class, as a sop designed to placate voters and weaken political resistance. Nonetheless, when the new Congress met in 1935, FDR asked for and received a slew of social legislation, including Social Security and the National Labor Relations Act. Another important piece of legislation approved by Congress that year was the Emergency Relief Appropriation Act with its $4.8 billion price tag. Out of this law, in May 1935, the Works Progress Administration (WPA) emerged, with Harry Hopkins as its chief administrator. Although there was speculation that it might duplicate projects already in operation under Harold Ickes's Public Works Administration (PWA), Hopkins molded the WPA into a much more comprehensive employment agency under the ideal first utilized in CWA work relief.[5]

The WPA undertook its awesome task through the determination of Hopkins. After taking over the agency, he promised that the government would not "refuse responsibility for providing jobs to those whom private industry does not hire." He told the American people that the WPA would improve the quality of life for most citizens, and, in a speech broadcast over CBS radio in June 1936, he promised that the WPA would prove democracy's ability to win the battle against unemployment. He placed this confrontation clearly within the ideological debate of the times, linking the ethic of hard work and individualism that had built the country to the fact that Americans would not to choose "the easiest way, but . . . the most courageous, intelligent way." By utilizing traditional means for improvement, jobs would spring forth, security would be provided, and wealth be insured.[6]

Of all the programs initiated under the banner of the WPA, Hopkins had especially high expectations for the arts projects. He felt that those "less tangible" projects might provide the most worthy contributions, perhaps helping to establish "in some ways a new base of American life." For all the construction of the many work projects of the WPA, Hopkins also needed something that would garner regular media coverage. He hoped that the arts projects would provide this important element. On August 2, 1935, he announced the creation of the Federal Arts Projects, or Federal Project One. Designed to replace any existing arts projects, the new federal directors—Holger Cahill for art, Hallie Flanagan for theater, Henry Alsberg for writers, and Nikolai Sokoloff for music—were given the charge to create a nationwide arts program utilizing those on relief rolls and, further, to meet the artistic needs of the American people. From the outset, as Richard McKinzie convincingly argues, FDR was also interested in protecting the arts through his sense of noblesse oblige, and therefore funding would come directly by presidential letter on a yearly basis. On September 8, 1935, Roosevelt allocated $27,315,217 for the risky task of employing the nation's artists and inherently rediscovering and defining American culture.[7]

Hopkins wanted to get the arts projects operational as soon as possible because he saw the ideological role they could play in the recovery. The Crash had signaled the end of one era and the start of a new one, and within this context both the government and the people searched for meaningful symbols on which to base their new pattern of living, which Warren Susman has called a "satisfactory American Way of Life." It was apparent to many that the depression was as much about rebuilding and redefining America's national will as it was about economic recovery. There needed to be a reunification of the national "mission" with the American Dream, a term which came into vogue during the era. The successful New Deal programs were as concerned with psychological and social effects as they were with creating tangible economic results. The WPA especially hoped to strengthen the "American Way" by paying men and women for their labor, thus renewing their self-worth and restoring confidence in the government.[8]

It was with these high hopes and within this ideological context that the four arts projects were founded in 1935. While the individual directors understood that the Federal Arts Projects' primary task was employment, they also saw the larger, more culturally and politically complex task of defining cultural identity. Hopkins had asked them to be leaders in the national process of rediscovery. In the highly charged ideological and political atmosphere of the era, these arts projects exemplified both the pluralistic vision of FDR's New Deal and the cultural debate regarding classical versus modern, cultivated versus vernacular, or traditional versus avant-garde.[9]

Each project dealt with the debate differently and within its specific cultural history, yet the problem of what those employed should create lay at the core of all the projects. On the one hand, many felt that the artists should produce useful, nationalistic goods: government manuals, nationalistic murals, patriotic plays, and a musically literate audience. On the other hand, many held that the United States should follow the example of other nations and subsidize artists so that they might be free to create and develop whatever they wished. The first alternative alone would do little to ease the effects of the depression on the nation's artists, while the second opened the possibility of the government financing potentially subversive material.[10] What each project ultimately did with its charge reflected the attitudes and aims of those it chose to employ as well as the vision of its principal administrators. The government representative responsible for helping to shape how the arts projects balanced these alternatives was the man responsible for setting up Federal Project One and for selecting the national directors: Hopkins's assistant, Jacob Baker. An individualist often criticized for his leftist tendencies, he also wanted to use the arts projects as part of a greater cultural defining process he and others believed was underway.

To head the Federal Writers' Project, Baker selected Henry Alsberg. America's writers, like others, reacted to the Crash by casting off their earlier bohemianism and accepting the commitment to detail the struggles of the common man. Many felt that their writing was as vital to the survival and reformation of the nation as were the products of the engineer, banker, or businessman. Alsberg sought to utilize this energy in the FWP by making the American Guide series its principal project. These guides would fulfill the patriotic desire as well as allow the writers the creative outlet of interpretation. The FWP also encouraged fiction writing, and, working with private publishing houses, it did indeed release many works. It also tried to publish a small magazine dedicated to the nation's poets,

American Stuff, but its life was cut short due to political pressure. In fact, from its start the FWP came under scrutiny for supposedly harboring communists and fellow travelers. The FWP was pressured to tread lightly over political issues. It wanted to inform, but it also wanted to survive.[11]

When the Federal Art Project (FAP) was created in 1935, Holger Cahill was appointed its national director. His immigrant and impoverished background helped determine his vision for the FAP. He encouraged the artists to experiment with new ideas and saw in the FAP a chance to unite the artist with the community. He allowed more stylistic freedom and sought from his artists a vision of the American scene in terms not only of the contemporary but also of the romantic recent past, when society seemed to have more unified artistic symbols and images. He hoped to use the FAP to unite the American people under its art and sought a return to a sense of faith that he believed had to be supplanted by technology. "Art should belong to the people as a whole," he believed, and he would use FAP to bring art to the nation's citizens.[12] This meant producing an art that was for the people, and discouraging the search for masterpieces, which he believed belonged in a past propagated by businessmen and collectors. FAP paintings, murals, and posters were created to be displayed in public buildings; poster advertisements helped inform citizens of socially useful programs. As Marchal E. Landgren remembers, "Walking through the galleries was like taking a tour of the country." This meant at times portraying the less favorable aspects of America, which led to criticisms similar to those leveled at the FWP. Despite these attacks, the FAP survived by utilizing the balancing tactic of providing socially useful American art while at the same time protecting artistic freedom. Its massive Index of American Design project, for example, preserved the rich heritage of America's decorative arts and did much to ease criticism of the FAP.[13]

The Federal Theater Project (FTP) was the least successful of all the projects in this artistic/political endeavor. It too wanted to cater to the needs of the people, their communities, and the nation. National Director Hallie Flanagan brought with her an excellent reputation for creating socially relevant theater. While at Vassar she had earned notice as someone not afraid to take artistic risks, and she believed that theater, like all art, had to experiment in order to best reach its audience. Flanagan wanted to use the FTP to redefine and reinvigorate American theater, which she believed meant focusing on social relevance. The FTP's problem was that while Flanagan had one view of what America's theater should be and say, the government and politicians had another view.[14]

Prophetically, Flanagan believed the "theatre, when it's good, is always dangerous." Thus, while the other projects were able to sidestep much of the political pressure associated with being under the government's employ, the FTP seemed forever under attack by anti-New Dealers, conservatives, and others who feared that America's political institutions were being influenced by communists. When Martin Dies and his House Committee on Un-American Activities began to look for disloyal Americans in government employ, the FTP became their favorite target. By 1937, Flanagan's dream of socially relevant American theater had been seriously undermined by political pressures both within and outside the president's administration. Indeed, although both Hopkins and Roosevelt supported the FTP, they also stayed as far from it as possible so not to taint themselves or their other programs by association. Thus, while the FTP did serve the community, it lacked a balancing patriotic program to offset its social consciousness, and it suffered as a result.[15]

Nikolai Sokoloff's Federal Music Project faced similar pressures and challenges, and his activities form the core of *All of This Music Belongs to the Nation*. Within each of the other arts projects, administrators dealt with the problem of satisfying artistic demands without offending either the American public or its leaders. Some succeeded better than others. How did the Federal Music Project deal with the complex issue of art versus politics, especially when the music culture itself was divided over the role of cultivated as opposed to vernacular music, the role of modern as opposed to traditional music, and over the power of popular music? Would the FMP find projects that would insure the critics that it promoted America? Could it avoid the stigma of radicalism while at the same time encouraging experimentation? Would it be able to provide good music for the American people? What type of music would be chosen and who would choose? These were the issues that faced the FMP upon its creation, and they form the basis of this study.

During its tenure, the FMP employed more people than the other arts projects, reached more Americans through its artists' performances, and steered clear of political scandal. Many American composers heard their works performed on a regular basis, while others received the chance to conduct. African Americans, women, Mexican Americans, and other culturally neglected persons participated on a broad scale in order to fulfill the FMP's announced goal of proving that "All of this music belongs to the nation."[16] Yet, the FMP's leadership was essentially conservative. It held high the notion of the positive social benefits of cultivated music, which led to favoritism toward classically trained musicians over the more numerous popular players. This traditionalism tempered many of its seeming gains. Women musicians did receive benefits, for example, but in limited numbers, and the project avoided the question of parity in a field where women represented a significant percentage. Further, the

FMP's use of African American and other minority musicians most often included their being both segregated and stereotyped.

The Federal Music Project thus provides an excellent example of the cultural battlefield that was Great Depression–era America. In the larger context, the FMP's problems and means of addressing the fundamental questions of its existence mirror the cultural tensions concerning popular, vernacular culture in relation to its antithetical relationship with the traditional, cultivated culture. The FMP had to deal with these questions not only in a theoretical way but also in practical terms, as its existence depended on how well it could operate within the confines of politics, economics, and culture.

There are many people who have contributed to this project over the years. Some, like Ron Lora and Gerald Thompson, guided me through the early stages and helped me find the confidence to continue. Others, like Jeffery Livingston, Kenneth Noe, and John Ferling, read and critiqued specific chapters and gave me excellent advice, some of which I took, some of which we discussed further. Others who gave assistance include Paula Ashton and Elmira Eidson, who, with their departmental know-how, made sure that my day-to-day affairs were in order. The interlibrary loan departments at the University of Toledo and West Georgia College libraries went out of their ways to satisfy my requests for books and articles, most of which I wanted that day; I had to learn patience. Jennifer Jones, a student at the Indiana Academy, became my research assistant and helped to check notes, the bibliography, and create the index. Small grants from the University of Toledo history department, the West Georgia Learning Resources Committee, and Ball State University allowed me to travel to specific archives around the country. The assistance I received from the curators, directors, and staff at the National Archives, the Library of Congress, the FDR Presidential Library, George Mason University, Illinois Historical Library, Claremont Graduate School, Detroit Public Library, Wisconsin Historical Society, Indiana State Library, Louisiana State University Archives, and the Kentucky State Archives was invaluable. At the University of Tennessee Press, Meredith Morris-Babb and Scot Danforth deserve much thanks for keeping me on track throughout the project and guiding me through the paces of getting this manuscript into press.

Eight and six years ago joy came into my life and forever changed how I view my world. Zachary and Colin taught me that true happiness comes through love and acceptance. And, while it took several years to accept this lesson, I am finally on their path. And to Jean-Anne, you touch my soul.

All of these people, and many more, contributed to the final product by allowing my voice to be revealed in the book. I alone am responsible for any of its flaws, while we all share in any of its praises.

ONE

THE CONTRADICTIONS OF CREATION

When the FMP was created, Sokoloff and his staff outlined its five major goals. These included providing employment assistance for musicians on relief rolls, establishing high standards through classification of these musicians, stimulating community interest, creating an intelligent musical public, and demonstrating to the public the constructive work being done by the federal government to combat the depression.[1] Each of the FAP projects came up with its own goals, although each had employment and community interest as central aims. The music project, under Sokoloff's direction, felt its other goals, namely to promote and encourage the acceptance of cultivated music, was just as important. This policy of favoring high art over popular music would have serious ramifications, as those musicians not academically trained or who could not read music were less likely to gain employment in the FMP.

The plight of the America musician during the depression era was severe, so those who were able to read and perform cultivated music found themselves with an ally in Washington in Sokoloff. Many of the nation's professional musicians tended to perform in the popular realm, where hard times had begun in 1928 with the introduction of the soundtrack for the moving picture. Things worsened in 1929 as mechanized sound music machines replaced some twenty-two thousand theater musicians. In Washington, D.C., for example, over 60 percent of the theater musicians employed in 1930 were replaced by canned music the following year. The growth of the radio and recording industries in the late 1920s also meant unemployment for many musicians. Restaurants, pubs, hotels, and other employers of musicians and orchestras favored the cheaper canned sound of radio or the phonograph. Even the New Jersey Funeral Directors' Association recommended the cost-effective use of radio over live musicians. As late as 1937 the Chicago local of the American Federation of Musicians (AFM) prohibited members from recording because it put musicians out of work, as the AFM estimated that only 5 percent of the music heard in Chicago was produced by live musicians. Prohibition also created musical unemployment. Many night clubs and bars, where many musicians plied their wares, were forced by the Eighteenth Amendment to close their doors. This meant another estimated 30 percent of professional musicians were jobless. All of these factors contributed to the fact that unemployment for America's musicians rose dramatically in the late 1920s and early 1930s, even without the economic crash. The American Federation of Musicians estimated in 1933 that 12,000 of its 15,000 members in the New York City area were unemployed, and that two-thirds of the nation's musicians were out of work.[2]

The already critical unemployment problem for the country's musicians grew worse with the depression. With the economic collapse, some private opera companies, orchestras, and theaters were forced to fold or to curtail their seasons. With less upper- and middle-class support and fewer people attending each season, the funding drain forced some companies to close their doors. Commercial concerts of this sort dwindled from 3,750 in 1929–30 to a mere 2,600 three years later. Add to this the continued growth of sound movies and radio, and by 1934 the AFM was able to estimate that unemployment for America's musicians hovered near the 70 percent range, with those 30 percent employed making less than a decent living.[3]

Just as with the rest of America's unemployed, private charities provided inadequate relief for the nation's musicians, and the federal government was forced to step in. The first governmental aid targeted at unemployed musicians occurred under FERA from 1933 to 1935. FERA itself did not create musical projects, but in some instances it employed musicians. For example, FERA in Los Angeles formed Musicians' Project 8047 and hired 900 musicians on rotation for 300 jobs.[4] Aside from a few cases, however, little was done to aid the musician. The Civil Works Administration (CWA) instituted a program of federal work relief for America's cultural workers and white-collar unemployed under the Civil Works Service (CWS). This program employed musicians, but placed emphasis upon educational and recreational music. Also, no uniformity existed between music projects, as each state controlled its own program, and the CWA gave no direction or supervision. The confusion caused many problems and forced AFM president Joseph Weber to complain to Roosevelt that in as many as thirty-one towns, aid was denied to musicians on the grounds that the government did not allot the money specifically for music; in fifty-three other towns, projects were canceled almost as soon as they started. In all, the union president said, only 5,161 members received aid among over 8,000 who applied.[5]

When the CWA ended in March 1934, the states once again received FERA grant monies to be doled out at their whim. Most states quickly disposed of the expensive arts projects. When the June 1934 Emergency Appropriation Act made a special grant available to states that created professional and nonmanual projects, which included music, some states organized music projects to qualify for these special FERA monies. This led to the establishment of some new state orchestras, such as those in New Hampshire, Alabama, Idaho, and North Carolina. And, while the FERA music program did achieve some level of success in New York City, Minnesota, and San Francisco, it peaked in February 1935 with 9,000 employees in only 17 states.[6]

When FDR created the WPA in the spring of 1935, he hoped to avoid the problems he had faced with earlier legislation. Lobbying for the arts had begun earlier; for example, in February 1934, Hopkins and a host of dignitaries, including Mrs. Roosevelt, held a conference to discuss relief for musicians. Sponsored by the Federation of Music Clubs and held at the White House, those in attendance discussed and agreed on the benefits of a federally directed and controlled project.[7] Subsequently, in August 1935, Hopkins authorized the creation of a federally controlled and directed program called Federal Project One. Because of the widespread unemployment of American musicians, and with the aid of the many national musical organizations and the AFM, the Federal Music Project became one of the first of all WPA projects to be organized.[8]

Even before the FMP received funding, Hopkins appointed Nikolai Sokoloff to be its national director. Sokoloff's initial reaction to the appointment was to be overwhelmed, because "the need was so great, and the whole thing so pressing."[9] Born into a musical family in Kiev, in southern Russia, on May 28, 1886, by age five he had begun violin study under his father, Gregory. When the family emigrated to the United States in 1898, they sold his violin to help pay for passage. The following year, the thirteen-year-old Sokoloff entered the Yale University School of Music on a special scholarship. He remained there until age sixteen, when he left New Haven to become first violinist for the Boston Symphony Orchestra. He stayed in Boston for three years until 1907, when he left the United States to continue his study with Vincent D'Indy and Eugene Ysaye in France. After several years, the now mature Sokoloff made a successful concert tour of England and France in 1911, including a temporary conductorship of the Manchester Orchestra. He returned

Fig. 1. Nikolai Sokoloff, head of the FMP, directs the Illinois Symphony Orchestra in rehearsal. His emphasis of classical over vernacular music was a major problem within the FMP. Courtesy of the Illinois State Historical Library.

to America that same year to become Modest Altschuler's concertmaster for the Russian Symphony Orchestra. After five years with Altschuler, he left to organize a string quartet for the San Francisco Philharmonic. The success of this project subsequently led to his assignment as conductor. He resigned from this post in 1917 to go to France to help organize and direct musical presentations for the American Expeditionary Forces. When the war ended, Sokoloff came home to conduct a series of concerts for the Cincinnati Symphony. These proved so popular that symphony organizers in Cleveland invited him to direct their new orchestra. Sokoloff remained with the Cleveland Symphony until 1933 and is credited with helping make it a respected symphony orchestra. He retired from Cleveland at the young age of forty-seven to Weston, Connecticut. Shortly afterward he organized a small New York orchestra to give a series of outdoor concerts near his home. He continued this activity until Hopkins asked him to organize and direct the Federal Music Project.[10]

Sokoloff understood the potentially dangerous nature of his new job. The WPA was already under scrutiny, and in the future the attention given to the arts projects specifically would be great. He believed that the FMP had to project the best of America and its music and avoid at all costs any taint of radicalism or charges of anti-Americanism. Sokoloff believed the FMP's primary task would be to make music a part of the country's "accepted civic and cultural system." He felt, as had others before him, that a "nation without music is an inert nation."[11]

His appointment was not without opposition. Secretary of the Treasury Henry Morganthau's wife wrote to Hopkins to complain that Sokoloff lacked the "temperament and character for the position." She asked Hopkins to "thoroughly and impartially investigate his ability and character" and limit Sokoloff's power to lessen the harm he would do American music. Mrs. Morganthau was not alone in her disapproval of Sokoloff, as others attacked his lack of creativity and animosity toward American composers in calls for his dismissal. California's state directors called Sokoloff arrogant and high-handed and asked that the FMP be placed in the "hands of a native born American musician" who would better understand the American musician. Sokoloff only fueled the fire when he advised regional directors that the FMP would not "participate with every Tom, Dick or Harry who has no musical ability." Or, at the same meeting, by telling the state directors that "the American composer or artist will get no place playing stupid things," and that simply because a piece of music had an American author did not mean it was to be performed.[12]

Regardless, Sokoloff was put in charge of the FMP. Realizing the tenuous nature of his position, Sokoloff tried to ally himself with as many well-respected American musicians as possible. Central to its ongoing operation would be the district supervisors chosen to implement the program. By late October, Chalmers Clifton, Lee Pattison, and Guy Maier assumed regional posts.[13] Sokoloff and Hopkins also created a twenty-five-member advisory committee with the same purpose in mind. The committee included *New York Times* music critic Olin Downes, conductor and composer Walter Damrosch, George Gershwin, American Federation of Musicians president Joseph Weber, Philadelphia conductor Leopold Stokowski, Eastman School of Music director Howard Hanson, Chicago Symphony conductor Frederick Stock, and many others active in the musical field. One member of the advisory committee, Mrs. John Jardine, served as president of the four-hundred-thousand-member National Federation of Music Clubs. After her appointment, she asked her organization to mobilize its support for "the most vital project which can engage the attention of our organization."[14] Other musicians and organizations followed suit by advising their members to give full support to the FMP, including the American Federation of Musicians.

But the AFM responded cautiously to the FMP's overtures. Based upon the limitations of the previous relief efforts, the union wanted certain assurances that the project would benefit them. AFM president Joseph Weber and his members, numbering 105,013 in 1936, remembered the NRA experience. After giving immediate support to the NRA acts, the NRA codes encouraged the practice of paying musicians less than scale and became the codes of the employer, not the worker. When Hopkins announced the WPA's intentions, AFM's parent union, the American Federation of Labor, pressured Hopkins to stipulate that employment lists for the WPA would come from the "recognized unions."[15]

From the outset of the FMP, Weber negotiated with Sokoloff over the union's role. The first problem concerned who qualified for relief. According to presidential decision, relief could only be given to those persons listed on relief rolls as of May 30, 1935. But, since musicians were denied relief up to this point, fewer than five thousand were listed. Weber got the government to issue an extension for the musicians to apply until November 1.

The other problems were more difficult to solve, for they spoke directly to the two men's differing views on music. Sokoloff, Weber, and the FMP were part of the century-long struggle between cultivated and vernacular music. In the early nineteenth-century little distinction was made between the two camps, but as the century wore on, several factors encouraged a musical split. H. Wiley Hitchcock has argued that the rapid expansion of the United States led to a lack of appreciation for art music, as it was deemed unnecessary for the frontier. Once the regions were settled and businesses and governments established, however, the desire to detail one's social standing allowed for the introduction of the finer things, including cultivated music. Hitchcock has also pointed out that the immigration surge from continental Europe that began in the 1830s and lasted into the early twentieth-century weakened the grip of Anglo-American musical culture. Many of these new Americans brought with them the musical ideals of Romanticism. Under this musical movement, German composers like Beethoven, Schubert, Liszt, Wagner, and Mendelssohn changed the manner in which the composer and audience interacted. Art music required contemplation, appreciation, and education to be fully understood. One did not listen simply for diversion or pleasure, but had to become familiar with, as Hitchcock quotes John Sullivan Dwight as saying, "the beautiful and the infinite." Cultivated music required effort to be understood, and therefore it served to encourage the separation from the vernacular. Hitchcock defined the latter as "plebeian," "utilitarian" music served up for its "entertainment value." Cultivated music required reflection and was part of the greater awakening of the intellectual.

As the century neared its end and the impact of industrial capitalism began to be felt in American society, the gulf between the two musics widened farther. The new wealth created by rapid industrialization encouraged some to use music and art as symbols of social and economic standing. Attending a symphony or visiting a museum took on a much larger social role than it had in the past. Within the concert hall, the conductor's power also grew and his virtuosity was valued and his taste in music preferred. Since many of these conductors were either directly from Europe or trained there, they tended to favor the established "classics" of the recent Germanic period. In an earlier time, church music and parlor songs were absorbed into the cultivated tradition, but in the period of the late nineteenth-century the symphony orchestra became the symbol of the complexity of art music. The vernacular was dominated by gospel, spiritual, and minstrel songs throughout much of the century. In the latter part of the century and into the next, new vernacular music, spurred on in part by the impact of the cultivated tradition, in the form of brass bands, ragtime, and, a bit later, jazz, came to symbolize the popular. While this new vernacular music stressed musical competence in performance, the fact that it was played for entertainment, amusement, and dance made it less respectable. While more people came to consume the vernacular music, the cultivated music held onto its lofty position by establishing conservatories, journals, and concert halls. These served to reinforce the notion that cultivated music was good music—

for it required discipline both to listen to and to perform, an understanding of history, and an acceptance of European-based culture. Since American culture, especially American music, tended to encourage mass production and consumption, and therefore to cater to the lowest musical denominators in entertainment and dance, those who favored the cultured music of the classics used their choice to make social as well as musical distinctions. To attend the symphony or appreciate art music meant one was cultured, educated, and able to recognize the best of humankind's existence. In comparison, visiting a dance hall, a cabaret, or watching a parade involved entering the mass domain.[16]

Sokoloff came to the FMP determined to use the project to promote and protect what he considered good music—that is, cultivated music—largely without consideration for either the plight of the unemployed musician or for the American audience, both of whom seemed largely to favor the vernacular.

Sokoloff wanted the FMP to provide musical relief by creating symphonies, chamber music groups, and other "serious" musical organizations. Weber, on the other hand, argued that, outside of the large urban areas, few musicians of symphonic quality would be found. The AFM wanted the project to dedicate more monies to the rank-and-file unemployed musicians—namely, those who played "popular" music. The union also disagreed with the FMP pay scale, which penalized those who lacked "serious" music credentials with lower wages. After much debate, Weber persuaded Sokoloff, and the project decided to pay all musicians the same wage (music teachers were paid at a lower scale).

Sokoloff and Weber also disagreed about the weekly work load. Sokoloff wanted to increase the work week from five to eight performances, but the union pressured him not to increase the hours. However, when Weber was summoned to the White House and told that, as of January 1936, hours would be increased and that any musician protesting the increase would forfeit relief status, the AFM agreed to the change. With the debate over serious versus popular still simmering, Weber believed he had given Sokoloff some input and asked his membership to support the FMP.[17]

Getting musicians onto the project payrolls went slower than expected, although it occurred faster than it did with the other arts projects. Sokoloff complained to Assistant WPA Administrator Jacob Baker that the regional directors had difficulty getting things activated; by November 1935, only 915 persons were employed. As the new year began, however, things picked up. The Ohio project, for example, had only one employee in November, but by June 1936, 578 musicians were employed, giving 2,136 concerts. The FMP eventually employed over 40 percent of the total Project One workers in Ohio. Out in the western district, the situation was similar, as 4,000 musicians were on the rolls by June throughout the 11-state region.[18]

It was in 1936 that the FMP blossomed throughout the United States. Tulsa, Oklahoma, organized a FMP symphony in 1936, as did the Illinois Symphony Orchestra and Philadelphia's Civic Symphony Orchestra. Thirteen cities and towns in Wisconsin formed units, and several more asked for future consideration, given that within a month the FMP had produced 147 concerts for 168,826 persons. After only six months of operation, the FMP became the largest employer in the Federal Arts Project with over 15,000 workers.[19]

One of Hopkins's directives dictated that the project operate in as many places—big and small—as possible. The key to the arts projects' success would be in their widespread exposure. The San Bernadino, California, unit is a good example of the lengths the project went to in order to perform. Several guitar players and fiddlers were organized in the spring of 1936 as a novelty group that made regular appearances at local baseball games to play nationalistic tunes and baseball songs. When the season ended, so did the sponsorship by the ball team. However, because of the group's popularity, an arrangement with the Orange County schools was made, and the musicians made regular visits to the schools dressed as cowboys to play traditional western ballads. The unit's sponsorship lasted throughout the school year. In Cleveland, Ohio, one FMP unit took the thankless job of performing for a parking-lot opening in Cuyahoga Falls. While performances such as these were small scale, they reinforced the project's belief that "music has no social value unless it is heard."[20]

There was initially some apathy regarding the FMP's emphasis on art music. Frances McFarland of the FMP educational section wrote Sokoloff that the children enrolled in the New York City music education classes preferred radio and Broadway tunes and "thought it American to cultivate and patronize cheap music." Sokoloff and his staff realized that most Americans preferred the popular tunes available, but held fast to the notion that if these same people were exposed to better music, they would naturally choose cultivated music over popular music. The people simply lacked an understanding of the beauty of art music, but once exposed to it, as McFarland wrote, "the masses of people will absorb what is best, given the opportunity." Sokoloff and the FMP claimed success in this endeavor much in the same way the military might claim success on the battlefield: by using numbers. The people came, and to the administrator this was proof of their support for art music. By August 1936, thirty-two million Americans attended thirty-six thousand FMP performances throughout the nation.[21]

The people heard the FMP's performances laced with the best of American and European music. The Old World classics proved the most popular, since many people were familiar with them. But Sokoloff wanted to avoid the accusation that the FMP was un-American, so the project announced it would give American composers the first shot at performance. The FMP sought to expose the best music to the American people. Much of this music, it was hoped, would come from American composers, although the national staff realized that, when they listened to classical music, the American public continued to favor the European classics developed over many centuries. The FMP hoped to reveal the undiscovered genius of American music. Sokoloff understood that "no great numbers of these [American compositions] contain lasting value," but he believed the FMP might clear the way for a national idiom or for, perhaps, a classic. While Sokoloff was criticized for not being a supporter of American music, he argued that the American people must be trained to see the value of cultivated music, American or otherwise. He agreed that "the hour for the development of American music has struck," but believed that much education had to take place before good music would become a part of American life.[22] Because of this, in 1936 Sokoloff announced that a "wealth of creative talent" had been uncovered and the "long anticipated dawn of American music" had come into being. The American compositions most performed in 1935–36 came from the pens of Victor Herbert, John Philip Sousa, and George Gershwin—all Americans.[23] This nationalistic tactic was noticed, and many observers recognized FMP's attempt to promote American music as nationalism, and as better "propaganda . . . to tell the world we know what benefits have arisen from President Roosevelt's efforts," as a Detroit critic put it.[24]

The project employment rolls also emphasized FMP's favoritism toward Americans. Only citizens of the United States qualified for the FMP. Hans Blecheschmidt, a world-renowned composer and conductor, was denied admission to the FMP in early 1937 because he had not applied for citizenship papers. California state director Harle Jervis said that "no exception can be made to employ . . . all those who are not fully naturalized citizens." Sokoloff even refused aid to the great Toscanini because he was "not an American." Preference, the national director said, must be given to native Americans or citizens—"Until we take of those who belong to this country, we cannot" extend FMP services to foreigners, no matter how great their talent.[25]

In an extension of these efforts to emphasize the patriotic qualities among the music and musicians it supported, the FMP also tried to avoid any taint of scandal, especially as it related to radical affiliations and activities. The AFM, from which many on the FMP payrolls came, had a long-standing policy against radicalism in its ranks, and this policy helped eliminate many possible controversies before they started. New York City director Chalmers Clifton wrote to Sokoloff in early October 1935, asking for advice concerning "the agitation of communistic and radical leaders" who were disrupting some of the project's activities. The national director told Clifton to fire anyone involved. Unlike the other arts projects, which encouraged experimentation and tolerated some radicalism as part of the artistic process, Sokoloff believed he had received a mandate from the president and Hopkins to make the FMP an organization Americans would be proud of, one which would lead the people into a new realm of musical appreciation.[26]

The FMP tried from the start to distance itself from its more radical sister projects, primarily by using its Office of Information, headed by Harry Hewes, to disseminate pro-FMP American stories. When something happened that could be tied to the FMP's allegiance to America, the Office of Information either distributed the news itself or excerpted it as part of a more general story. For example, *Current History* ran a favorable story on the FMP in 1938 that came directly from Hewes's office. The article detailed the project's favoritism toward American composers and said other nations were recognizing the importance of the FMP's work. Hewes called on his friend Bruce Bliven at the *New Republic* to run pro-FMP stories. He told Bliven that the informed reader of the *New Republic* would want to know more about "one of the greatest forces for social culture that these United States have known." The letter came as a follow-up to an information packet sent earlier to Bliven that featured photos, statistics, and news releases. The packet emphasized that future historians of American culture will claim the years 1935–36 as halcyon days for American music and will give the credit to the FMP. The *New Republic* ran several supportive articles.[27]

The publicity that Hewes collected and distributed showed up in local, state, and national publications. Most music magazines—*Musical America, Musician,* and *Etude*—featured regular stories on the FMP. Sokoloff contributed pieces to *Musical America, Etude,* and was featured in interviews in a number of other monthlies. *Musical America* gave especially detailed coverage to the project, perhaps because its editor, A. Walter Kramer, was a member of Sokoloff's National Advisory Committee.[28] The AFM's *International Musician*, whose president sat on the national board, also gave detailed coverage. In fact, one of the strongest articles of support appeared in the union's journal. Written by Prof. Andre Polsh, head of the Syracuse University School of Music, he argued that

Fig. 2. Modern ensemble of Herrin, Illinois. While not the primary focus of the FMP, some popular units were funded. Courtesy of the Illinois State Historical Library.

no country could prosper without its own song. Support and "love of his country" could come to a child early through "the spell of the song." He rhetorically asked if there was "ever a nation that was not stirred by its nationalistic anthem?" Polsh believed the project needed to supply American children with American music to tap this valuable patriotic musical asset, which would help inspire American composers: "Let us be the same nation that built America—America that was built in song, built by a courageous people, building for the future generations with a song upon their lips and in their hearts—the America of which Walt Whitman wrote: 'I hear America singing . . . her strong melodious song.'"[29]

Polsh embodied the type of enthusiasm the FMP hoped to capture throughout the nation. When the FMP began in late 1935, it was just a part of the general relief effort. But by the close of 1936 it had become a powerful governmental agency, separate in many ways from its sister projects, and with a formidable publicity campaign designed to minimize opposition. Friends of the project, like the magazines and Polsh, did all they could to show support. Sokoloff and his staff continued to maintain that few could object to the FMP if it stressed Americanness, commitment to the American citizen, and quality music.

Yet, some problems remained. Perhaps the most obvious was with Sokoloff himself. Not an overwhelming choice for his post, his treatment of underlings and those musicians labeled "popular" by the audition boards created a widespread belief that the director lacked empathy for the bulk of the unemployed musicians. For example, when asked how he felt about the new popular music, swing—which was providing employment to many musicians and reviving a nearly dead recording industry—he responded, "I like to dance when I am dancing but to compare it with music, why, it is like comparing the funny papers with the work of a painter."[30]

This type of attitude led many to complain that the FMP catered to cultivated music at the expense of the unemployed American musician. Further, some more radical musicians argued that this elitist music was part of the now-bankrupt culture that had created the depression. AFM president Weber even began to complain that he was asked to join the project's advisory team not for input, but for information. When Weber gave advice, Sokoloff would disagree. From the outset, Weber was concerned that the FMP's emphasis on "serious" music would not meet the needs of the majority of unemployed musicians, and he believed that "no matter how praiseworthy these cultural educational efforts are, they should not be the reason [for the denial of] relief to the vast army of musicians who cannot possibly be placed in symphony orchestras." He added that these orchestras never employed more than a thousand musicians nationwide in the past, and it was illogical to assume in the future this tendency would change.[31]

But Sokoloff and the project administrators were unmoved and held firm to the idea of creating, as New York City director Lee Pattison said, "a permanent audience for the support of really good music in this country." The paternalism of the FMP was evident, as most of the administrators agreed with Pattison when he argued that the people needed the "correct stimulus" to appreciate good music. To create this "latent taste," the "right teachers and leaders" should be employed and not the "unqualified pedagogues." Pattison added: "At no point are we prepared to sacrifice artistic standards for mass production, but we realize . . . the tremendous importance and responsibility of the task confronting us in the manner of educating the public musically, and supplying them with the correct musical outlets."[32]

Sometimes signals got crossed and units began without the national office's approval. For example, in Kentucky the FMP organized a folk music unit in early 1936. With few professional musicians in the rural counties, the unit collected some two hundred folk songs and fiddle tunes. However, due to the fact that the FMP was designed to rehabilitate and employ musicians, Sokoloff and the national office found it difficult to fund such an operation. Guy Maier even supplied the Office of Information with photographs of these Kentucky Mountain Minstrels, believing the photos would be excellent for rotogravure sections throughout the country. However, neither the photos nor the story reached the press, as Hewes believed Sokoloff might not want this project boosted. In July 1936, the unit lost its funding.[33]

The FMP did attract great numbers of spectators, which they equated with widespread support and acceptance. In an effort to offset criticism, accusation, and to distance itself from its already more experimental sister projects, the FMP stressed American musicians, compositions, and nationalistic musical activities. The country, the project believed, needed to be exposed to the best music, American and European, in order to secure these aims. But the FMP faced future problems, not the least of which was an administrator with limited musical vision and a government-sponsored project with a distaste for the "popular" American musician.

TWO

THE PEOPLE'S MUSIC, 1935–1936

The FMP's initial success in organizing music projects and the numbers these units attracted impressed the national staff. They were especially excited that so many made the connection between the FMP and the idea of a "people's music." This helped the project administrators believe they were well on the way toward the development of a musical democracy.[1] This association of the FMP with the people's music and the fact that the symphonies of the FMP were receiving the support of masses of American people encouraged the FMP to reach further into America's communities to perform in places and before people who had never attended a live symphonic presentation. During its initial years, the FMP hoped to prove its validity by making attendance numbers so large that no one could contest either the acceptance of the project or the cultivated music and musicians it chose to favor.

To many, the idea that the national government had become involved in the production of music proved exciting and challenging. They hoped the FMP would help Americans listen to, study, compose, and perform serious music more than at any other time in the country's history, leading to a musical awakening, long awaited but yet to arrive. The FMP wanted to be credited with this development.[2]

But government-sponsored music worried others. They pointed to the European experience and the tight control the governments of the USSR and Germany, for example, exerted over the production of art in their countries. Some feared that controlled, propaganda-oriented art that had developed elsewhere in the 1930s would be the end result of this project. The FMP sidestepped these fears by refusing to pay composers to compose. Composers were free to write whatever they wanted, submit their compositions to the audition board, and, if they passed, the FMP would perform them. The only stipulation the national office made was that American composers receive fair and equal consideration, and it "recommended" that at least one-fourth of all programs be music produced by Americans. Few saw the favoritism toward American composers as an artistic limitation. Most were pleased by the recommendation, as it had proved difficult for contemporary American composers to get new works on private symphony playbills. The FMP thought that by featuring American music, few would miss the project's nationalism and commitment to a cultivated, yet democratic, musical culture.[3]

Before it had been created, the FMP enjoyed reporting, American schoolchildren were ignorant of their musical culture. A Michigan study done in 1935 by WPA supervisor Karl Wecker pointed out that only 35 of the 739 music teachers surveyed responded that their communities had active musical scenes. Out of 13,526 children surveyed who wanted to take lessons, only 1,734 received instruction. The problem was nationwide, Guy Maier told the Music Teachers' National Association conference in 1936. An assistant to Sokoloff, he told the teachers that two-thirds of the 4,000,000 schoolchildren in the United States went without musical instruction of any kind and that "it is often pathetic to find whole audiences of children who have never seen an orchestra or a band in the flesh, not to speak of having the slightest acquaintance with . . . the clarinet, French horn, or oboe." The FMP's job, he continued, was to perform and instruct so that America could discover its national culture.[4]

Sokoloff and the surveys above both cited a lack of musical culture in the United States, a lack which they claimed injured children. Yet, by 1937 an active vernacular music scene was present throughout the country. Popular music, via the phonograph, radio, and many touring bands, brought jazz, swing, Tin Pan Alley songs, country music, and blues into America's homes and communities. But to the FMP, this was not the musical culture to be emphasized; instead, it was the culture the FMP hoped to replace. Sokoloff believed that most of the United States was musically "arid." The FMP, he announced, would sow musical seeds by performing wherever it could, allowing America's children to reap the harvests. He regretted that music education had suffered cutbacks during the 1930s, but felt that the project could bring back a "spark of life" by organizing mass musical lessons. He pointed to examples like the Mississippi education unit, which provided seventy thousand children with musical instruction, or the Oklahoma unit, which taught three hundred thousand children to play music in 1936 alone.[5] Instruction, however, was not a major goal of the FMP. Musical performance of cultivated music to help create a better all-around American citizen was its primary goal. Sokoloff believed he had a democratic vision, making good music, which reinforced that "music is a public right and obligation."[6]

The project's main tactic to attract audiences was to give free or nominal-charge concerts (usually no more than twenty-five cents). In cities this opportunity may or may not have been a big deal, given the variety of recreational opportunities which existed, so the FMP focused much of its attention on the smaller areas between the East and West Coasts. These middle America performances drew hundreds of thousands of people. In Huntington, West Virginia, for example, the project gave 428 concerts to nearly 150,000 persons during its first 16 months of operation; in Shamokin, Pennsylvania, the project gave 325 concerts to 180,000 persons in 17 months. From 1936 to 1938 in Pueblo, Colorado, an FMP orchestra of only 13 musicians gave 284 performances in halls, orphanages, and hospitals to almost 200,000 persons. The Utah state FMP sinfonietta performed 139 times in 23 different towns in 1936.[7] The FMP units attracted these numbers not by waiting for the people to come to them, as a private orchestra might, but by going to the people. FMP units played many concerts in hospitals, orphanages, and other places not frequented by symphony music. They joined in any and all civic rallies or community activities in an effort to, as the Iowa state administrators reported, bring music to people in "all walks of life."[8] In urban areas like New York City, FMP units played for almost any event, from the dedication of a playground at Williamsburg Bridge Plaza to the July Fourth celebrations at the Soldiers' and Sailors' Monument.

Many of these activities went unheralded in the press, but struck a chord with the people. As one letter testified, the thrill lay in the concerts and music, which proved that the "American masses really do enjoy musical classics when it is within their power to listen." This was exactly the type of connection Sokoloff hoped the FMP would make. When the former mayor of Hartford, Connecticut, wrote a favorable letter to the FMP, he hit on another FMP goal: integrating music into community life. The mayor said the project kept the balance in Hartford between baseball, swimming, and active sports with more passive educational activities, including art and music. Sokoloff and the national staff hoped that this integration would enable the American people to link their appreciation of the FMP to support for the WPA and Roosevelt. "This is the first time," one letter read, "that the government has had anything to do directly with the fostering of the fine arts, and, if for no other reason, I am going to vote for the present administration at the next election."[9]

One venue regularly used by the FMP was the public schools. The Omaha unit gave weekly school concerts throughout Nebraska from October 1936 until May 1937, reaching over 130,000 youngsters. In Indiana, the FMP units gave 177 educational concerts in 1937 in Indianapolis and Evansville alone, reaching 55,420 schoolchildren, while in 1936 the Delaware unit performed before 22,000 students.[10] The project's school activity resulted in numerous letters from schoolchildren and teachers throughout the nation. The FMP's 1936–37 Children's Music Appreciation Drive in Nebraska yielded 2,000 letters of approval from students, parents, and teachers. The Kansas City, Kansas, superintendent of schools thanked the FMP for its work in the schools and said that the project added "immeasurable value" to the students' educations and to the "cultural development of the community." The 1936 concerts in the Hartford, Connecticut, area schools were so successful that the state superintendent requested the FMP to expand its concerts in 1937 to include all the public schools in the state. Interestingly, parents began to request that the FMP perform the same material for them, so they might "absorb some of the knowledge and benefit the children received and . . . made known at home."[11]

The project hoped that if it gave regular concerts at schools, the children would more likely discuss the concerts at home. The parents, upon hearing about the FMP concert, might want to attend a performance for themselves. The Kansas City, Kansas, unit combined its emphasis on public school performances with a weekly radio show on Wednesday evenings over station KCKN. Teachers made the programs part of the children's lessons and homework. They were to listen to the broadcast, which might encourage their parents to tune in also. As the children went, the project hoped, so would their parents.[12]

Going to the schoolchildren brought results. Parents began requesting concerts, especially at their churches. One member of a Mississippi Baptist church visited by the FMP orchestra wrote to Sokoloff to thank him for the opportunity to "look into the faces" of those making the music. When the Minnesota unit performed at a Minneapolis Lutheran church for a series of concerts in 1936, the local press appreciated not only the high quality of music but also the fact that the United States government had "made culture a part of its official business." Music, the editorial continued, had become a "state responsibility." Out west, a rector from Pasadena, California, thanked the federal government for the "admirable" program an FMP dance band had presented at his church and pointed out the great cultural and community value his members placed on the project.[13]

The project used other creative means to reach the adult and voting audience. In Miami, where the city's many neighborhoods lacked adequate hall space, the FMP and the Recreation Department built a mobile eighteen-by-thirty-two-foot stage to travel from outdoor park to outdoor park. The mobile stage came equipped with its own sound system

Fig. 3. Illinois Valley Blue Coats marching in Peoria, Illinois, parade. The FMP tried to integrate itself into as many American communities as possible by participating in local festivals. Courtesy of the Illinois State Historical Library.

and a twelve-foot backdrop painted in modernist collage fashion.[14] One Boston FMP unit decided to attract adult audiences by going to where they congregated the most—the train stations. The North and South stations enjoyed regular FMP concerts during the rush hour, and busy commuters often paused to watch and chat with the musicians.[15]

The project also used the radio. The expansion of electricity in America played a major role in the advances of the radio. In 1917 roughly one-quarter of America's homes had electric energy. By 1940 this number had increased to 40 percent. Many technological innovations came with the electrification of America, especially the radio. From radio's inception in 1920 until 1925, the number of radio stations in the United States increased from one to 571 with 2.75 million listeners. By the end of the 1920s, electricity and devices like the radio had become virtual necessities in America's homes. During its infancy, music made up over 60 percent of broadcast time. With the development of network hookups by the National Broadcast Company in 1925 and the Columbia Broadcast Company in 1926, live musical broadcasts could be heard from coast to coast. By 1931 these networks numbered seventy-nine for CBS and sixty-one each for NBC's two networks, Blue and Red. In the depression era the radio became one of the central features of the American home and helped the growing entertainment industry. And, as Warren Susman has argued, the introduction of national programs into American homes during this era helped build a consensus of thought, values, and ideals.[16]

The potential of the radio to promote cultivated music appreciation was part of the larger debate concerning the usage of this new and important medium. Frank Biocca has outlined the debate that took place in the 1920s over whether the radio waves should be used for educational and socially uplifting purposes, and therefore feature cultivated music, or be used to cater to the whims of the consumer, and therefore play popular music like jazz and Tin Pan Alley songs. The debate sounds much like the general debate surrounding the popularity of jazz in the 1920s, as the guardians of Victorian culture tried to prevent this African-American music from spreading in the face of widespread white and black acceptance. Using a variety of methods, from having internationally known composers broadcast over the radio to a well-designed media campaign, by 1927 classical music was featured more than popular music on the radio. By 1930 this trend was overturned, and programming featured popular music over classical music at a rate of two to one. The blame, from the point of view of the opponents of this shift, lay with radio and its desire to make money rather than uplift listeners. As an article in the *Etude* put it in 1932, radio featured music by "badly trained moron[s] . . . [who] are piped over the air to millions of homes . . . that are a menace to music, every sensible person knows."[17]

By the time of the creation of the FMP, Roosevelt's administration already understood the potential importance of the radio and had used it for political advantage. Both NBC and CBS cooperated with the president by giving the administration free air time to both inform the public and to protect their viability: since radio stations had to renew their federal licenses every six months, cooperation insured survival. Also, NBC's vice-president Frank Russell and CBS's Henry Bellows were allies of FDR and the New Deal. By 1934 radio had become the central organ from which to build support for the New Deal. NBC provided over 250 free hours of broadcast time during that year alone. In 1935, CBS produced a series entitled *Of the People, by the People, for the People* designed to re-create the great moments in Roosevelt's short but exciting tenure. In a cooperative venture, the Office of Education advised high school civics and government classes to listen to and discuss the program. The demand for radio time grew so intense that Stephen Early, Roosevelt's press secretary, began to screen the administration's potential radio material so that time would be reserved for those programs and productions best suited for its use.[18]

The FMP believed it had much to offer via the radio. Not only could it perhaps use its power and influence to return classical music to the forefront of programming (a very distant possibility), it also could transmit good music to rural areas where producing live shows was unrealistic. This latter goal was much more attainable than the goal to overtake popular music on the radio, and in 1936 the project initiated a program of recording the best of the FMP's symphonies and sending these recordings to any station that requested them. Under the personal supervision of Sokoloff, the FMP recorded more than three hundred fifteen-minute vignettes of symphony, concert, and Negro chorus music. Local stations donated the air time for the broadcasts, and their listeners heard "live" FMP radio programs. The Oregon FMP unit's series of concerts over station KGW-KEX in 1936–37, entitled *The Builders of Tomorrow*, detailed the many positive undertakings of the WPA in Oregon. The *Indianapolis Times* told its readers that the twice-weekly FMP radio concerts represented the only "serious music emanating from Indianapolis."[19]

Sokoloff and his state directors wanted to renew community interest in art music, whether by radio or live performance. They hoped that through their activities some towns might want to create or revive their symphony orchestras, thereby employing musicians. Des Moines, Iowa, provides a case in point. Through 1936 and 1937, the FMP gave regular concerts in the city that proved to be popular with the people. Civic leaders, spurred on by the FMP, organized a civic symphony in the fall of 1937, and the former FMP unit became the privately funded Des Moines Orchestra. The city of Hartford, Connecticut, whose orchestra had folded in 1920, organized a symphony under FERA in 1934 and under the FMP in 1935. The popularity of these orchestras encouraged local leaders in 1938 to form the privately funded Hartford Symphony. Similar situations and results occurred in Buffalo, New York, Tulsa, Oklahoma, and other American cities, as the partial list below details.[20]

The creation and growth of these symphonies served to justify the project's belief that "community interest will grow when the community is being served." By giving concerts throughout local areas, from schools and churches to men's clubs and auxiliary meetings, the FMP became an essential part of many American communities. Many citizens in these areas wrote to the national office to thank the FMP for all its work and became the central feature of Sokoloff's justification that the people, if given the choice, favored cultivated, quality music over popular, cheap music. An Ohio educator wrote that of all the things in his community—

Table 1

Listing of Places Where the FMP Rejuvenated or Created Symphony
Orchestras

Rejuvenated	Created
Des Moines, Iowa	Bridgetown, Connecticut
Hartford, Connecticut	Lynn, Massachusetts
Buffalo, New York	Manchester, New Hampshire
Tulsa, Oklahoma	Providence, Rhode Island
Omaha, Nebraska	Akron, Ohio
Toledo, Ohio	Jackson, Mississippi
Portland, Oregon	Paterson, New Jersey
Syracuse, New York	St. Petersburg, Florida
San Diego, California	Worchester, Massachusetts
Utah	Richmond, Virginia
	Oklahoma City, Oklahoma

the chamber of commerce, local government, men's clubs, church—the
"greatest instrument for community good" was "the Music Project." The
FMP became "one of the most important elements in Detroit's musical
life," wrote one resident, while the Detroit Police Department issued a
report late in the 1930s that suggested that juvenile delinquency dropped
almost 90 percent in those areas where the FMP dance band performed.[21]
The Richmond, Virginia, Parent-Teacher president, G. Randolph Smith,
wrote to the national office and thanked the FMP for music fit for the
whole family. The FMP orchestra could strengthen the moral, familial
bond by allowing families to attend regular uplifting concerts featuring
the "best music" in Richmond. The citizens of Phoenix, Arizona, voted
municipal funds to increase the size and performance capabilities of its
FMP concert unit, calling it good for all the people of Phoenix. In Eunice,
New Mexico, businessmen linked a good band to good business. If a town
had a good orchestra, both the community and the town prospered. The
Eunice businessmen gave their full support to the FMP.[22]

Newspapers and magazines also praised the FMP. Roscoe Wright
concluded in an article for *Current History and Forum* that the people
were impacted by the WPA and took activities like the Music Project

seriously mainly because of their emphasis on community involvement. The local Asheville, North Carolina, newspaper reported that the people "got more enjoyment . . . from the concerts of the North Carolina Symphony . . . than from anything of like cost that the government could have provided." Examples from papers from around the country included phrases like "eminently worthwhile activity" and "something the public agreeably accedes."[23]

The project's initial years went relatively smoothly. Few attacked a relief effort designed to provide employment for out-of-work skilled musicians who at the same time offered local communities high-quality, low-cost concerts. The FMP performances became one of the few quality forms of entertainment in many communities, especially those mid-size cities in the Midwest, South, and Southwest. The FMP wanted to get community support by going to the people, starting in the schools and then reaching out to the adults, by playing almost anywhere. The project tied its activities to the ongoing musical renaissance that began in the early part of the century, spurred on in part by the piano industry's desire to increase sales. Even though the depression slowed this growth, by 1938 the country seemed to be in the midst of a musical rebirth. The project wanted the people to know of its role in this process.[24] The FMP provided the music "that carries the singing spirit in its varying moods and wide range of tone and feeling," wrote an enthusiastic project administrator. George Albee wrote in the *Ladies Home Journal* that "the FMP deserves credit" for the musical renaissance.[25] The project wanted a response, and it was the people who wrote to their newspapers, sent letters to the state and federal offices, and supported the FMP through their continued attendance at musical events.

But despite these successes, the problems of mission and service continued to plague Sokoloff and his staff. The debate concerning favoritism toward classical musicians did not go away, nor did the call for more popular, recreational musical projects. Some private musicians, teachers, and conductors also complained about unfair competition. ASCAP filed suit against the project over the project's use of the radio without due compensation. The New Deal coalition, so strong up to that point, began showing stress cracks in 1935, which by 1936 became major fissures. Rural, conservative, and anti–New Deal legislators allied themselves in opposition to the president, forcing cutbacks and investigations. The economic recovery and the European situation made artistic boondoggling projects open to attack. Add to all this the vocal and widespread charges of communist subversion within the WPA and Federal Arts Projects, and one can imagine the problems the FMP would have to face in the coming years.

THREE

EXPANSION, CURTAILMENT, AND ATTACK, 1937–1938

Many problems helped weaken Roosevelt's power in Congress after 1935: the growing world military threat, increased budgetary restrictions, congressional scrutiny, and charges that FDR had moved too far to the left. All of these, plus the continuing economic troubles, fragmented the supporters of the WPA and undermined the FMP's ability to set long-range goals. With the existence of the entire FAP threatened during 1937–38, the FMP embarked upon a program to prove its social worth and loyalty by expanding its performances to include even more Americans. Through concerts and other special attractions, the FMP hoped to build a network of supporters that would allow it to continue to bring quality music to American citizens, regardless of politics.

The years 1937–38 were tense and confusing times for America. Events in Europe and East Asia began to occupy more of Roosevelt's and Washington's attention. Mussolini's invasion of Ethiopia and Hitler's repudiation of the disarmament clause of the Versailles Treaty, both in 1935, heightened Roosevelt's fear of the fascist threat in Europe. Asia also appeared on the verge of total war in 1937 as Japan invaded China and in December fired upon the American gunboat *Panay*. The deteriorating situation forced the president to conclude that these could be the "last days of . . . peace before a long chaos." Roosevelt continued to monitor the situation throughout 1936, and he finally outlined the administration's view of the situation in the 1937 "Quarantine the Aggressors" speech. Although restrained by the isolationist sentiments of both Congress and the American people, the president asked for increases in the defense budget and a relaxation of strict neutrality laws. When Spain fell to Franco's fascist forces and the Nazis took over Austria in 1938, Roosevelt asked Congress for an additional five hundred million dollars for defense.

Isolationists and other critics attacked this request, calling it a ploy to avert attention from the administration's failure to stimulate recovery.[1]

Roosevelt knew that foreign policy decisions would change budgetary considerations at home. At the same time that he began requesting more monies for defense, cutbacks elsewhere had to be made. The pressure to cut spending had begun in the latter part of 1936, when the administration hoped the economic recovery might bring some relief. From 1933 to 1937 unemployment declined from 25 to 14 percent and farm prices rose to 1930 levels, and some in the administration saw this recovery as a chance to reduce federal spending and balance the budget. Led by Secretary of Treasury Henry Morganthau, the process of cutting the federal debt began—it was cut from $4.3 billion in 1936 to $740 million two years later.[2] As the budget was cut and relief rolls were reduced, an unexpected recession in 1937 reversed the economic upturn, catching the administration off guard. The decline forced four million Americans back into the ranks of the unemployed, bloating the rolls to 18.7 percent. The recession had political effects as well: with 11 million unemployed, stock prices down 43 percent, and industrial output at 1933 levels, it appeared to some that four years of the New Deal had failed to stimulate recovery. This bad economic news, coupled with Roosevelt's court-packing battle and a series of sit-down labor strikes, caused Roosevelt to suffer a considerable loss of his middle-class support during 1937. Additionally, the president's unwillingness to tour in support of liberal Democrats in the elections the next year resulted in a power vacuum of sorts, with the New Deal coming under increasing attack from its opponents and one-time supporters.[3] In an effort to offset some of this criticism, an April 1937 memo asked all department heads to submit a reduced expenditure report as soon as possible. Collection of revenue by the government declined by nearly five hundred million dollars in 1937, and, combined with the additional monies requested for defense, Roosevelt felt all the agencies had to tighten their belts. Roosevelt felt that "every effort should be made to offset this loss as far as possible by a reduction in expenditures" and that some controls needed to be put on spending before the already growing deficit got out of control. Roosevelt specifically mentioned that the "PWA and WPA projects have got to be curtailed."[4]

This was hardly good news for the arts projects. They knew that the first to feel these cutbacks would be the nonproduction units, for their cuts had begun earlier. In July 1936, Roosevelt cut all WPA projects by one-fourth and the Federal One budget by one-third. Although he had promised earlier in January that no cuts would be made, the president asked that Hopkins submit a detailed listing of each WPA project's community involvement in order to justify its allocation.[5] The cuts forced the reduction of personnel by 25 percent and stipulated that no alien be employed when an American citizen could be found for a particular job.[6] Many politicians had questioned from the very start the necessity of spending government funds to support artistic creativity. The high wages paid to the artists did little to sway opinion, and many saw their wages as unfair in comparison to other relief workers. In Ohio, for example, unskilled workers received twenty-three to sixty-four dollars less a month than those employed in the arts projects. Hopkins tried to avert attention from the wages and onto the many quality plays, concerts, books, and paintings already produced and enjoyed by the American people. To him, this proved the WPA and the arts projects were "real democracy in action."[7]

The WPA and FMP were thus forced to cut back at the same time that there seemed to be a greater need for them. The annual budget vote, the attitude of the country toward Roosevelt, toward the WPA, and toward the arts projects all affected funding. Making things more difficult, the money for the arts projects could only be released by presidential letter, which covered from one to six months. When FDR cut the WPA in 1937, he initially advised those in white-collar projects, like the FMP, that their expenditures were out of balance with the rest of the WPA and their sponsors' contributions less than those on the construction projects. After much lobbying from Hopkins and Acting Budget Director Daniel Bell, Roosevelt allowed for below average sponsorship for some white-collar projects. But, early in 1938, these same projects were informed by presidential letter that no worker could exceed a total cost of a thousand dollars. Since this would reduce the potential wages of most of those in the FMP, AFM president Weber protested to Roosevelt that such an action would eliminate the project's ability to provide relief. The president ignored Weber's and others' pleas. The FMP was forced to slash employment by 5,000 from its 1936 peak of 15,842. Things worsened when Congress added a clause to its 1938 allotment that limited the employment term of WPA workers to 18 months. By 1939 only 5,449 musicians remained on FMP payrolls.[8]

These cutbacks and rulings forced the FMP to try to increase its sponsorship revenue. During 1938, private sponsorship in the entire WPA had increased to 20.8 percent, but the administration wanted to see even higher rates. The nonproductive units were especially pressured to seek more sponsors to relieve some of the cost to the federal government.[9] For the FMP, the pressure to increase local sponsorship also helped to reinforce its desire to favor cultivated over vernacular music. Its traditional sponsors, schools, churches, and civic organizations, wanted the FMP to provide safe, good music for its citizenry and thus discouraged dance band activity in favor of classical and light classical concerts. Popular music could be heard anywhere; the sponsors and the FMP wanted to uplift rather than entertain.

If budget problems were not enough, the reports of communist infiltration in the arts projects also encouraged the FMP to continue to favor "serious" music over popular music. The American Communist Party, under the leadership of Earl Browder and with the full support of the Soviet Union, embraced the Popular Front stance in mid-decade. The party slogan of "Communism Is Twentieth-Century Americanism" signaled the party's decision to work within the existing political system to achieve its goals. By 1938, the American Communist Party had tacitly allied itself to the Democratic Party and FDR in order to promote prolabor activity. This new approach swelled party rolls to eighty-two thousand with another half million in affiliated or front groups. Regardless of the Popular Front image, many Americans did not trust the communists or their supporters. They continued to hold onto their traditional, middle-class values. These were the people the FMP hoped to get support from.[10]

Some New Deal critics pointed to the WPA—especially the arts projects—as an example of communism's infiltration of the government. The first volley was fired at the arts projects in early November 1936, when New York's National Emergency Council director George Combs accused Federal Project One of harboring subversives and making a "conscious attempt [to] bring political and social matters to the public who resent this type of propaganda."[11] For some, the arts projects were perfect examples of the administration's coddling of communists. The *Saturday Evening Post* attacked "the radical domination" of these projects, which it argued was involved in trying to "destroy the mythical bourgeois class." The *Post* also pointed out that those on the arts projects' rolls who "tried to oppose the tide of Communism" were ousted and shunned. One disgruntled white-collar employee, working in the Historical Survey department, wrote to the president in 1937 of an "Episcopalian" who had been discharged in favor of "communists" who "threaten[ed] to murder the president of the United States." These charges held much political sway, and although Hopkins tried to convince the president that these reports were "either elaborate distortions of the true fact or else actual fabrications," critics used the popular stereotype of the radical artist to continue their attack on the New Deal.[12]

The most notorious of the Red hunters during this era was Martin Dies and the House Un-American Activities Committee (HUAC). He and his cohorts, Congressmen Joe Starnes of Alabama, J. Parnell Thomas of New Jersey, Noah Mason of Illinois, Arthur Healy of Massachusetts, John Dempsey of New Mexico, and Harold Mosier of Ohio, repeatedly pointed to the arts projects as hotbeds of pro-Red ideology. Thomas, a Republican, announced prior to a series of hearings held by HUAC that he was convinced not only of communist influence, but also of the existence of a vast "New Deal propaganda machine." Committee Chair Dies went into the proceedings also convinced that the "WPA was the greatest financial boon which ever came to the Communists in the United States. Stalin could not have done better by his American friends and agents."[13] Dies believed FDR was using the excuse of the depression and relief programs "to socialize the country."[14]

HUAC was given political ammunition when, in June 1937, Ralph Easley wrote to President Roosevelt charging the WPA with communist infiltration. Easley, chairman of the National Civic Foundation, said he had studied the arts projects employees in New York City and found that 86 percent of them belonged to the pro-Red Workers' Alliance, and 34 percent were actual members of the Communist Party. After the letter was reprinted in the *New York Times,* FDR could not stop HUAC from investigating.[15]

Beginning in August 1938, the committee began to allege that there were communists on Federal One's payroll, mostly within the Theater and Writers' Projects. Testimony by disgruntled employees hurt the credibility of the projects. A former FTP employee, Wallace Stark, testified that Theater Project head Hallie Flanagan had certain pro-communist sentiments and charged she had hired communist personnel directors. When he was transferred to direct the *Living Newspaper,* Stark told the committee, his new bosses "advocated the overthrow of the government type plays," and, because he did not agree with these kinds of "social-problem plays of revolutionary nature," he was fired. Hazel Huffman also charged Flanagan with being pro-Red, testifying that communistic-type plays were the FTP norm. Francis Verdi testified that when the FTP reduced its payrolls in 1937, those belonging to the pro-Red Workers' Alliance did not lose their jobs, regardless of their qualifications. William Humphrey told the committee that he had played the role of American Communist Party head Earl Browder in the FTP production of *The Triple A Plowed Under,* but left the play because he felt the propaganda was "along Communistic lines." Leo Dawson brought samples of communist literature regularly distributed at the FTP headquarters in New York City, one entitled "Back the President—Jobs and Recovery—Workers' Alliance—Communist Party—Federal Theater Project." These testimonies against the FTP should have been taken less seriously, for, as John O'Connor and Lorraine Brown point out, those who testified had had a hard time in the FTP simply because they had little talent.

But these types of stories only fueled the activity of HUAC. Dies himself produced a front cover from Browder's book, *The People's Front*, with 103 FWP employees signatures, thus proving they were "avowed Communist Party members." Jerre Mangione explains in his *Dream and the Deal* that members of that New York City unit had signed the book to honor the retirement of Edwin Banta, whom they assumed to be a member of the Communist Party because of his role in the Workers' Alliance. He was in fact an informer, and the signatures became damning evidence of pro-Red sympathies.[16]

It became obvious that certain material caught the committee's attention. For example, the children's play, *The Revolt of the Beavers*, which detailed the events in Beaverland where working beavers revolted against an oppressive Boss Beaver and lived happily ever after, came under attack as communist propaganda. And, while a New York City psychologist explained that few children understood the political or social messages and just liked the good beavers, Dies and HUAC agreed with the *Times* reporter Brooks Atkinson's assessment: "Marxism à la Mother Goose." Stark told the committee that he wanted to produce plays about Lincoln, Theodore Roosevelt, and other great Americans, but had received no support from the FTP. Too many plays, books, and paintings, the committee decided, contained subversive and un-American ideas, and HUAC used the testimonies to document the level of communist control of the arts projects. The committee's full report to the House in 1939 concluded that "foreign governments are influencing, if not directing, policies and activities of certain organizations of the United States and are using the[m as] fronts to advance their cause and interests."[17]

The suspicions raised by Dies forced the administration to fear that the communist taint might spread throughout the entire WPA and affect the president's ability to pass other legislation. As a result of HUAC's findings in 1938, the House Subcommittee on Appropriations began to investigate the WPA and the arts projects. The subcommittee wanted to determine the WPA's cost-effectiveness and investigate Dies's charges. Many in the House knew that to ignore Dies's findings might suggest to the American people that the federal government indeed sponsored and paid for pro-communist activity. Given the fact that white-collar workers and the artists earned more than the rest of those employed by the WPA, and that they worked fewer hours and indoors, many Congressmen were feeling the heat from their constituents.[18]

The subcommittee seconded HUAC's charges that the arts projects employed some communists and fellow travelers. An ex-editor on the FWP, Oscar Goll, testified that the Writers' Project produced and distributed the communist bulletin *The Red Pen* and estimated that 60 per-

cent of FWP directors were Communist Party members. Another testified that "one-third of the FWP's managing supervisors [were] either
Communist Party members or Workers Alliance stooges." Asked if this
infiltration applied to all of the arts projects, he replied that "of the *three*
[emphasis mine] I would say that the Art Project is least dominated by
the Communists."[19]

Throughout all the investigations, the FMP escaped even guilt by
association. Although some challenged it because it employed so many
musicians with foreign-sounding names—not the least of whom was the
Russian-born Sokoloff—the FMP's tendency to emphasize "acceptable"
music and the conservative nature of the project distanced it from the
other more radical and innovative arts projects. While the other projects
allowed for some artistic experimentation and encouraged some avant-
garde activities, such was not the case for the FMP. The Music Project
sought to provide employment over composition, which encouraged the
propagation of acceptable musical standards. Thus, while the other projects
faced accusations of communist influence, very few questioned the Americanism of the music division. When the subcommittee once again investi-
gated the WPA for subversive elements in 1940, the FMP was excused
because "there was nothing of particular [radical] interest in this Project
to report."[20]

The FMP, under Sokoloff's leadership and with the aid of his regional directors, favored cultivated music that had already won acceptance from listeners and was labeled by all "cultured" people as good.
Even those compositions from the lighter side, like those by Sousa or
Foster, had by the 1930s become acceptable as part of a concert of quality music, for they exemplified the growth and development of America's
musical legacy.

The project was also fortunate that in the private sector, many musicians disapproved of the radical, anti-American ideas promoted by other
artists for several reasons. Perhaps most significant, most professional
musicians were either members of the AFM or worked within the union's
governance. Within the AFM and its parent, the American Federation
of Labor, ties to radical organizations were not tolerated. For example,
in order to dissuade industrial unionism earlier in the 1930s, the AFL
resorted to anti-communist propaganda, a tactic it used later in the decade to discredit rival trade union leaders. The lack of sympathy for radi-
cals spread to the AFM. To this end, the AFL told all of its members
that the communists were responsible for "disorganizing" all of labor by
infiltrating union affiliates and using the workers to destroy the union.
This led to a frustrated rank-and-file membership and played right into
the hands of the American Communist Party.[21]

The AFM did not tolerate radical subversion within its ranks. A resolution at the 1935 convention called for the purge of all communists from the union's membership rolls and asked that no AFM member be allowed to play "The Internationale." In 1937, David Lasser of the Workers' Alliance of America invited AFM delegates to its convention, but the union refused, implying that the Workers' Alliance was part of a greater communist threat.[22] Nearly eleven thousand AFM members received aid from the FMP between 1935 and 1939. Therefore, that so little radicalism took place in the FMP comes as little surprise. The national staff in Washington knew the problems any taint of radicalism might have caused on the project, and early in its tenure it advised that anyone espousing radical or communist ideas be immediately fired. The FMP wanted the American people and its government to recognize it for its ability to give free or low-cost concerts of good music, for educating and uplifting the American people through cultivated music, and for rarely stepping outside its musical boundaries and into politics. Perhaps unconsciously, the project tapped what came to define much of American culture in the 1930s: it was politically conservative, individualistic, and decidedly middle class.[23]

The policies and practices that allowed the FMP to escape HUAC and congressional criticism opened it up to attack by many of the nation's private musicians. The depression hit musicians ahead of the rest of the nation, as sound movies, radio, and the loss of philanthropic donations forced many out of work. After bottoming out in 1931, live performance bookings began a slow climb through 1934. As the Music Project came into existence, the demand for live music in the private sector had risen from 2,650 bookings in 1933–34 to 3,150 in 1935. Private engagements continued to climb so that by the 1937 season, private concert bookings were up 104 percent from the 1929–30 season. The popular swing music explosion that began in 1935 and gathered momentum through the rest of the decade did much to aid this musical employment renaissance. Led by Benny Goodman and by Fletcher Henderson's arrangements, the swing era provided immediate employment for thousands of musicians, both on the road and in the recording studio. In fact, largely as a result of the swing movement, the moribund recording industry also underwent a revival, providing more employment opportunities for musicians. Critics used these figures to argue that the private music industry could absorb those on the FMP's payrolls. Other musicians accused the FMP of unfair competition because it charged less admission and took business away from the private sector. The FMP needed abandonment, went their argument, for it ran counter to the American tradition of free enterprise. The AFM kept up its criticism of the FMP as well, arguing

MAMMOTH
Symphony Concert

ERNO RAPEE

Conducting

275 MUSICIANS
of the W. P. A. Federal Music Project

SOLOIST
BRUNA CASTAGNA
Leading Contralto
Metropolitan Opera

■

MADISON SQUARE GARDEN
50th Street and 8th Avenue

WED.—July 29—8:30 P.M.

Tickets On Sale:	General Admission:
Mad. Sq. Gd.—CO. 5-6800	4500 Seats at 25c
Macy's—LA. 4-6000	RESERVED SECTIONS
Wanamaker's—ST. 9-4700	7000 at 40c 55c 75c
L. Bamberger—Market 2-1212	3000 at $1.10 and $1.65
(*Newark*)	*Tax included*

258

Fig. 4. Erno Rapee concert. In an attempt to swell attendance figures, these types of mammoth concerts were a regular FMP feature. Courtesy of the National Archives.

that the swing movement proved that the American people favored popular music over cultivated music and that the FMP needed to change its audition standards to allow more rank-and-file members into the federal fold.[24]

Sokoloff and his staff, aware of the budget restrictions and cutbacks, the congressional scrutiny, and the charges of favoritism and elitism by many out-of-work popular musicians, made a concerted effort to expand its musical activities and thus silence the opposition. Sokoloff told Ellen Woodward that in 1937–38 the FMP would try to "bring to a wider public the cultural and educational benefits of the project, especially the underprivileged." Cultivated music needed to be heard throughout the country in order to make friends for the FMP and the WPA.[25]

Building on the momentum of the second half of 1936, when 25,000,000 persons attended 36,000 FMP concerts, attendance increased in 1937 by 7,000,000 people. Willem van Hoogstraten, the summer director of the New York Philharmonic, wrote that the FMP brought "music within the reach of the masses of people who cannot afford opera or the usual symphony orchestra" and made cultivated music available to "all of the people." In 1938, with cutbacks in both funding and employees, the FMP still was able to give 57,600 performances to 34.5 million Americans. Radio helped bolster these numbers, as project broadcasts increased to 4,493 in 1937. In Philadelphia, for example, the FMP gave 28 radio performances to what they estimated to be 5,000,000 listeners in 1937. In New York City, the project broadcast an average of 75 hours a week in September 1938 over station WNYC.[26] The Indiana FMP gave over 51 broadcasts in 1937 to what the FMP estimated to be 153,000 listeners, while the Charleston, West Virginia, project reported that in a two-week period during 1938 it broadcast 78 FMP concerts over station WSAZ. It could not even attempt to estimate the audience.[27] By the fall of that year Sokoloff boasted that the streamlined project operated in 42 states and New York City, and, by using these sometimes bloated attendance statistics, he argued that the FMP was meeting the musical needs of the American people without catering to their lowest musical denominator.[28]

By using this musical blitzkrieg approach in 1937–38, the FMP hoped it had proved its value to the WPA's administrators and to the American people. It wanted more press like the kind it had received from the *Milwaukee Leader,* which wrote that the FMP gave people hope and showed them a government sensitive to their physical and mental health. Supporter Gail Martin in Salt Lake City pointed out that the value of the FMP lay not in the exposure it gave to the American composer, but to the audience. "Instead of being limited to the aristocracy," quality music "could be enjoyed by anyone sufficiently motivated to walk or spend the cost of carfare to the school auditorium." And, even though the composition performed might have been written by Haydn for the elites in Austria, under the auspices of the egalitarian and American FMP, it was made available to all people. This is exactly the type of press the FMP encouraged.[29]

Regardless of its expanded activities and attempts to distance itself from its radical sister projects, the FMP still felt the brunt of the anti–arts projects reaction. Budgetary restrictions, some of which were necessary but others designed to punish the arts projects, made it difficult for the FMP to meet its musical and employment obligations. The project did its best by expanding performance numbers and re-emphasizing what it had always stressed—cultivated music, American composers, and the American people. "This was the people's music," announced the *San Francisco News* in 1938. The men, women, and children who went to watch the FMP after work and school were the American public and represented the potential for quality, affordable cultivated music in the country.[30] Or, as Harris Pine wrote in the AFM's *International Musician*, the FMP and its emphasis on tradition, order, and high standards helped "unify the hearts of America and make them beat as one for the common good of all."[31]

FOUR

THE ONLY RESPONSE:
EXPANDED EXPOSURE

"Music is a public right and obligation," Sokoloff proclaimed in 1937. Over the next two years he encouraged many project-sponsored ventures in order to introduce music into America's communities. The FMP's hope was that if the American people heard good music performed by American musicians, their patronage would guarantee their continued survival. The FMP and Sokoloff wanted even bigger numbers in 1937 and 1938 and asked that all units get involved wherever and in whatever capacity they could in the local communities. The battle was for survival.[1]

The summary of operations for 1938 lists over 57,000 performances to some 34,496,117 Americans. Radio presentations topped 2,831 broadcasts to millions of listeners. The larger music units in the eastern cities had little trouble attracting huge crowds. During the first six months of 1937, for example, the Philadelphia FMP gave 1,130 performances to over 683,565 persons. In smaller market areas like Kansas City, the project was able to give 69 concerts before 100,000 listeners. The Madison, Wisconsin, unit's attendance increased over 50 percent in 1938, as over 2,000,000 persons attended 3,186 FMP concerts in 247 different statewide communities. Even West Virginia averaged 1,466 persons in the 25 FMP concerts it put on during the last two weeks of August 1938.[2] These numbers were used by Sokoloff and his staff to detail the FMP's community acceptance and to justify its credibility.

The FMP's basic organizing tactic was simply to join existing local celebrations, rather than starting from the ground up. This insured both large attendance and good press coverage. In one of the few instances in which vernacular music was featured, the project's Negro dance band helped celebrate the 1938 Grand Island, Nebraska, Harvest of Harmony celebration. The Omaha FMP concert orchestra was the star attraction as it led an estimated 12,000 people in a parade. When the parade ended, the project dance band played for a massive Jitterbug contest. Another way the project improved its popularity was to perform compositions written by local citizens. In Ames, Iowa, the project showcased local talent weekly and did much to make the town feel connected to the rest of the nation. The Lewiston, Maine, residents also received weekly project concerts, which featured Maine composers peppered between compositions by Sousa, Foster, and Berlin.[3]

The FMP even sent out traveling orchestras to reach into areas not normally serviced. The Oklahoma City project, conducted by Victor Alessandro, organized a tour for the sixty-piece orchestra throughout the southern and western parts of the state designed to bring live, cultivated music to people who might never have heard or seen an orchestra. Virginia's FMP unit was created as a traveling unit because it lacked enough classically trained unemployed musicians. During its first three years of operation (1935–38) this unit gave concerts in fifty different locales. Northern California's orchestra was organized for the same purpose. It played in small communities like Taft, California, where in 1938 the FMP "made history . . . [as] the first symphony concert heard" in the town. Administrators pointed out that successes in towns like Taft encouraged other small towns to contact the FMP for concerts. Colorado's traveling FMP symphony's itinerary for the latter part of 1938 included a thirty-town tour of Colorado, Nebraska, and Wyoming, which most assuredly brought the first live cultivated music to these regions.[4]

The project did not ignore large-scale activities, like the opening of the Theater of Music in New York City. Using the closed Gallo Theater on 54th Street, the FMP's Theater of Music opened on January 24, 1937, with a fifty-cent concert featuring Sokoloff and the one-hundred-piece Federal Symphony Orchestra. The project wanted to make the facility the central auditorium for the presentation of music to the people of New York. Lee Pattison, the city's FMP director, planned on having the project perform something of "genuine musical interest each day of the week." Every other Sunday was reserved for the Federal Symphony, but the rest of the week was open to almost any programming. The theater became the place to hear the Madrigal Singers, attend Composers' Forum-Laboratory meetings, attend opera openings, and take part in a host of other activities. On February 7, 1937, the theater began a series of twenty bimonthly concerts dedicated to tracing the evolution of dance rhythms from medieval times to the present. The project hoped the variety of programming would capture the attention of the city's population, and because of its diverse activities, bring even more people in under the FMP umbrella.[5]

The project even gave limited support to folk festivals. While Hopkins had requested that the project help promote a national folk festival, little was done to make it a reality. Given Sokoloff's attitude toward vernacular music and musicians, it should come as no surprise that so little was done to preserve and promote the nation's folk music. The project believed its responsibility was to give employment to professional musicians who had been trained at conservatories and who had the best chance of private employment off the FMP's rolls. Therefore, little value was placed on the family-trained folk artists, as they were not seen as professionals. Bowing somewhat to pressure, the FMP allowed some units to sponsor folk-type festivals, which usually featured the participants dressed in the costumes of their native lands and singing songs from the old country. In Baltimore, the FMP unit joined with the American Legion in the annual Federal Interalles des Anciens Combattants festival in 1937. And, while the WPA orchestra played the national anthems of eleven countries, including those of Czechoslovakia, Poland, and the United States, eleven young girls dressed in their native countries' costumes spoke messages of peace in their European tongues. The festival concluded as participants joined hands to sing the national anthem.[6]

While the project gave grudging approval for these European-type festivals, it made little effort to participate in rural folk festivals. It appeared that some folk traditions were better than others. The FMP did participate in Virginia's state folk festival, where tall tales were told and where mountain music, sea chanties, spirituals, and even symphony music were played, but the FMP did not advertise its involvement. The annual Ashland Folk Festival in Kentucky also received some budgetary assistance. These "singin' and gatherin' days" worked in conjunction with one of the few active FMP folk units, directed by Jean Thomas. Informal at best, the event included folk songs and the telling of stories in the folk tradition. Sokoloff's office sent congratulations to Thomas and pointed out that in the future the materials she and the FMP collected could "find themselves in the libraries of the world beside the folk-lore of the French, the Germans, the Scandinavians, and the Russian peoples."[7]

The project did try some unusual, nontraditional activities. In 1936, for instance, the FMP tried to create a listing of American composers' homes, famous places, and memorials, and sent out letters and questionnaires throughout the country to discover where the great composers had been born, raised, and educated. Calling itself the Organization of American Music Shrines, it wanted Americans to associate Spillville, Iowa, with Anton Dvorák, or Peterborough, New Hampshire, with MacDowell. Aside from the letter and questionnaire, however, lack of interest led to little else being done on this project.[8] Another activity involved the employment of blind musicians. One of the first musicians employed by the

Fig. 5. Advertisement for FMP show in Reading, Pennsylvania, in 1936. Another attempt by the FMP to integrate itself into the community. Courtesy of the National Archives.

Detroit unit was blind pianist Wilson Murch. The Capitol Dance Orchestra of New York City was the most famous of the FMP's activities for blind citizens. Organized in 1936 from a nucleus of five, by 1938 nine blind musicians gave regular concerts over WNYC municipal radio. Acknowledged as one of the more popular FMP dance bands, this unit gave over five hundred live performances throughout the New York City area until 1939. The musicians believed that the project had rescued them from oblivion and poverty and had given them equal treatment. Like most other Americans, these musicians wanted "jobs we are equipped to handle . . . [the] Federal Music Project is a fair project and ours is a fair job," said Oscar England, unofficial leader of the group.[9]

The rehabilitation of blind men into contributing members of American society provided valuable publicity, as did the FMP's other conversions. When in 1936 Harry Hewes received a letter from Louisiana director Rene Salomon detailing the discovery of a man named Lang at an Algiers, Louisiana, transient camp, the information director knew he had a good story. According to Salomon, while entertaining the men in Algiers, the director of the FMP band noticed this man Lang singing along. Afterward he approached the transient and recommended he join the FMP, to which he soon transferred.[10] The symbolism of the story—a transient saved by FMP—impressed Hewes, and he encouraged the project to develop a radio play about the incident in 1937. The FMP play begins in a transient camp four days before Christmas. Fifty men, dirty and with the "appearance of depression derelicts, hopeless and beaten," sit at a long dinner table eating and listening to the New Orleans FMP concert orchestra before them. As the orchestra finishes Franz von Suppe's *Poet and Peasant Overture,* a man with grimy hands and broken shoes rises up and shouts "Bravo." The music supervisor, a bit disturbed by the outbreak, asks the transient about his knowledge of music. The filthy man, who had to dig ditches to qualify for a meal, replies that he used to sing. The script drips: "The supervisor looked at the derelict, hard-boiled. If this man was [going to] bluff, he was going to call it. 'What is your voice?' he demanded. The transient pushed back his heavy plate and looked the supervisor squarely in the eyes and answered, 'I was a basso cantate.'" The transient soon joins the FMP and prepares for the Christmas gala, although now described as a clean-shaven and well-dressed man. His performance is well received by the audience, which includes his much-relieved and proud wife and children. As the radio play closes, the narrator describes how this former transient soon found private employment as a singer and became a contributing American citizen.[11] The project saved the man, his family, and, in a larger sense, all of American society by giving a transient a chance to be a part of America.

The sponsorship of Stonewall Jackson's Own Band also qualified as an unusual project activity. Organized in Staunton, Virginia, in 1845 as the Mountain Sax Horn Band, Stonewall Jackson later incorporated the band into his Virginia Regiment during the Civil War. After the war, General Grant gave special orders at Appomattox to allow the band's members to keep their instruments. Later, they marched in Grant's funeral, the Chicago Exposition in 1893, and other national events. The effects of the depression, however, made many of the band's members consider leaving northern Virginia to find work. Local residents wrote to the state FMP director for help. Informed of the situation and of the importance the community of Staunton and all of Virginia placed on the band, Sokoloff authorized the formation of a FMP unit in Staunton for the nine musicians. The director saw the Jackson band as a perfect vehicle to demonstrate the project's determined effort to preserve the Americanness of the country. Federal money kept the Stonewall Jackson Band alive, and, soon after receiving FMP authorization, the band began playing throughout northern Virginia.[12]

These unusual activities were vital to the FMP's survival, but the project still held to its traditional view that accepted events, like the annual National Music Week held during the first week of May, would be its bread and butter. Organized after World War I by Charles Tremaine's National Bureau for the Advancement of Music and underwritten by the piano industry, the project considered its participation vital. It expanded its role in 1937–38 to include more units and Americans. This type of festival, featuring the best of classical and light classical fare and playing before guaranteed crowds, was a sure cure for the increased pressure from both the Administration and the public to show the worth of the arts projects.[13] During its 1938 involvement, the FMP sponsored events in forty states and featured six thousand musicians. In Lewiston, Maine, the project kicked off Music Week with a concert dedicated to great American and Maine composers. A lecture by Prof. Seldon Crafts of nearby Bates College followed, providing the details of Maine's contribution to the world of music. He ended his presentation by saying that, with continued FMP assistance, Maine would produce many more great American musicians.[14] In New York City, a full slate of concerts was offered during the week, including a gala in Central Park before over twenty-five thousand people. Sokoloff ventured up from Washington to open the festivities at the Manhattan Theater on May 3. Noted American composer Howard Hanson conducted the federal orchestra in an evening dedicated to the best of American music. The week ended with a capacity-crowd concert at Carnegie Hall that featured the works of Copland, Piston, Harris, Nordoff, and Shuman—Americans one and all.[15]

Aside from its Music Week activity, the project also organized a wide variety of musical celebrations on its own. Independence Day concerts were a yearly staple. Other events were planned as they came up. For example, in 1937 the project organized a pageant to honor Mark Twain in his hometown of Hannibal, Missouri. Over 3,200 persons attended. In St. Louis, the FMP Symphony performed its rendition of America's greatest songs, including "The Battle Hymn of the Republic," Hopkinson's "Washington's March," and an original composition by local Francis Blackstone entitled "History of America." Afterwards, in cooperation with the WPA's Recreation Project, a pageant entitled "Our America Yesterday and Today" was presented. The eight historical episodes traced how sacrifice and hard work had made America great. The closing episode had all 652 participating boys and girls singing Roosevelt's theme song, "Happy Days Are Here Again," to full FMP accompaniment.[16] In Memphis, Tennessee, the FMP band played in honor of those killed in the First World War as a Gold Star mother placed a wreath at the National Cemetery. In Huntington, West Virginia, the project led an impressive parade on Armistice Day, while out West the Phoenix FMP unit led the 1938 Navy Day parade to honor those seamen killed during America's wars. These scattered activities, although small in terms of attendance, were an important component of the FMP. By performing at any and every occasion, but especially at patriotic celebrations, the FMP wanted to detail its loyalty to the people, Congress, and the president.[17]

Many of the project's activities revolved around patriotic themes during these years. Given the growing tide of resentment Federal Project One was generating as a result of charges of communist activities, the FMP wanted to make doubly sure that its music was used as evidence of its loyalty. One of the more ambitious patriotic activities undertaken by the project involved the 1937 sesquicentennial celebration of the American Constitution. In the city where the delegates had met 150 years earlier, the FMP joined a Philadelphia-wide committee to organize the anniversary celebrations of Constitution Week, September 9–12. The FMP provided the music for the Mass of Thanksgiving celebrated by Archbishop Dougherty before one hundred thousand people, and several concert bands performed throughout the city to honor the document. In a program designed to coincide with the celebration in Philadelphia, the Westchester County, New York, unit performed a variety of American musical selections. The review from the *White Plains Argus* underscored the FMP's aim in participating in these type of events: "Even to the average American who seldom demonstrates his nationalism . . . music probes his inmost being and stimulates the happiness we all feel in being part of the heritage of this great country."[18]

Of all the activities the project was involved in during these sensitive years, the creation of the American Music Festival represents the project's most ambitious undertaking. Organized in 1938 by Sokoloff and Woodward to showcase FMP units performing American compositions in over one hundred cities and utilizing more than six thousand musicians, the three-day gala would focus national attention on the FMP. Sokoloff wanted the programs to be "All American." The celebration peaked on Washington's Birthday, when programs across the country played music of the Revolutionary era and songs written in honor of the father of the country.[19] Sokoloff hoped the American Music Festival would bring attention to works by American composers. In an effort to broaden its appeal and to underscore its loyalty, the project sought out official sponsors for the events. Sokoloff's staff asked the United States Senate to officially designate February 1938 as American Music Month. "It is not the business of Congress to undertake such a matter" read the official denial.[20] Spurned at the national level, the project administrators decided to focus on receiving state and local support. Ohio's governor, Martin Davey, a critic of Roosevelt and the WPA, nonetheless urged the citizens of his state to attend the concerts in Akron, Cincinnati, Columbus, Canton, Dayton, Cleveland, Toledo, and Zanesville. In his official proclamation he emphasized that Americans had ignored the fact that "much of the world's finest music has come from the creative genius of Americans." Gov. Frank Murphy of Michigan hoped the festival would "foster and encourage in our people a deeper appreciation of this nation's contribution to the music of the world." A. Harry Moore asked the people of New Jersey to "wholeheartedly" support the three-day festival, for the "aim of the . . . festival [is] both nationalistic and cultural" and should be observed by all in accordance with their normal celebration of Washington's Birthday.[21]

Many mayors also issued proclamations of support and set aside the three days in February for the festival. The mayor of Long Beach, New York, told his constituents to "lend their efforts in paying tribute to the American composer," while the mayors of Philadelphia and Milwaukee agreed to install large, illuminated signs across their city hall facades honoring the American Music Festival. In Wisconsin, civic pride between Wausau and Manitowoc surfaced when the latter's advisory committee asked the mayor to issue a proclamation of support before "other Wisconsin cities [get] ahead." In response, the mayor of Wausau quickly encouraged his townspeople to support the nationalistic American festival.[22]

While the planning and support stressed the aesthetic value of American composers, the true thrust of the festival was its nationalism and promotion of the FMP. In Mississippi, the project dedicated the whole month of February to the study of American music. In small towns like

Fig. 6. Playbill for New York City Festival of American Music, 1938. To promote its patriotic appeal, and to distance itself from its more radical sister projects, the FMP embarked upon a number of nationalistic presentations. Courtesy of the National Archives.

Vimville, McComb, Cleveland, and Highland, the FMP units performed all types of American music, which the local paper, the *McComb Daily Enterprise,* understood were "not a toy . . . but a force to be reckoned with." In West Virginia, the local Charleston paper equated the recent upsurge in cultivated music with the FMP, noticing that more people attended concerts as a result of the American Festival. On the West Coast, the *Portland Oregonian* linked the festival to the rediscovery of the state's musical heritage. The paper asked the people to look within themselves and discover the songs of Oregon and all the West. For the first time ever, the Wilmington, California, Women's Club opened its doors to the public by sponsoring an Americanization Day program featuring talks on Washington, Lincoln, and the flag. The WPA concert band provided music for the event, presenting a full program of American songs.[23]

The festival also played to the rural areas of the country. Designed to honor President Washington and American composers, the American Festival wanted its presence to underscore its value to the community, state, and nation. By using George Washington as a symbol, and by featuring local American composers, the FMP and the festival attempted to rally popular support. The FMP utilized the city hall of Lewiston, Maine, to give a Washington-era performance to a capacity audience, while the public schools throughout the state of Oregon made arrangements for the FMP to give American concerts in their schools all during the festival. In small towns like Niagara Falls, New York, where five hundred persons jammed the local music hall to hear Victor Herbert's *American Fantasie*, Edward MacDowell's *Woodland Sketches*, and other American compositions, and Erie, Pennsylvania, where the FMP performed the songs of America—"Columbia," "Dixie," "The Girl I Left Behind Me," "Tramp Tramp Tramp," "Johnny Comes Marching Home," "Yankee Doodle," "The Star Spangled Banner"—Americans heard the songs of their country. Across the rest of the United States, the project favored places like Cambridge, Ohio, Oshkosh, Wisconsin, Wheeling, West Virginia, Clarksdale, Mississippi, and Omaha, Nebraska, with musical performances. In these towns and many others like them, the FMP gave concerts that honored the father of the country, paid homage to the American composer, and brought small communities into the federal web. Whether or not these towns and cities recognized the link between the FMP and Americanness, their participation and encouragement gave the FMP the support it needed.[24]

The tactics utilized in this festival were simple and fail-safe. First, by connecting the festival to the father of the country, a man no loyal citizen would dare attack, the project used nationalism and the fear of the communist label to offset opposition. Few people would criticize the festival, for to do so would seem like attacking America itself. The project chose this mode of celebration exactly for this reason—opposition would be minimal. The second tactic involved musical programming. Most communities emulated the unit in Little Rock, Arkansas, which featured local composers and songs. That unit showcased three compositions, entitled *Arkansas Rondo, Arkansas Traveller Fantasie,* and *Arkansas Senator,* as the central themes of its American Festival. The compositions reflected themes about that state and utilized Arkansas folk songs and images. Not classics by any stretch, they served their purpose by making the program relevant to the people of Arkansas. Cleveland, Ohio, and Grand Rapids, Michigan, featured their composers. Memphis, Tennessee, showcased a local black composer. While most festivals throughout the nation dedicated a portion of their programs to Negro music, Memphis used the festival to honor its native son, W. C. Handy. The FMP concert orchestra's rendition of "St. Louis Blues" reportedly brought all in attendance to their feet with applause.[25]

The last tactic called for the utilization of good music the populace was sure to recognize and enjoy. Two composers' names figured prominently on nearly all American Music Festival playbills: John Philip Sousa and Stephen Foster. Sousa's marches and rousing nationalistic brass ensembles moved audiences to clap, sing, and demonstrate their enthusiasm, and they were the highlight of celebrations in Phoenix, Memphis, Toledo, and many other communities. Only Stephen Foster was played more often. Orchestras featured his antebellum and Civil War–era music on nearly every Festival playbill, featuring his famous songs, "Swanee River," "Beautiful Dreamer," and "Old Folks at Home." The Superior, Wisconsin, unit dedicated a whole performance to Foster songs, while four youngsters under FMP educational guidance in South Carolina played his tunes on their harmonicas as their contribution to the American Music Festival.[26] The FMP knew that Sousa and Foster were very popular. Neither had produced music that was included in the cultivated music category in the traditional sense. Foster's skill came more from his songwriting ability, especially his parlor and minstrel songs, and Sousa's marches were designed to be entertaining and popular—hardly the stuff of serious music. Yet, the project and Sokoloff used these two Americans more than any other because, on the one hand, they detailed one aspect of America's musical development, and, on the other, they were well liked by the American people.

The American Music Festival was a shrewd move on the part of Sokoloff and the FMP. By using George Washington, local composers, and the music of Sousa and Foster, the 1938 festival was a tremendous success. The concerts, which featured some of the "best type" of music, proved so popular with the audiences that the administrators immediately began planning for the second festival in 1939. However, due to continuing budget cutbacks and a lack of national leadership, the festival died after only one year.[27]

Through its success, the American Music Festival reinforced the FMP's determination to portray itself as an organization dedicated to performing quality music for America and its people. During 1937–38 many events were planned and executed with this purpose in mind. With the increased scrutiny by Congress and the nation into its sister units' radical affiliations, the economic limitations imposed by Washington for the FMP's survival, and the attacks by conservatives and private musicians over unfair competition, the project's course of action during these years reflected its administrators' concern for the future. Positive response to the FMP, the national staff reasoned, was dependent on the FMP continuing to emphasize quality music, professional standards, and American themes. The project tried to avoid any music that might be misunderstood and therefore challenged as potentially un-American; it relied on tried and tested classics, placing them on existing festival playbills, or organized their performances around patriotic celebrations. In this way, the FMP reinforced its reliance on cultivated music and conservative musical selections. As a result, the project was spared the ideological attack its sister projects underwent. The lessons learned during these years would not be lost on Sokoloff and the FMP, as they would try other more grandiose activities to attempt to display the best music for the American people.

FIVE

GETTYSBURG:
AN OPERA FOR THE PEOPLE

One of the more interesting of the Music Project's activities in 1938 was the production and promotion of a nationalistic opera, entitled *Gettysburg*. The success of the American Music Festival in 1938 indicated that nationalistic programs had made the FMP acceptable in many American communities. The FMP hoped to create similar excitement with the 1938 opera, *Gettysburg,* as many communities planned to hold celebrations and commemorative assemblies in 1938 to honor the seventy-fifth anniversary of the battle and Lincoln's speech at Gettysburg, Pennsylvania. The federal government planned to bring the remaining Civil War veterans to Gettysburg to join President Roosevelt at a gala celebration from June 30 to July 6. On Independence Day some 150,000 people did turn out to hear the president's speech, including 2,000 Blue and Gray veterans and 50 from the battle itself. Roosevelt equated Lincoln's struggle and the Battle of Gettysburg to the problems America faced in 1938. While Lincoln struggled with weapons of steel and lead, Roosevelt battled with reason and justice in order to "preserve," just as Lincoln had, "a people's government for the people's good."[1]

Several months prior to this battlefield celebration, in March 1938, the Los Angeles Music Project's audition board heard an exciting new libretto and score for an American opera entitled *Gettysburg* by Morris Hutchins Ruger and Arthur Robinson. Gastone Usigli, conductor of the Los Angeles FMP orchestra and a member of the audition board, believed the authors had touched on a "vital theme for American opera." He and the others read the book and in the end were convinced that Ruger and Robinson had written a truly significant piece of American music. Of course they were pleased that the music had been written in time to coincide with the large patriotic celebrations planned throughout the country for Gettysburg.[2] Written in commemoration of the seventy-fifth anniversary of the Gettysburg Address, the audition board decided that the opera was the perfect vehicle to communicate the project's nationalism and its determination to encourage native compositions. Holding high hopes, the project's administrators believed they had discovered a national opera that could tour throughout the country under the FMP banner.[3]

That the FMP in Los Angeles placed such expectations on this as yet unperformed opera was unusual given the relatively small role opera played in the project's operations. The history of opera in the United States during the period leading up to the creation of the FMP pointed to opera's ongoing difficulty in sustaining an American popular base for its craft. The operas of Strauss and Puccini represented a modern approach, which stressed melody and drama easily identifiable to those in the audience. Their operas focused as much on the acting ability of the performers as on singing. Most significant, these modern operas placed the story in the here and now, dealing with relevant issues that were easily understood by the audiences. Despite these changes, opera continued to struggle, and, under the weight of declining patronage during the 1930s, even large successful companies, like the New York Metropolitan Opera Company, found it more and more difficult to keep their doors open. American audiences traditionally had lacked enthusiasm for opera for several reasons. Some saw it as too foreign, while others chafed at the de facto class barriers erected by museums, symphonies, and opera. Many felt uncomfortable in the cultivated environment. The costly ticket prices, fine clothes, and perception that serious music and opera were for the best of society discouraged many and put opera out of the reach of some Americans. The "serious" arts directed their energies toward a distinct social class, assuming those in attendance brought some background, education, and understanding to the presented material.[4]

One of Sokoloff's primary goals for the FMP was to introduce cultivated music to Americans. In order to bring the people into the opera, the project had to break down these barriers. The FMP had to prove that opera was for everyone, not just the wealthy. Carnegie Hall and the high-class opera house clientele were negative symbols for the people to identify opera with, and, partly because of this identification, the Metropolitan Opera had had a hard time selling its tickets for the 1937 season. The FMP broke away from the elite opera stigma by featuring dramatic, fast-paced, and melodic pieces. The FMP used devices not unlike those used in the Theater Project's *Living Theater* experiment, namely projections, loudspeakers, shorter operas, the placement of characters in the audience, or simply the use of a narrator to help guide understanding. Utilizing these devices, and making English the language of performance, encouraged 18,000 persons to attend FMP-sponsored opera on four May 1937 nights in Los Angeles and Long Beach. Best of all the changes was the price. Since it was a government project, the FMP could make opera cheap enough to attract people. Despite a ban on new operas (because of their expense) by the federal office in early 1937, a later ruling allowed for the production of operas if sponsorship covered all nonlabor costs. This would make the tickets cheaper, bring in larger crowds, and potentially make the FMP some money.[5]

One reason why opera was not considered vital to the FMP was that it was very expensive to produce. Thus only four opera units were in operation as of December 1936, employing 512 persons. Even after the sponsorship decision of 1937, the project sponsored and produced only 831 operas before 581,351 persons through 1939. Compared to the symphony and concert orchestra's 77,670 performances before 55,000,000 people (even if the numbers were inflated), one can see that opera played only a small part in the project. In the western district, where *Gettysburg* was to get its performance, Los Angeles and San Francisco produced a few operas, but only San Diego made opera a regular, profitable feature.[6]

While small in number, the FMP gave several American composers the opportunity to perform their operas and reached out into America to produce this art. Homer Gunn, Frederich Hart, and Mary Carr Moore all had their operas, or parts of them, showcased by the FMP. In fact, by December 1936 sixteen new American operas received performance by the project.[7] Aside from opera units in large urban areas like New York City, Boston, or Philadelphia, the FMP produced operas in Newark, New Jersey, Portland, Oregon, Cleveland, Ohio, Tampa, Florida, Omaha, Nebraska, San Bernadino, California, and many other smaller communities. In California alone, the FMP gave 274 FMP operatic performances by 1938. Opera held a small but attractive position in the minds of the project administrators.[8]

Most of the operas highlighted by the project contained symbolism relevant to the audiences of the 1930s. Seth Bingham's May 24, 1936, premiere of the folk cantata *The Wilderness Stone* by the New York City unit was one such case. Using Stephen Vincent Benét's "John Brown's Body" as the central theme, it was described by the FMP as an "important step in the fusion of native American music and literature." The cantata was divided into thirty-nine musical episodes and followed the lives of Jack Ellyat and Melora Vilas as their love is tested by the rigors of the Civil War. The story ends as the two are reunited and begin raising a family. With themes of sacrifice and courage, combined with the patriotic appeal produced by focusing on the Civil War, Bingham's work was well received by project administrators.[9]

The FMP also presented more "modern" operas, like Frederick Hart and Tillman Breiseth's operetta, *The Romance of Robot.* The opera satirized a society where the modernist efficiency of logical decision making and organization replaced individual initiative and humanity. Accepted for performance in New York City in June 1936, the one-act opera by two inexperienced composers took over ten months to rehearse, cost far more than expected, and needed the infusion of dance talent from outside project rolls. The opera opened and closed on Monday, April 12, 1937, at the Theater of Music on West 54th Street. The plot and music were, according to ardent FMP supporter and *New York Times* critic Olin Downes, simply "neither original nor very well done." The story concerned a scientist/dictator of a future world where machines rule and humans serve their every need. The scientist, in an effort to detail the superiority of machines and, by extension, the superiority of his own mind, creates a perfect man in the Robot; yet, in doing so he also sows the seeds for his society's destruction. Once created, the women of this dominion worship the new man by singing "we adore you man of steel, we adore the way you feel, humbly at your feet we kneel." The women try to seduce the perfect man but find him cold to their advances, for he lacks the soul to love. This creates tension in the perfect future, and, in order to prevent further questioning of his authority, the scientist decides that "no sacrifice is too great for Robot. . . . I'll show the world I can create a man capable of falling in love." He then gives the machine his soul. Almost immediately the scientist realizes his mistake, for now that his "soul is gone," he is filled with "frightful emptiness." And what happens to the Robot? He falls in love with a songbird (which is really a beautiful woman trapped by the gods in the bird's body), and, even though she might lose her ability to sing if she pledges her love to Robot, the operas ends as they profess their undying love for each other and, in a way, attack the modernists who favor science over humanity. The Robot sings near the end that "I am the spirit of our modern age, Free from traditions of old, Called the new mechanist, forced to be hard, Made to be brutal and cold. Robot, they called me, the great man of steel." *The Romance of Robot* did not venture outside New York City as an opera, although several selections were performed later in San Francisco. As an opera for the FMP it lacked a unifying national symbolism, and, more important, its music was much too "modern" for the project. Machine sounds, bells, sirens, buzzers, and other noises that were mixed into a music best described as frenetic did little to enamor *The Romance* to the FMP's national staff. While the show was interesting, the music and presentation were far too avant-garde to appeal to either Sokoloff or a mass American audience. Also, given the complicated nature of its message, it ran the risk of being misconstrued the way so many FTP plays had been for those looking for evidence of anti-Americanism in the FMP. *The Romance* was just not safe.[10]

A similar situation took place on the West Coast. In San Francisco, Ernst Bacon, Phil Mathias, and Raisch Stoll attempted to create a play with music entitled *Take Your Choice.* Presented at the Columbia Theatre from December 2 to December 7, 1936, the two-act musical took satirical shots at fascism, communism, militarism, the newsreel, crooners, advertising, and the self-made man. The central characters, Eustace Jones, the Leftist, the Boss, Bootblack, Cop, and Bluebird of Swing, were designed to challenge the modern mind-set of the era. In the hospital scene, for example, three doctors fight over the prognosis of a dying patient. Doctor L(eftist?) proclaims that "Marx's diagnosis proves I'm [the patient's] savior," while Doctor S(talin?) states a purge is needed before any recovery can take place. Doctor D(emocracy?) finally interjects: "Gentlemen! While you fight the patient may be dying," and chastises them for their reliance on rhetoric and failure to treat the problem. Doctor D is shouted down, and he and the patient leave. A substitute is found to replace the departed patient and the scene ends with a chorus chanting "the operation must go on." While reviews were encouraging—one San Francisco critic labeled it "a show which has all the elements necessary to become a theatrical hit"—it did not get the support of the project administrators because it, like *The Romance,* could have been used as fodder by those who wanted to attack the FMP. Even though its music was much more within the project ideology and modeled after popular melodies, its political content made it a dangerous experiment.[11]

These examples help explain why, when Ruger and Robinson submitted their score for *Gettysburg* in 1938, the FMP was so excited to get it performed. The score and libretto for *Gettysburg* concerned the great battle and Lincoln's courage, two themes with which most Americans could easily identify, and some in the FMP believed they had found the perfect opera to detail the American objectives of the project.

Gettysburg's composers had little experience in the production of opera. Ruger, born in Superior, Wisconsin, in 1902, had graduated from Columbia and Northwestern Universities and had studied under Isador Philipp. At the time *Gettysburg* was submitted, he was a Los Angeles public school teacher. His works included *The Jefferson Academic Overture, The Maid of the North,* and *Variations for Piano,* but he had never before attempted to write an operatic score. Robinson had fewer credentials. Born in New Haven, Connecticut, in 1894, he had worked as a newspaper sports and editorial writer, as a staffer at *Collier's Weekly,* and as a playwright at the Wharf Theatre in Provincetown, Massachusetts. But he had never attempted a libretto.[12]

Despite the risks of producing an opera written by inexperienced composers, the audition board authorized *Gettysburg* for performance. The opera featured what music critic Gilbert Seldes called real Americans and legends like Abraham Lincoln, a man most citizens of the United States admired. In his own lifetime, Lincoln fought and was martyred to preserve the Union. Musically, he had always proved a popular symbol because of his rough-hewn appeal to the common man. Most music that used him as its central theme also used certain symbols to convey the message, including rails, greenbacks, Negroes, flags, and eagles.[13] During the 1930s Lincoln's image was popular on many fronts, from Robert E. Sherwood's Broadway hit *Abe Lincoln in Illinois* to Carl Sandburg's multivolume biography. The movies found Lincoln a favorite symbol, as studios used him, or at least Lincolnesque traits, to engender popular support for their Hollywood productions. Lincoln was the perfect personification of the common American who had worked hard to rescue the country from a national crisis.[14]

The year of its submission also played a major role in the opera's acceptance. Aside from the seventy-fifth anniversary of Gettysburg, the arts projects were under pressure for their supposed leftist tendencies and lack of patriotism, and a popular image like Lincoln would prove excellent public relations for the FMP. The authors themselves provided another asset in this regard, as Ruger counted among his ancestors both a signer of the Declaration of Independence, Robert Morris, and a general at the Battle of Gettysburg. Robinson, for his part, was a decorated World War I veteran.[15] Aside from these factors, *Gettysburg* met the central qualifications for performance with the project: it was written by American citizens, it stressed American themes, it was cultivated music, and it might become popular.

The FMP initially presented a condensed version on May 10, 1938, at the Belasco Theatre in Los Angeles. The opera received much pre-performance publicity from the local newspapers. The *Los Angeles Times* encouraged its readers to attend this "epoch-making music drama," while the *Los Angeles Examiner* announced that the opera would dramatize the "hopes, fears, and high nationalistic feelings aroused by the clash." Even small local papers and ethnic papers ran stories on the opera, including *La Parola Degli Italiani* and the *Magyarsag,* a local Hungarian tabloid.[16] *Variety* thought the opera might "click" and have a bright future and help the project. Rising star Ralph Bellamy even took a hiatus from his current movie, *Carefree,* in order that he might help stage *Gettysburg.*[17]

May 10 arrived, and 750 persons, including some Civil War veterans, filed into the theatre to hear Gastone Usigli lead the Los Angeles Federal Orchestra in accompaniment of the opera. The four musical episodes took place on Cemetery Ridge right after the battle and focused on how the local people of Gettysburg dealt with the battle, the war, and America. The opera climaxed when Charles de le Plate sang the Gettysburg Address. But the most spectacular feature of the performance was the racially mixed chorus of 200 singing from behind a thin backstage curtain.[18]

Gettysburg also experimented with the stage lighting and with arrangement techniques, much the same way as the FTP's *Living Newspaper* had. Representative symbols arranged to the music were projected onto the back screen and allowed everyone in attendance to view them. When soloist James Jones, in the role of Aaron the Negro, sang his solo, *Gettysburg* broke established operatic tradition by having him sing from behind a thin, backlit curtain while wearing the costume of his character, instead of center stage in tails, as was often the case for concert versions of opera.[19] It was the final ensemble, however, that caused near "pandemonium." In this highly nationalistic finale, entitled "That These Dead Shall Not Have Lived in Vain," a raised American flag brought the audience to its feet, as they "arose to applaud, every nationality under the sun seemingly joining in."[20]

Most critics agreed with columnist Florence Lawrence's assessment that *Gettysburg* qualified as "one of the most important demonstrations of [the FMP's] value to the community." Carl Bronson focused on the ability of the composers to capture Gettysburg's "patriotic themes" and added that some of the veterans of the battle in attendance had tears in their eyes. Other critics believed the opera had "greater artistic possibilities than the old [European] form." A month later in Salt Lake City, FMP supporter Gail Martin wrote of his hopes for a national *Gettysburg* tour.[21]

Not everyone was as optimistic. The *Daily News*'s Sara Boynoff questioned whether the programmatic music would stand up to a full opera. Frank Mittauer cited the composers lack of musical continuance and originality and warned that Ruger's repeated usage of hymns, folk melodies, and bugle calls would "prove pretty dull stuff in a two-hour opera." Fay Jackson of the *California Eagle* called *Gettysburg* the "Federal Flop." Ruger and Robinson, she wrote, relied on "high school community songs dipped in a broth of chromatics." And using the flag at the end was simply a grandstand stunt designed to get applause.[22]

Regardless, the project's coordinators liked the opera. In May's report on its activities in California, the southern California administrators highlighted *Gettysburg* as the star of their activities and forecasted a September full-length premiere. They also mentioned the possibility of the Chicago project presenting the opera in November. The administrators further decided that the opera merited a second presentation. This encore performance would utilize the best feature of the first—its nationalistic appeal—and leave no doubt as to *Gettysburg*'s intentions. The project decided to showcase the opera at the same time Roosevelt would be at the battle site, on America's Independence Day. There was some effort to try to get the opera to actually be staged at the battle site on the Fourth of July, but the FMP opted instead to air parts of the opera nationwide over the radio. *Gettysburg* seemed perfect for the radio. It had national appeal and history on its side. Commemorative July Fourth assemblies would surely invoke the spirit of Gettysburg, and the Music Project's opera would be part of a nationwide celebration of the event.[23]

The Los Angeles Music Project attempted to publicize the event, but newspapers in the Southern California area, which had earlier given the project free or low-cost publicity, curtailed this practice. This lack of publicity greatly reduced the potential audience in the Los Angeles vicinity, and *Gettysburg* received little buildup in the California papers. Out-of-state publicity fared worse, as no advance notice of the broadcast occurred. The Los Angeles newspapers, the *Daily News, Times,* and *Examiner,* briefly reported that excerpts of the opera would be performed on the Fourth of July, but failed to mention the radio broadcast. Only one West Coast paper, the *San Diego Sun,* carried any advance notice of the broadcast, and only San Diego's NBC affiliate, KFSD, gave courtesy announcements prior to the show date.[24]

At eight o'clock on the night of the Fourth, Los Angeles radio station KECA broadcast *Gettysburg* from the El Capitan Theatre to the nation over NBC's Blue Network. The opera was also broadcast to Canada and by short wave to Europe. This hookup potentially reached millions who, under normal circumstances, would never have heard the opera. At the same time, in order to maximize the value of the opera, the Los Angeles Music Project presented a simultaneous outdoor showing of *Gettysburg* at Griffith Park. The radio opera featured California baritone Emery Darcy as the voice of Lincoln for the Gettysburg Address, and a piece not heard at the May 10 concert called "We Are Coming Father Abraham" was performed. The opera's dedication, read over the air, outlined the aspirations of the performance: "It seems appropriate that a new, indigenously American opera should receive its first performance by such an intrinsically American institution as the Federal Music Project. Accordingly, we should like to dedicate this premier . . . to the government which has allowed us to try to express, in music and drama, our almost religious adoration of the genius of Abraham Lincoln."[25]

Unfortunately for the project coordinators, the opera seems to have gone generally unnoticed on the Fourth of July. But *Gettysburg* had gen-

Fig. 7. Front cover from the program of *Gettysburg.* In another attempt to display its patriotism, the FMP produced the "All-American" event in 1938. Courtesy of the National Archives.

erated enough favorable reactions for Usigli and other FMP administrators to want to produce the opera in its entirety. The Hollywood Bowl had recently instituted a policy to "hear America first" and had begun to sponsor events promoting American music. Artie Mason Carter, founder of the amphitheater and promoter of American music, believed that "American grand opera should be given its premier in the Hollywood Bowl."[26] The Los Angeles Music Project lobbied for and won the right to use the Hollywood Bowl's facilities for *Gettysburg.* The administrators of the project continued to tout the Ruger and Robinson piece as the "genesis of a new American opera" and pointed out that the opera would mark the first time an American opera had its premiere in the Bowl. The project administrators were proud of this coup, calling it "one of the most outstanding accomplishments" of the project.[27]

As it had before its first showing, the September 23 Bowl premiere of *Gettysburg* received vast advanced promotion. Beginning in early September most of the Los Angeles dailies regularly featured stories about the composers and stars. The Independent Publishers, Authors, and

Composers' Association (IPACA) agreed to co-sponsor the event and offered to help secure nationally known opera stars for the opening.[28] Harry Hewes, always in search of good publicity for the FMP, sent a letter to editor and friend John Selby at the Associated Press, asking him to personally review *Gettysburg,* as it qualified as an "authentically grand opera [that] has moved critics on the Coast to warm praise."[29]

The Southern California FMP office issued a five-page release for all papers on September 17. Included was the cast listing, and IPACA had made good on its word. The all-American cast included Coe Glade, Anne Jamison, Tandy MacKenzie, Emery Darcy, and Kenneth Spencer. Charles de la Plate, the only FMP employee to make the main cast, won a small role as the chaplain. The release suggested that because of *Gettysburg's* positive response on the West Coast, IPACA, the American Opera Association, and the FMP might co-sponsor the first all-American opera festival, with *Gettysburg* as the main attraction.

Most of the local dailies ran stories lifted directly from the release. Other papers added their own commentary. The *Daily News,* which reported that the conductor, Gastone Usigli, who had earlier faced pressure because of his foreign birth, was truly an "American citizen by adoption" and that all the principals in the opera were American. The *Hollywood Citizen News* noted that the Los Angeles Junior Chamber of Commerce Music Foundation had selected *Gettysburg* as its musical protégé, and featured an interview with the foundation's president, D. W. Pierce. He pointed out the importance of the opera's nationalistic element at a "time when war fever is rampant in Europe" and labeled *Gettysburg* a "triumph to American culture" that expressed "the tremendous essence" of America.[30]

"With searchlights fingering the star-spangled sky and silent surrounding hills," the *Examiner* reported on September 23, *Gettysburg* received its world premiere at the Hollywood Bowl. A moderate, informal audience of four thousand to eight thousand, who had paid from fifty cents for general admission to two dollars for reserved seats, filed into the amphitheater. The program that was handed out repeatedly emphasized the Americanness of the opera. Emblazoned across its back were lines from Robinson's libretto that foretold the theme of the opera: "This is my own, my own native land." The event had a myriad of co-sponsors, true to the federal policy of defraying the cost, including the IPACA and the Los Angeles Junior Chamber of Commerce. Post 534 of the American Legion also helped sponsor the event, coincidental with the organization's national convention in Los Angeles. It was hoped that many of the visiting legionnaires would attend *Gettysburg's* opening.[31]

Gettysburg dealt with the individual tragedies that took place in the town after the battle and during the retreat of Lee's army. A modern opera, it featured a series of vignettes that symbolically dramatized all those engulfed by the war. It abandoned plot in favor of simplicity, lack of contrast, and little dialogue. The story, though not inclusive, revolved around the character of Jenny, played by Coe Glade of New York. Unsettled by the loss of her husband in the battle, this young war widow goes amongst the dead soldiers, collecting shoes to give to the living.[32]

Throughout the work Ruger utilized classic American favorites, like "Dixie," "We Are Coming Father Abraham," and numerous army bugle calls. While the bitterness of the war is the dominant theme, the spirit of the piece comes at the climax, the Gettysburg Address. It was projected from behind the audience seemingly right out of the Hollywood Hills. Robinson planned this effect, hoping it would make the speech sound as if it were coming from out of "space and time, out of the night and stars." Sung offstage from behind a screen by Bowl veteran Emery Darcy, the stage was resplendent with people, lights, and color. Small illuminated crosses filled the scene, dominated by one large cross in the center with a backdrop of mountains made alive through varying colored lights. The Gettysburg Address reached its crescendo as the chorus, orchestra, and Darcy—as well as the lights and visual scenery—grew more brilliant, ending with the closing of Lincoln's speech.[33]

Responsibility for most of the stage techniques, including the dramatic lighting and curtaining, went to Adrian Awan. He had created for *Gettysburg* a two-part stage, one realistic and one spiritual, which could give the illusion that the characters rose up out of the Bowl and disappeared into the hills beyond. Awan also used the lighting to create dramatic effects for the principals, who carried farm implements through most of the opera and sang before the audience at a three-fourths angle so that the lighting crew could better illuminate them. This effect was made more dramatic because the singers looked upward to the stars, from which, later in the program, the voice of Lincoln came.[34]

A racially mixed chorus also played a prominent role in the production. Functioning as the commentator for most of the opera, the members of the chorus remained behind a sheer curtain on the spiritual stage level. When needed, such as during the Gettysburg Address, they wore the costumes of townspeople and sang on the realistic level. The African-American members were part of the Carlyle Scott Chorus, on loan to *Gettysburg* from the popular and profitable Federal Theater Project's folk play, *Run, Little Chillun,* written by Hall and Johnson.[35]

Gettysburg tapped into the feelings of many in the American audience of 1938. Robinson used biblical imagery to convey his points, naming his characters Ruth, Aaron, and David. Aaron prays aloud to the Lord, asking Him to wave His mighty "sword an' put dis world to peace."

David also begs for aid, asking God for both victory and peace. As the widow Jenny goes about removing the shoes from the dead, the biblical passage in which Moses is before the burning bush and is told to remove his shoes is sung by the chorus.[36] Robinson's point is plain—just as the Hebrews had to struggle to survive in the Old Testament, so too did Americans during the Civil War and in the modern age. *Gettysburg* was tied to America's millennial mission and concerned with how the divine rights of equality and justice were not given freely, but were earned with blood, sweat, and tears. To an American audience suffering the worst economic crisis in its history, combined with the growing unstable military conditions in Europe and Asia, the message rang clear. Nothing came easily, and for America and its citizens to remain free and happy, they had to endure the individual sacrifice necessary to justify the future. Gettysburg in 1863 was an example of the courage it took; *Gettysburg* of 1938 sought to rekindle the type of virtue necessary to rebuild America and preserve its freedom.

While many had high hopes for the opera, reviews proved less than positive. While the *Herald and Express* reported that the triumphant opera should be heard in every city and exported worldwide as a "lucid and noble expression of American ideals," most other reviewers felt that Ruger and Robinson had tried to tackle too much with too little. The *Evening News* tore at the nationalistic appeal and religious evocation, believing that these techniques did little to "alter the basic fact that *Gettysburg* contained too little action to be good drama and music somewhat below the standards demanded of good opera." Others believed the opera was seriously lacking musically and represented more a sermon than an opera. One reviewer, Alfred Price Quinn, told his readers that the opera proved so listless that he sat in the "audience like a bump on a log and did not even realize when the opera had finished." The national magazine *Musical America* also criticized *Gettysburg* for its lack of plot and musical theme. The monthly advised its readers that *Gettysburg* added little to "opera in general, and even less to American music."[37]

The hopes pinned to *Gettysburg* were quickly forgotten. Even though some people, like noted musicologist Hans Blecheschmidt, thought the opera was great and believed Ruger to be the long-awaited great American composer, *Gettysburg* faded away. In Washington, Harry Hewes had initially hoped that the New York City unit would produce *Gettysburg* at the Hippodrome in February. Local Los Angeles newspapers had earlier predicted the opera would go on the road, starting its tour in San Diego and San Francisco and then continuing across the country. The Chicago FMP unit had made plans to produce *Gettysburg* sometime in November of 1938.[38] All of these plans were canceled.

Despite the pre-performance hoopla and excitement, the opera was below normal standards and not performed again simply because it was not quality work. The negative reviews from the Bowl debut ended any chance *Gettysburg* might have had as a national touring opera. An exchange of letters between Hewes and New York City FMP information director Glenn Tindall in October exemplified the post-premiere sentiments. Hewes asked Tindall if the New York Project still planned to produce *Gettysburg* in February, which Hewes had formalized with the approval of Sokoloff. Tindall responded that he had discussed the matter with Director Clifton and that, "in as much as *Gettysburg* has not had favorable reviews, [the New York City FMP] sees no reason for producing it in this sophisticated 'milieu.'"[39] This is not to disparage either Ruger or Robinson, for they produced *Gettysburg* to the best of their abilities and should be commended for their dedication. But, for both, it was a first attempt, and as with all first tries, making mistakes is almost inevitable.

The question then becomes why the project risked so much for *Gettysburg.* The men and women who made up the Federal Music Project's audition boards had spent most of their lives studying the great music of the world. Why did they produce and promote *Gettysburg* so strongly? Did they really believe that the work, which in hindsight appears so marginal, could be the genesis of a new American opera? The audition board surely realized the mediocre nature of the opera and under different circumstances probably would not have promoted it so doggedly. But 1938 was a turbulent year for the world, the United States, the WPA, and the Federal Music Project. As an example of this pressure, in 1937 *Musical America* reported that some people were attacking the Los Angeles FMP for its support of "non-Americans."[40] Faced with increasing animosity, cutbacks, and congressional attacks, the project had to make a show of its patriotism and community appeal. Obviously, the production brought little financial return to the project, but it did help quell any charges of anti-Americanism in the Music Project, and, when Dies's committee began naming "subversive" elements in the arts projects, the Federal Music Project was spared. *Gettysburg* alone did not stem this tide, but it was what the opera represented in the Music Project that held back the cries of un-Americanism and communism: cultivated music, favoritism toward American composers, and American themes.

SIX

EVALUATION AND PARTICIPATION: AMERICAN COMPOSERS AND THE FMP

The period from 1937 to 1938 represents the mature period of the Federal Music Project's activities and provides an opportunity to evaluate specific musical participation within the FMP. Going into the depression era, the development of an indigenous art music had progressed steadily, if slowly. While many American compositions had been written, acceptance of them was slow in coming. For example, from 1919 to 1925 only 5.3 percent of the compositions from thirteen private orchestras in the United States were written by American composers. By the end of the nineteenth century, orchestras, which had developed along the same lines as museums, parks, and theaters, catered to a predominately urban audience and favored the best classical music from Europe, especially of German origin. European-connected classical culture led to a type of cultural elitism in the selection of compositions, musicians, and especially conductors. Well into the twentieth century, many of the conductors and principal musicians for the major orchestras came from Europe, which reinforced the public's belief in American musical inferiority.

The development of American music found renewed spirit in the early part of the twentieth century. The German school of music that had dominated the American scene for so long and had emphasized the composition styles of Beethoven, Brahms, and Schumann began to decline, largely as a result of anti-German sentiments during World War I. There were other musical forces at work prior to this, namely, the attraction of French impressionism and the newer approaches to composition that utilized aspects of the vernacular. By the end of the Great War, the more academic German hold over American composers had lost much of its influence.[1]

This trend gathered momentum after the war, when many American artists went to Europe, and particularly to Paris, in order to experience the best of European culture and escape what they saw as a culturally bankrupt American society. But this environment fostered a rediscovery of their American heritage and, later, when they returned to the United States, a redefinition of American culture. Composers were among those who fled to Paris. In America, according to critic Harold Stearns, the composer was treated with "good-natured contempt." Aaron Copland, George Antheil, Roy Harris, Roger Sessions, and Virgil Thomson all went to France to study. When they returned home, the gulf between those composers who continued to look back to the nineteenth-century European tradition and the modernists who wanted to create a music of and from the twentieth-century widened. Some, like Howard Hanson, continued to write in the classic European style, while incorporating American themes. Others, like Aaron Copland, tried to combine the best of the Old World with samples of the new vernacular-based music of the twentieth century. Still others, perhaps best represented by George Antheil, tried to recreate and redefine musical composition in relation to the changes brought about by the machine and technology. The debate between all three of these groups, however, tended to ignore the audience. Much of the music lacked popular appeal, and, as the world tumbled into economic depression, these American composers found themselves with few interested patrons. As Copland recalled, during the 1930s he began to feel that he had a duty to try to speak to and for the American people. When expatriate composers returned home in the late twenties, they did so with a renewed sense of purpose—to expose America to cultivated music by utilizing American themes and melodies. This was not the only movement present, as some composers held fast to the German academic ideal. But by the mid-1930s many American composers saw the need to speak to and, at times, for the American people. Art music had to be freed from its ivory tower to help define the responses to the crisis of the depression.[2]

One of the first attempts to re-create the ideals of Paris in the United States came in 1928 when Aaron Copland joined with Roger Sessions to initiate the Copland-Sessions Concerts in New York City. Composers met to perform their work and have it critiqued by those in attendance, especially in terms of its relationship to the audience. When these concerts ended in 1931, Copland and Sessions organized the Yaddo Festival for the summer of 1932. They hoped this festival of American music would reveal the breadth and depth of American cultivated music, so long hidden from the mass public view. The festival brought together an impressive list of younger American composers, including Copland, Harris, Blitzstein, Piston, Sessions, and Bowles. When it ended, these and others left renewed and determined to introduce American music to larger audiences.[3]

Shortly before Yaddo, some American composers joined together to form the Composers Collective in New York City. Formed out of the Pierre DeGeyter Club, named for the man who wrote the "Internationale," and dedicated to finding a socially useful music, the collective began in 1931 to discuss the technical aspects of creating the new mass music. They hoped to create a mass song type modeled after those written by German composer Hanns Eisler. Membership included Marc Blitzstein, Elie Siegmeister, and Henry Cowell. Another member, who would later turn up in the Resettlement Administration and in the FMP, Charles Seeger, explained the purpose of the organization: "The social system is going to hell here. Music might be able to do something about it. Let's see if we can try. We must try."[4] For all its desire to widen the appeal of its music, initially the collective frowned on both the people and their vernacular music. The members of the collective saw 'popular' music, like hillbilly, blues, folk, or jazz, as too common and simple. When the great folksinger Aunt Molly Jackson visited, the collective refused to let her perform because it considered her a musical illiterate.[5]

The collective's problem was the larger problem of the American composer. Many saw the time as ripe for the emergence of a truly American art music, but disagreed over which direction this music should take. Some, like Roy Harris, believed that American composition had reached the stage when America's "musical destiny awaits action," but was at a loss to describe how to achieve this end.[6] Meanwhile, as America's composers struggled for definition, attendance at symphonies continued to decline as the depression worsened. The experimental and dissonant modern music of the 1920s and early 1930s had alienated many concertgoers. This "art for art's sake" music lacked the social commitment necessary in the troubled thirties, and some, like Aaron Copland, believed that the American composer had to change and "speak directly to the American public in a musical language which expresses fully the deepest reactions of the American consciousness to the American scene." To Virgil Thomson this meant utilizing the country's "own genuine musical heritage."[7]

A change was afoot, all agreed, but what about method? How to speak to the American people when they obviously knew so little about "serious" music? This debate was the cornerstone of the Composers Collective's existence, namely, how to write songs the people can understand while having little respect for their taste in music. After several failed attempts to write the mass song they sought, the collective reversed itself in 1935 and began to accept as valid, for political and cultural reasons, the vernacular music of the American people. As a political organization under the direction of the Workers' Music League of the American Communist Party, the DeGeyter Club and the Composers Collective operated from 1931 to 1935 under certain restrictions imposed by the Communist International. One of the more strictly defined directives was that the composers not base their new songs in the defeatism of folk music or in the elitism of serious music. "Proletarian" music had to be politically correct, musically progressive, and provide a marching anthem for the people. Music that might conform to these nearly impossible restrictions went uncomposed. In 1935 the Communist International changed its focus to the Popular Front, in an effort to cooperate with the New Deal and the people's culture. This change in emphasis allowed the composers in the collective to use vernacular music in their compositions. This is not to say that the collective forced composers to write or not to write certain things, or that every member of the collective followed the Communist Party line, but the organization did exert certain social pressure to insure musical conformity and added another wrinkle to the ongoing debate concerning popular versus classical music.

Outside of the collective, many American composers had, by 1935, come to the same conclusion. Even with the collective's input and the potential radicalism existent in the 1930s art communities, Alan Levy reminds us that, in cultivated music, American composers "showed themselves liberals, not leftists." This would be important in the functioning of the FMP. Collections of folk songs from Alan Lomax, George Pullen Jackson, and Carl Sandburg captivated many composers who saw in the melodies a chance to break the barrier between the highly trained composer and the audience. In the earlier period, the composer served himself and the people had to agree; in the post-1935 period, the composer wrote to serve the people.[8]

One of the most ardent of the new supporters of folk music was Charles Seeger. He advised the composer to leave the cities, suburbs, or large estates and see the nation. The "digestion of this experience . . . will [show him] he has learned a new language." To Seeger, this new language would rely less on the complex strains of art music and more on the simplicity of folk music. The music of the proletariat was "a rising, progressive factor," he wrote, and the era of bourgeois music had lost its "positive social value." Hanns Eisler agreed, saying that "modern music will be possible only when there is a new modern style, pertaining to all, and useful to the public."[9]

The divisions and debates amongst the American composers were incorporated into the FMP when it was created in 1935. Seeger, for example, joined the FMP in 1938 and administered the underfunded folk and social music division. Other composers saw in the FMP an excellent chance for them to have their compositions performed: by March of 1940 7,332 compositions by 2,258 American composers had been featured by

FMP orchestras. The project realized that few of these would have lasting value, but felt that the introduction might lead to a wider appreciation of American music. "It is possible," Sokoloff believed, "that the American compositions heard . . . have [produced] as many enduring works as Europe had produced in any similar period." The FMP hoped to discover "a rich symphonic literature" by favoring American compositions over foreign works.[10]

However, Sokoloff's support of American compositions over European classics was, at best, lukewarm. His musical preferences ran toward nineteenth-century German compositions, and he was generally uninterested in the work of the modernists or the new Americanists. During his tenure as national director, while the FMP generally promoted American compositions and composers, Sokoloff did not think it necessary to perform "a composition simply because it is written by an American." Standards had to be maintained, and in Sokoloff's mind this meant nineteenth-century standards; therefore, "the American composer or artist will get no place playing stupid things."[11]

Even given Sokoloff's attitude, the project was able to help American composers. Ferde Grofe said the FMP inspired "the dawn of a musical culture" that used "our own ideals, history and folk-habits." Howard Hanson wrote to Sokoloff to express his gratitude to FDR and the FMP for their "protection and encouragement of American musicians." Daniel Mason Gregory called the project "one of the best things that has ever happened to our native musical art" because of the diffusion of the orchestras throughout the country. This, combined with the FMP's stress on democratic, mass-appeal musical entertainment made "the WPA movement one of which the significance is not yet sufficiently appreciated, but which is nevertheless making history." Charles Wakefield Cadman saw the project as the "finest constructive force that has come into American musical life." New York Post critic Samuel Chotzinoff and British critic James Agate commented on the project's ability to present quality music to the American people. Agate even called the FMP "the highest cultural force in America."[12]

The central reason for such praise came in the face of the sheer volume of American compositions presented by the FMP. After only one year of operation, FMP orchestras played 3,849 American pieces, ranging from eighteenth-century American composers long neglected to contemporary artists outside of the noted musical circles. While many cultivated composers had their works performed, some repeatedly, the most frequently performed compositions came from the lighter pens of John Philip Sousa, Victor Herbert, Stephen Foster, and George Gershwin— composers who utilized vernacular traditions in their compositions and who by the 1930s were intrinsically identified with American music.[13]

The FMP orchestras favored older, accepted compositions, but in order to better meet the needs of the contemporary composer, the project organized the Composers' Forum-Laboratory in New York City in October 1935. This new FMP activity held its meetings at the Midtown Community Center and sometimes attracted five hundred persons. The first forum, held on October 30, presented the music of Roy Harris. The goal of the forums, according to the director of the New York City Laboratory, Ashley Pettis, was to help develop a "more definite understanding and relationship between the composer and the public [in order to remove] the barrier which has always existed between the composer and the people who are or should be the consumers of his goods." The format for the forums began with a presentation of a modern composer's work, followed by questions from the audience and a general discussion. Afterwards, a copy of the work was sent to Washington to be included in a Library of Congress Index of American Composers and music. The best of the laboratory's presentations were then sent to units throughout the country and performed by the FMP orchestras.[14]

The New York City forums met with such outstanding success that the laboratory expanded its activities the following year. The second series opened in October 1936, and thirty-six composers, including William Schuman, Henry Hadley, and Lazare Saminsky, had their works presented. Interest in the forums continued to grow. In fact, late in 1937, the FMP presented the Composers' Forum-Laboratory over radio station WQXR on Saturday afternoons. The 5:30 to 6:00 weekly shows featured the works of Marion Bauer and Goddard Lieberson, among others, and the laboratory hoped to introduce the awakening American composer to the people. During the New York City forums' existence, over a thousand compositions from sixty-six different composers were heard, adding significantly to the body of American music.[15]

The success of the New York City forums encouraged the FMP to introduce the idea to other cities in the United States. Over the next three years, composers' forums opened in Philadelphia, Chicago, Detroit, Cleveland, Milwaukee, Minneapolis, Los Angeles, San Francisco, Boston, Jacksonville, and Tulsa. These composers' forums utilized the works of local residents. Boston featured New England composers, Chicago featured midwesterners, and San Francisco featured those from the West Coast. While smaller than the New York City laboratory, these forums gave unknown and local composers from all over the United States the chance to have their work performed and then critiqued by peers.[16]

Many American composers praised the forums for their activities. Some, like Roy Harris and William Schuman, saw the labs as a chance to outline the difference between European and American music. Both viewed American music as more rhythmic and quick paced, as opposed to the highly intellectual European music—American music "feels;" European music "thinks." Harold Morris enjoyed the fact that the forums brought "about the closer contact between composer and the public." Traditionally, composers had their works privately screened with little input from untrained listeners. The forums, on the other hand, introduced the American people to the composition process, and this, according to Marion Bauer, helped develop "an interest in American music on the part of many people who hardly realized that there was such a thing." Bringing "the man in the street" into the process proved invaluable to the composer, for, as William Schuman said, it inspired him to write more pieces.[17]

The labs became a training ground for the development of American music. FMP orchestras would play the successful forum compositions around the country, fulfilling its aim to give "more impetus to creative orchestra work in America than a hundred years of the kind of recognition accorded American composers by the established American orchestras." Sokoloff established a network of FMP orchestras to perform the successful works, and, within the project's first six months, Sokoloff announced that over one-third of all compositions performed by the FMP came from American composers. By April 1939, the project's orchestras had performed 6,772 American compositions.[18]

Many of these compositions came from contemporary American composers, some of whom were associated with the FMP. Sokoloff's final compilation in 1939 emphasized that of the 2,034 American composers who had their works performed, 301 were at one time employed by the FMP as musicians, conductors, or arrangers. The works of Sousa, Victor Herbert, Stephen Foster, and Henry Hadley were the most popular, followed by compositions by Ferde Grofe, Charles Sanford Skilton, M. C. Cake, and Charles Wakefield Cadman. African-American composers Clarence Cameron White and Nathanial Dett also had many of their works performed.[19] The FMP provided a forum for the premiere of new works. Paul Frederic Bowles introduced five symphonic works before the composers' forum in New York City in 1936. Virgil Thomson, who wrote the scores for the Resettlement Administration's *The Plow That Broke the Plains* and *The River,* had several pieces premiered by FMP orchestras. No orchestra would perform Ernest Bloch's 1933 *Sacred Service* until the FMP showcased it in San Francisco in 1938. Frederick P. Search conducted his choral-symphony premiere, *Rhapsody: The Bridge Builders,* with the San Francisco FMP in September 1937. These are just a few examples. But the project did not solicit works nor pay composers for their work, because, as a 1937 internal memo explained, "all works of art produced on the Federal Art Project[s] remain the property of the

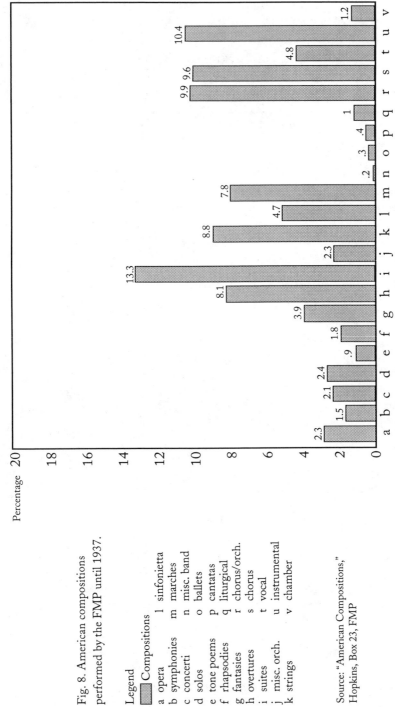

Fig. 8. American compositions
performed by the FMP until 1937.

Legend

[Compositions]

a opera   l sinfonietta
b symphonies   m marches
c concerti   n misc. band
d solos   o ballets
e tone poems   p cantatas
f rhapsodies   q liturgical
g fantasies   r chorus/orch.
h overtures   s chorus
i suites   t vocal
j misc. orch. u instrumental
k strings   v chamber

Source: "American Compositions,"
Hopkins, Box 23, FMP

Federal Government." With pressure from ASCAP and other copyright difficulties, the FMP decided it was too difficult to pay composers for each piece. Also, the project did not want to have to deal with issues of artistic freedom or problems from Congress over what was being produced. This policy did not stop the flow of compositions, as evidenced by the fact that by 1939 more than 60 percent of the American compositions performed by the project came from contemporary composers.[20]

While many nationally known composers, like Hanson and Thomson, had works performed by the FMP, the bulk of the American compositions played by the FMP's orchestras came from local, relatively unknown composers. The national office wanted the local units to solicit compositions from these composers for two reasons: first, it would introduce some composers who might not have gotten involved with the project; second, it might create a larger audience. For example, in Philadelphia, the FMP enticed locals to attend the Philadelphia Civic Symphony Orchestra's performance of over twenty Philadelphians' works during the 1937 season. The tactic worked, and the orchestra played regularly for capacity crowds.[21] The FMP's utilization of local composers and compositions was most successful in areas that lacked regular symphony music. The Oklahoma final report declared that "wherever possible, the works by Oklahoma composers [were] given preference." The state unit performed sixteen local compositions, the majority coming from composers residing in Oklahoma City. The Oregon project featured the work of eleven locals and boasted two popular world premiere performances: Dent Mowry's *At the Tomb of the Unknown Soldier* and Frederick W. Goodrich's *The Call to Worship*.[22]

One of the more difficult project tasks was to assign native conductors to its orchestras. American conductors in private employment were a rarity. The *International Musician* protested as late as 1937 that no American had been named conductor of a major symphony orchestra since Eugene Ormandy had been appointed in Philadelphia. The project wanted to give American men and women equal opportunity to conduct an orchestra on a regular basis. The FMP believed that by encouraging young conductors like Victor Alessandro, Izler Solomon, Franco Autori, Henry Aaron, Richard Horner Bales, Dean Dixon, and Ralph Rose, many of them might find jobs with American orchestras based on their project experience. Once in charge of a private symphony organization, they could then use their positions to place more American works on playbills.[23]

The FMP used its position to introduce a new generation of American-born conductors. In Oklahoma, both the Tulsa unit (1935–37) and the Oklahoma unit (1937–40) employed young American conductors.

Victor Alessandro was given the podium for the Oklahoma Symphony Orchestra at the tender age of twenty-three. The FMP administrators gave him the position because of his youth, vitality, and his "policy to perform the work of an American composer on each program." He stayed with the Tulsa unit until it disbanded in 1937. When a new unit was created in Oklahoma City, Alessandro's assistant conductor, Ralph Rose, assumed the podium. Just twenty-six years old at the time, Rose grew up in the Midwest and was seen as a local boy done good. His initial series of concerts were well received in Oklahoma City, and soon afterward he led the unit in fifty-one school concerts and an eight-city tour of Oklahoma, all before April 1938. Police Lieutenant Charles Roth was named both the conductor and music supervisor of the Toledo, Ohio, FMP orchestra. A department member for eighteen years, in his spare time Roth had conducted the private civic orchestra. The highlight of his tenure with the project came in 1936 when he led the federal orchestra before Eleanor Roosevelt at the civic auditorium. When the Illinois FMP symphony was searching for a conductor, it wanted a Chicagoan, but through Sokoloff's intervention the job went to Izler Solomon, who was not an Illinois native but had worked in the Midwest and had a good reputation in Chicago. By 1939 he had become quite well known; both *Time* and *Modern Music* commented on his able direction and ability.[24]

The project selected these and many other conductors because they would encourage a larger American musical renaissance. For this reason, Sokoloff did not ask the help of established conductors like Arturo Toscanini. When Sokoloff testified before the Sirovich committee in 1938, he explained why he had not invited the great Toscanini to conduct. "He is not an American," the national director said, and "until we take care of those who belong to this country, we cannot [help him]." Government monies and conductorships, Sokoloff concluded, "should go for Americans first."[25]

During its existence, the project did as much for the American musician, composer, or conductor than any other federal organization before or after its tenure. By 1937 even the president sided with the FMP policy of favoritism toward the neglected American composer, indicating that "the good work will go on until every symphony orchestra in the land includes in its program a fair representation of American compositions." At the same time, FDR's lack of personal commitment to either the FMP or the American composer was an indication that, outside of speeches, he would have little to do with their promotion.[26]

In order to preserve what it had accomplished, the FMP undertook the task of listing every American composer, their compositions, performances, and critiques from colonial times until 1939. Although it never reached completion, the Library of Congress holds the Index of American Composers, which contains 7,300 titles of compositions from 2,258 American composers, on over 20,000 index cards. The goal of the Index, to outline the breadth of America's musical culture, was also the FMP's.

In return for the FMP's assistance, many classical musicians agreed with *San Francisco Chronicle* critic Alfred Frankenstein when he praised the project for "giving the American composer a break." For perhaps the first time, many American works were being performed by orchestras "under an American conductor, with a guest soloist who is also an American." Jacob Weinberg wrote to Sokoloff in 1935 to praise the FMP's policy of performing American compositions: "This policy is undoubtedly of greatest importance for the growth of our musical culture." The composer of *Shanewis* and *Thunderbird Suite,* Charles Wakefield Cadman believed that "the Federal Music Project . . . is serving as a vital stimulating factor . . . in the perpetuation and furtherance of a high type of music which is so important to any nation's cultural and ethical progress. A vital musical evolution has taken place in every community it has reached. I am for the Federal Music Project with all my heart and soul." America was developing an acceptance, many believed, for the better music. There was a certain defensiveness in many of these comments, particularly in light of the fact that another musical force, jazz, was undergoing yet another revival in the form of big band swing music. Composers, like Sokoloff and the FMP, hoped the momentum they had created for art music would continue to grow. William Grant Still, who had once been a jazz arranger, said in 1937 that the project had to continue to lay the basis for "the formation of a remarkable culture—a culture as fine as any possessed by the ancients."[27]

SEVEN

EXPOSURE, NOT EQUALITY: BLACK MUSICIANS AND THE FMP

One of the clearest examples of the FMP's difficulty with the ideals of the democratic, pluralistic vision promoted by the New Deal can be seen by examining its employment of African-American musicians. A government agency like the FMP believed it had a certain responsibility to all the unemployed, not just to the white majority, and from the outset the FMP sought to employ, publicize, and include black Americans in the whole of its national agenda. African Americans received the opportunity to create, perform, and conduct as the FMP employed many black musicians as part of its work relief efforts. Yet, these same musicians were often segregated, stereotyped, and often denied the same credibility and pay of their white FMP cohorts.

For many whites, the Crash had ruined their lives and made them poor. For much of the black population, however, the poor far outnumbered the middle and upper classes before the Crash, and the status of those left behind remained unchanged. For much of the United States' black population, the worst depression in the country's history had a leveling social effect. "The country had been in the throes of the Depression for two years," Maya Angelou wrote of Stamps, Arkansas, "before the Negroes in Stamps knew it. I think that everyone thought the Depression, like everything else, was for whitefolks, so it had nothing to do with them."[1]

The northward migration begun by the southern blacks during and after World War I continued during the 1930s. In the cities where they migrated, the depression had already forced one-quarter of the population out of work and afforded little opportunity for new employment. According to a National Urban League study done in 1931, "Negroes . . . are suffering more severely than white people in the present crisis of unemployment" with black jobless rates sometimes running four to five times

greater than their population percentage. In industrial centers like Detroit, Philadelphia, and Chicago, black male unemployment during the
early 1930s ran upwards to 60 percent. Blacks who qualified for relief
ranged from Pittsburgh's 32 percent to New Orleans's 67 percent. Workers outnumbered jobs, and discriminatory hiring practices made black
employment even more difficult. As Harvard Sitkoff notes in *A New Deal
for Blacks,* "On the eve of The New Deal, a specter of starvation haunted
black America."[2]

Despite this, the depression may have actually eased some racial tensions, as economic problems overshadowed the race question. While de
facto and de jure segregation remained a part of the daily experience for
most African Americans, during the 1930s many experienced increased
opportunities in health, housing, and education. A shift in politics also
took place by 1933–34, when the majority of black voters went Democratic. As late as 1932, 70 percent of the African-American vote had gone
to the Republican Party. Norma Daoust points out in her study of the
voting shift in Providence, Rhode Island, that because of the Democratic
machine's ability to dispense patronage to the local black community,
combined with the increased relief efforts of the New Deal, blacks turned
away from the GOP and toward Roosevelt. By 1936 the Democrats captured 75 percent of the black vote, largely due to the benefits of Roosevelt's
New Deal. His comfortable manner, physical handicap, and ability to
make everyone feel personally involved also endeared Roosevelt to the
black community.[3]

However, the initial years of the Roosevelt administration did little
to ease the economic or social problems that black Americans faced in
the 1930s. FDR's lack of activity on racial matters surprised few, for in
the past he had shown little concern for such issues. Much like the president whose name he invoked throughout his tenure—Lincoln—Roosevelt's
commitment to the black American tended toward symbolic gestures over
active legislation. The point here is not to suggest that either Lincoln or
FDR were unsympathetic and inactive, but, given their times, their par-
ties, and their Congresses, their gestures did little in and of themselves
to attack the specific problems of race relations in America. The Hundred Days legislation failed to address the black American population,
as the emphasis on local "grass roots" control permitted discrimination.
The National Industrial Recovery Act (NRA) was, in the words of General Hugh Johnson, "a complete failure," as the industrial codes made it
possible for black workers to earn less money and to be restricted to unskilled jobs. To many blacks, according to a Virginia newspaper, the
NRA's Blue Eagle looked more like "a predatory bird instead of the feath-
ered messenger of happiness." The black press suggested that the initials

NRA might actually mean "Negro Removal Act." John Davis of the *New Republic* pointed out that the agency fostered segregation in the work- place and entrenched the "belief that Negro labor is inherently . . . less effi- cient." He reported one black textile worker as saying, "Before the Blue Eagle we was just one-half living, but now we is only one-third living." Davis's attack was followed by a poem entitled "Ballad of Roosevelt," by Langston Hughes. In it, Hughes paints a desperate picture of the suffer- ing incurred by the nation's blacks and chastises FDR for his continual promises but little action:

> 'Cause the pot's still empty
> and the cupboard's still bare,
> And you can't build a bungalow
> Out o' air—
> Mr. Roosevelt, Listen!
> What's the matter here?[4]

Discriminatory practices occurred in other New Deal agencies, such as the Agricultural Adjustment Administration (AAA), Tennessee Val- ley Authority (TVA), Farm Credit Administration, and Resettlement Administration. The TVA's model town of Norris, Tennessee, for ex- ample, housed black workers in temporary barracks while their white counterparts stayed in substantial homes. The TVA's vision of the fu- ture placed blacks within the same subordinate roles they had tradition- ally occupied. The Federal Housing Administration encouraged residen- tial segregation by detailing in its operations manual the negative effects of desegregated housing. Before 1936, blacks made up only 6 percent of the CCC rolls, despite the fact that their unemployment percentage was double that of whites. In many southern areas, where blacks were the unemployed majority, CCC rolls still carried twice as many whites as blacks. Within his own cabinet, FDR had only one staunch supporter of equal rights, Secretary of the Interior Harold Ickes. The activities of the first New Deal did little for the black American and has led one observer to label the era "an old Deal, a Raw Deal."[5]

The beginning of the second New Deal in 1935 signaled a change in FDR's attitude toward black Americans. Although never committing himself until 1941's Fair Employment Practices Act, he began to use a variety of techniques to encourage more minority participation in the New Deal's programs. His wife, Eleanor, proved one of his best tactical weapons to support yet not commit to the black population. In black newspapers and magazines, photos and stories about the first lady were common- place as she endorsed civil rights activities, the abolition of poll taxes, and a tough antilynching law. She attended the conventions of the NAACP and other black organizations, raised money, ate and mingled with black Americans. These activities received widespread coverage and enabled blacks to view her as an ally near the president. In fact, the NAACP's Roy Wilkins concluded that it was because of Eleanor, not Franklin, that the black communities supported the Democratic Party.[6]

Spurred by Mrs. Roosevelt's activity, others within the administration began taking the initiative. Francis Perkins of the Department of Labor started to insist that CCC rolls include more black youths, and by 1938 their numbers increased to 11 percent. During the CCC's nine-year term, about one-quarter of a million blacks served, 10 percent of whom worked in integrated camps. The National Youth Administration's (NYA) head, Aubrey Williams, used his position to pay equal wages and reserve at least 10 percent—and later 20 percent—of the NYA's rolls for black students. Other federal agencies followed suit, actively lobbying for increased black participation in government works agencies. Because the post-1935 New Deal stressed federal administration, the Washington staffs had more control over employment practices and loans, and they used this power to increase black participation. This activity allowed Roosevelt, in a burst of optimism, to announce in 1936 that the United States had "no forgotten men and no forgotten races."[7]

The WPA, the largest of the post-1935 agencies, was under a presidential stipulation that it not discriminate because of race or creed. FDR spoke plainly about equal employment before the NAACP in 1938, saying "that no democracy can long survive which does not accept as fundamental to its very existence the recognition of the rights of its minorities." Harry Hopkins, who strongly supported equal opportunity, wanted his agency to be nondiscriminatory because he understood that blacks "lost out faster than white workers. A fact surprising to no one familiar with the chronic insecurity of [blacks], or the small margin upon which they are forced to live." This inequality was not limited to unskilled labor, as educational opportunities for blacks also proved inadequate. In a speech at Columbia Teachers College, Hopkins stressed that "special emphasis has been laid on making WPA services available to this race" by employing and enrolling blacks in educational projects.[8]

Within the WPA, Hopkins wanted fair hiring practices. Any news of discrimination drew Hopkins's ire and quick retribution. Studies have shown that most blacks employed on WPA projects did receive proper job classifications and earned equal wages. In his study of WPA operations in Mississippi, Larry Whatley concludes that because the local administrators understood that the federal government allocated the money and wanted racial harmony, the locals promoted harmony as well. By

1939 over one million blacks were employed by the WPA, which led to a strong sense of voter loyalty. As Studs Terkel records one worker as saying, "It made us [blacks] feel like there was something we could do in the scheme of things."[9]

The support of the WPA and other agencies built a strong base of support for the New Deal among the nation's black population. When anti–New Dealer Edgar G. Brown attacked the New Deal in the Washington newspapers in 1942 for its desertion of the black American, Congressman Arthur Mitchell of Illinois responded without hesitation. As an African American, Mitchell viewed FDR's administration as a positive step toward racial equality. "It is not necessary," he told Congress, "for me to stand here and defend the New Deal in its attitude toward the Negro . . . [for] it is known throughout the world that under this administration the Negro has been given the best and highest opportunity that he has received since he came to the land of America." Representative Mitchell outlined the positive nature of the WPA, PWA, NYA, and a host of other federal agencies.[10]

Congressman Mitchell saved special commendation for the arts projects, and cited their efforts to both employ and introduce African-American culture to America. This, he argued, proved that "the Negro has a greater opportunity in this country than he has anywhere else in the world." Within the Music Project, 1,774 blacks out of a total of 14,922 musicians were employed during 1935. The figure represents almost 12 percent of the total FMP employment rolls for the year and corresponds to general population percentages. Throughout the FMP's existence, black employment rarely deviated from this percentile. For comparison, in 1937 the FWP employed only 106 African Americans out of a total work force of 4,500. The majority of those 106 were employed in New York City, Chicago, and New Orleans.[11]

The FMP formed black concert units from coast to coast. New York and California boasted three all-black units each, while Illinois had four; Ohio, Pennsylvania, and Missouri had two, and seven other states had at least one. In most cases these units were outside the larger project umbrella. For example, the Colored Orchestra of Milwaukee played in 15 cities throughout Wisconsin from 1936 to 1939 and averaged over 1,248 persons per concert. But they rarely played for whites, and when they did they did so under segregated conditions. The FMP's black units would usually perform before black audiences. Despite this, the black units were still a valuable asset to the FMP, not only for administrative and aesthetic reasons but also for economic ones—the black units were profitable.[12]

The major problem facing the project was part of its paradox, namely, how to expose the black FMP units to the white community without upsetting traditional racial attitudes. In music itself racial barriers were strongly entrenched by the time of the FMP's creation. While ragtime and jazz had exposed some of the musical contributions of African Americans, the American people by and large were reluctant to recognize this cultural addition. It would take the swing revolution, which deemphasized the blackness of jazz, to bring about some racial parity and acceptance in the 1930s. Led by Benny Goodman, Glenn Miller, Artie Shaw, and Tommy Dorsey, the swing bands achieved great popularity using arrangements by African Americans, including Fletcher Henderson, Duke Ellington, and Erskine Hawkins. Although swing came from African-American jazz and its sound was developed by black bands in the late 1920s and early 1930s, the originators, like Duke Ellington and Count Basie, who were also part of the swing movement, earned about half as much money as their white counterparts. Black musicians, in white or black bands, also earned less than their white colleagues. To its credit, swing did encourage racial integration and helped introduced many great black musicians to the American people, but the music, while rooted in black jazz, remained in the cultural control of whites.[13]

For the African-American composer of "serious" music, the obstacles to success were even more severe than they were for jazz musicians. Few blacks could afford to attend the expensive white conservatories, and those who did graduate from a college obtained low-paying teaching jobs at segregated colleges or high schools. Left with few alternatives, the black composer dedicated less time to his art. According to Carl Diton, these underprivileged yet talented composers lacked the patronage reserved for white composers from white supporters, and they went without and lived on one-third less. Clarence Cameron White thought it was a tragic situation for young blacks eager to contribute to the development of an American musical vernacular. They faced, he believed, the white patron's de facto discrimination.[14]

For the cultivated black musician, there were few opportunities to perform in white orchestras. Gifted black violinist Clarence Cameron White and pianist Hazel Harrison never performed before a white audience during the 1930s. A more familiar episode of racial discrimination in music occurred in 1939 when the Daughters of the American Revolution refused to allow Marian Anderson to sing in Constitutional Hall before a white audience. Even though she was recognized as a great singer around the world, her color made it impossible for her to perform before whites in the United States. *Musical America* joined with Eleanor Roosevelt and others to label the action as un-American. Anderson's career, they believed, symbolized "what it means to be born in America, where there are no oppressed minorities, no second class citizens."[15] Editorials aside, in

American musical society, both popular and serious, blacks did not receive equal opportunity to perform, learn, or earn.

The FMP's administrators did recognize the value of utilizing blacks within its organization. As a profession, musicians represented a significant and respected part of the black community. According to census data, almost 10 percent of the total number of blacks involved in professional employment were musicians. Only two other groups passed them in numbers—clergymen and teachers. The encouragement of this respected profession might quell some of the criticism leveled against the arts projects for coddling the wealthy, elite artist and would continue to build support for the New Deal.[16] In a larger sense, allowing blacks onto project rolls helped prove one of the central aims of the FMP—the rediscovery of American culture. Sokoloff, who took his cue from Hopkins, declared that the "WPA music projects are for all sexes, creeds, races, and colors. . . . Thoroughly American in spirit, the FMP considers only ability to perform and discriminates against no race."[17]

The FMP wanted to show that it believed the compositions by Still, White, Diton, and Handy were important parts of America's cultural heritage. But it was the black musicians' ability as lyric dramatic artists that especially pleased the FMP. All black performances of *Il Trovatore*, *Fra Diavolo*, and Verdi's *Aida* were popular and profitable on both coasts. The FMP choruses sang traditional Negro spirituals, while the popular dance bands attracted attention in Richmond, Virginia, Omaha, Nebraska, Toledo, Ohio, and Oakland, California. Sokoloff encouraged the units in all project areas to make themselves more appealing to the minorities in their towns.[18]

The black projects' popularity guaranteed their continuing existence. The American Folk Singers, a Massachusetts black unit, thrilled Boston-area audiences with spirituals and choral works by Brahms, Tchaikovsky, and Dvořák. The Miami WPA Black Choir of one hundred voices sang Jubilee hymns on Easter morning to untold thousands of Miami church-goers in 1936. In New York City, the Juanita Hall Melody Singers' popularity served as a rebuff to anyone who charged that the FMP was engaged in race discrimination. According to the educational division, in the summer of 1935, Hall and nineteen other black singers auditioned for the FMP. "They were in desperate need," the report read. "Some were so weak from hunger that Miss Hall doubted whether they would be able to sing." Because of the unusual nature of the group (rarely did the FMP allow group auditions), it took eleven weeks before the Melody Singers were added to the rolls. Once aboard, the group became one of the most popular of all New York City WPA performers.[19]

In the South, the black units also met with widespread approval. Vir-

The Michigan W. P. A. Music Project

Announces

The Lucy Thurman Music Hour

WITH THE

Michigan W. P. A. Concert Band

CARROLL McINTYRE, Conductor

DOROTHY GREEN

SOPRANO

EDGAR YOUNG

Cornet Soloist

LUCY THURMAN BRANCH Y.W.C.A.

THE DATES:	DEDICATED TO
Sunday, March 9th,	Marian Anderson
" " 16th,	Nathaniel Dett
" " 23rd,	Paul Robeson
" " 30th,	Clarence Cameron White

All Programs at 2 p. m.

Admission Free

Fig. 9. Concert announcement, Detroit, Michigan. The FMP tried to engrain itself into the community by showcasing African-American composers and performers. Courtesy of the National Archives.

ginia FMP director Wilfred Pyle acknowledged the Richmond Colored Orchestra as the most "cosmopolitan" of all the units and applauded the musicians' versatility. The colored orchestra could play Beethoven and swing in the same concert, and it appealed to both "high-brow" and "low-brow" audiences. Formed in 1935, by 1937 the Richmond unit had given 249 performances before more than 66,442 persons. The Kentucky Spiritual Singers crowded local auditoriums and churches with an average of nearly 1,000 persons per show. In fact, the unit proved so popular that efforts were made to secure a recording contract for the singers. The North Carolina black units, under the direction of Nell Hunter, presented a "March of Song" festival in Charlotte in late 1936 that depicted the progress of black Americans. These Charlotte singers presented one of the "most elaborate programs ever undertaken" and attracted large and enthusiastic audiences. The selections ranged from the primitive "Bamboula Dance" to the spiritual "Swing Low" and the modern "Exhortation."[20]

In the Midwest, the black unit's repertoire included both popular and orchestral music. In Chicago's *Music News,* critic Cooper Holsworth identified the Negro Dixie Orchestra as one of the outstanding musical organizations in the whole city. The band's talent lay in its ability to "jazz" up classics with trumpet solos, cross rhythms, clarinet cadenzas, and tinhats. On the day Holsworth visited, the band warmed up with the *William Tell* Overture, and he reported that "they were off on a spree of dizzy glory." Holsworth advised his readers to attend a swing concert by the Dixie Orchestra, no matter the distance they had to travel. The white Detroit Civic Symphony broke new ground in 1938, when two young Chicago men, Joseph Cole, a baritone, and Clyde Winkfield, a pianist, became the first black soloists with the orchestra. The next year the orchestra encouraged all "the colored citizens of Detroit" to attend a special presentation of William Grant Still's *Afro American Symphony* at a local high school.[21]

Farther west, in Nebraska, the Omaha FMP band attracted both swing and spiritual audiences. At the 1938 Grand Island Harvest of Harmony celebration, the black unit shared top billing with the Omaha Concert Orchestra and received glowing reviews for its ability to swing one minute and symphonize the next. The celebration climaxed when the black FMP unit provided the music for a jitterbug contest before five thousand onlookers. In Omaha itself, the black concert band regularly filled school auditoriums for its performances. The people of Parsons, Kansas, also had a popular black music project, with the high school auditorium serving as the podium for the first concert by the black students of the FMP educational unit there.[22]

On the West Coast, the black music units achieved great notoriety. The August 1938 concert conducted by William Grant Still drew the highest attendance for the FMP in the Los Angeles area for that season, and the gate receipts, $888.53, were the largest of the year. The concert featured Still's *Lennox Avenue* and the FMP Colored Chorus. RCA later signed this same Carlyle Scott–conducted FMP chorus to a recording deal. As a capstone to the group's success, their contribution to the Federal Theater's production of *Run Li'l Chillun,* which began in July 1938 and continued for 114 performances, enabled the FMP to share in the show's $19,787 gate receipts. For an FMP unit of any color, this amount was extremely large. Another California unit presented a successful black production of *Fra Diavolo* at the outdoor Greek Theater after a promising season in Los Angeles theaters. Up the coast in Oakland and San Francisco, many viewed the Colored Chorale of Oakland's FMP as the most interesting and professional of the Bay Area's music activities.[23]

Much akin to the rest of the FMP, the large scope of the black performances made the project an important contributor to the exposure of the African-American musical heritage. Aside from performances in larger cities like New York, Boston, Philadelphia, Chicago, and Los Angeles, the FMP sponsored all-black units in smaller towns and cities. The residents of Hope, Arkansas, were privileged to get an FMP all-black unit in 1937, and the unit, which also taught music, had four FMP members and 134 students. Both accomplished and budding musicians gave regular and popular performances in the Hempstead County, Arkansas, area. North Carolina's chorus and Ralph Isaac's twenty-one-piece Kansas City all-Negro FMP unit also gave frequent, popular performances. Both received widespread support, praise, and acknowledgment for their musical productivity and versatility. The New Orleans unit sponsored an annual Negro Music Festival in June, and when in 1936 the National Colored Sunday School Congress met in that city for its convention, the FMP's all-black unit provided the daily entertainment. In Richmond, Virginia, the Negro concert orchestra performed for schools, hospitals, orphanages, YWCAs, prisons, old-age homes, and the War Widows group. The three-hundred-voice Savannah, Georgia, unit gave spiritual concerts in local black churches. In Duncan, Oklahoma, the FMP organized a black music educational unit designed to give free lessons to "adult Negroes who would otherwise be unable to study music." Both Detroit and Akron boasted of their black FMP projects, identifying them as among the most popular of their cities' musical activities.[24]

Many of the programs given by these black units stressed patriotism and community worth. Project concerts usually began with the "Star Spangled Banner" and concluded with "America the Beautiful." In St. Petersburg, Florida, the black FMP chorus scheduled evenings of nationalistic music throughout the month of February 1938, in conjunction with the nationwide celebration of Washington's birthday and the American Music Festival. In Albuquerque, New Mexico, the all-black Federal Glee Club mixed patriotic songs with "Go Down Moses," "Dixie," and "Carry Me Back to Ol' Virginny" before the appreciative residents of the United States Veterans Hospital.[25]

Despite their popularity, scope, and patriotism, the FMP also stereotyped and segregated its black units from the rest of the project. Regardless of the positive impetus provided by Hopkins, Aubrey Williams, and Eleanor Roosevelt, the black American in the 1930s could expect only a certain amount of equality. In the musicians' unions, from which the project had taken some direction, the policy of segregation was firmly entrenched. The first "colored" local of the AFM was formed in 1902 in Chicago, and by the early 1940s over fifty other separate locals had formed across the United States, many of them in the North.[26] While some hoped the FMP could destroy the racial barriers in music, stereotyping dominated any effort to detail the black contribution to the musical culture. A critic in St. Paul, Minnesota, proved an excellent example as he waxed enthusiastic over FMP involvement with black musicians. "For years," he wrote, "I have listened to speeches about the democratization of music, many of them made by people who hadn't the faintest idea how to set about its achievement. And now the thing has happened, almost overnight, through the agency of a project . . . so wise, so civilized, so humane that most of us can only wonder why it wasn't undertaken long ago." The writer added that "nothing was as moving as hearing 'Let My People Go' sung by members of a race whose physical bondage is still a thing of living memory." This portrayal was a standard one for the black unit being publicized by a white critic—the black units were seen as talented, but should be left within their own domain. The Vicksburg, Mississippi, black FMP unit serves as another example of stereotyping. While recognized in the area as one of the most popular choruses, reviewers characterized their performances by emphasizing how these "Joyous Negroes," using the rhythm "so typical of the Negro race," created an "atmosphere of the Deep South that could not have been imparted in any other way."[27]

One of the most prevalent of the stereotypes involved the black American's putative inherent love of song. The Cambridge-based black FMP American Folk Singers were respected throughout Massachusetts; their well-attended concerts inspired patrons to indiscriminate applause. Yet, when describing conductor Thomas Johnson, race superseded praise. Portrayed as a "worthy example of his musical race," he, "like so many of his light-hearted, music-loving people, loved to sing." Many of the young blacks enrolled in Mississippi's Music Education unit needed to be taught that the "spiritual is the heritage of their race," according to the state's administrators. Being young, they preferred the popular music of the radio, and the educational unit impressed upon the young black musicians the distinction of their race—the spiritual. Once the young students adopted their racial ancestry, the educational unit's methods proved a "splendid example of what a little of the right sort of training will do for a group of music loving people."[28]

The stereotyping could be even more elaborate. Not only could black Americans sing, but their performances conjured up an image of their subservience and subordination. "Southerners in the audience," read a *Las Cruces (N.Mex.) Sun* review of an all-black project chorus at a local church, "needed only to close their eyes and vision cotton fields with the sound of the Negro workers coming sweetly over the hoary fields." Interestingly enough, one of the regular engagements of the FMP's Richmond, Virginia, black concert orchestra was at the Confederate Old Ladies Home.

Sometimes the white units tried to feature black music, as when the Oklahoma City Federal Orchestra, a white unit, played the blues to local audiences. Normally, a reviewer wrote, the blues concerned a "negro girl . . . couched in a corner in a bedraggled print dress . . . damp as moss from bawling over the guy who took a run-out powder on her." The Oklahoma Federal Orchestra tried to retain the sadness of the blues, the review continued, while adding dignity to the score. In Louisiana, state director Rene Salomon believed symphonic music was unattractive to black Americans because of their ignorance. In order to capture these music-loving folk, he organized a festival on the black side of town where the "typical 'nigger' [could] attend, either in shirtsleeves or overhauls."[29]

Racial stereotyping was only part of the problem; segregation was the other. In the North, the de facto segregation forced the black FMP to play for blacks in black neighborhoods. Occasionally, black FMP units crossed the color line to play for whites, usually as part of a greater musical extravaganza. The black units received frequent requests to perform spirituals, yet always as a part of a bigger event. William Haddon, the state director for the Massachusetts FMP, attempted in late 1936 to break up the black spiritual units and place many of their members into the white choral groups. Boston's NAACP president, Irwin Ponch, protested, believing that the transferred blacks would only be used as token performers. While it might seem that Haddon planned to integrate, the blacks in these new choral units were set to appear separate from the rest of the choral group, and they were to participate only when singing Negro spirituals. NAACP pressure forced Haddon to scrap the idea. Wisconsin allowed its black federal dance band to participate in National Music Week if it would perform "Negro Spirituals and Old Southern Melodies." In New York City, the audition board took great pains to point out that it had lowered the audition standards to allow the Juanita Hall Melody Singers to perform.[30]

The black FMP units faced much stronger segregationist tendencies in the South. Oklahoma's music educational unit set up two hundred separate music education units throughout the state in order to comply both with Oklahoma statutes for segregated music schools and with the United States Office of Education mandate that black music schools be

Fig. 10. Jubilee Singers of Chicago, James Mundy, conductor. While the FMP was quick to utilize African-American musicians, usually it preferred these musicians to perform for their own people or within the racial boundaries of the era. Courtesy of the Illinois State Historical Library.

equal to the white schools. To further complicate matters, the Oklahoma FMP also established segregated audition boards for black applicants, based on the belief that their talents would be inferior and more raw. Oklahoma was not alone in this activity, as most states in the South established two FMP educational and audition units, and some went even further by submitting to Washington separate monthly reports from both the white and the black units.[31]

But the black FMP units were popular, and the southern FMP administrators quickly made arrangements to allow whites to attend their performances. A section of the hall or auditorium would be reserved for the white patrons. Usually, as in a 1937 Tampa performance, whites held reserved floor seats while blacks were restricted to balconies. Nell Hunter's popular North Carolina FMP chorus performed for over seven hundred people, including two hundred whites seated in a special roped-off front section, in Asheville, North Carolina, in September 1937. The Norfolk, Virginia, black orchestra proved so popular that the Norfolk Symphony Orchestral Association made an effort in late 1936 to allow blacks to join and attend concerts. The organization wanted eight hundred black members, and for a season-ticket price of two dollars the black members could attend all performances and view the orchestra from the reserved balcony. The black FMP unit responded accordingly, reserving a special place in its audience for white patrons. In New Mexico, the administration of the FMP and the residents of the town of Roswell needed a larger hall for the black unit to perform, as the small auditorium did not allow adequate space to separate the races. This was not unusual for the region at the time; the racially mixed swing bands that toured the South in the 1940s faced similar seating arrangements.[32]

While the FMP did not give equal treatment to the blacks on their payrolls, some statistical observations reveal that the FMP gave the black musician opportunities to play music and the black urban dweller opportunities to hear music. While migration to the North accelerated after 1919, by the time of the WPA's creation, the South still contained three times as many black Americans. In Mississippi, according to the 1930 census, blacks represented 50.2 percent of that state's total population. Other southern states' percentages ranged from 16.9 percent in Maryland to 45.6 percent in South Carolina. Largest among the northern and midwestern states, New Jersey's black population accounted for 5.2 percent and Ohio registered 4.7 percent.

These percentages are important when considering FMP activity. California and New York state had three black units each, yet the percentage of blacks in the states accounted for only 1.4 and 3.3 percent of the population respectively. Illinois had four black units for 4.3 percent of that state's total population. In Massachusetts, Wisconsin, Nebraska, and New Mexico, the popular black units performed for 1.2, 0.4, 1.0, and 0.7 percent of each state's total population respectively. Yet, in the South, only Florida, North Carolina, and Virginia had active black units. Other states may have had small (three to five) educational FMP units, which did not give regular performances. In both the North and South the FMP organized around urban areas. In a state like New Mexico, for example, this meant that the black FMP units in Roswell and Albuquerque, which usually played only before members of their own race, performed for a possible total of 2,850 people in the state—0.7 percent of the population. Yet, the 793,861 blacks spread throughout South Carolina went without a unit.

In total, the employment percentage of the FMP for blacks hovered near 12 percent. But most of the blacks employed by the FMP worked in areas where the total population percentage fell far below the national average. In essence, in accordance with their state population density and percentile, black participation in the FMP in terms of performer to possible audience equaled or bettered the white units.[33]

Even though stereotyped and segregated, many of the black musicians agreed with Chicago musician William Everett Samuels when he said that "the WPA job was crucial" to his being able to support his wife and three children.[34] The black units of the FMP proved their musical worth time and again to the state administrators. Their popularity and versatility made them one of the few units to turn a profit, albeit a small one. The black units also never turned their backs on the federal agency, performing loyally at every occasion. Their repertoires remained American whether they played spirituals, slave songs, or swing. And, in spite of the era's forced segregation and racism, the blacks in the FMP proved themselves valuable to America as musicians, performers, economic units, and, most significant, as citizens.

EIGHT

STEPDAUGHTERS OF ORPHEUS: WOMEN MUSICIANS AND THE FMP

"WPA music projects are for all sexes," Nikolai Sokoloff announced in 1937. "Thoroughly American in spirit," he continued, "the FMP considers only ability to perform . . . [and] women play along side of men in the orchestras."[1] When the arts projects were created in 1935, Hopkins instructed that they give special consideration to the plight of the unemployed woman artist. By 1936, over 27 percent of the Federal Theater and Art Projects' employees were women, and the Writers' Project included over 40 percent women. But what about the Music Project? What were its policies toward women musicians, conductors, and composers?

The problem for the FMP was a complicated one, for it had to battle traditional opposition to women musicians, historical stereotypes of feminine frailty, and simple economic resistance. The project and its administrators proceeded cautiously in hiring women and never employed more than the 1936 high of 16 percent. Yet, the exposure the FMP provided to many women musicians, composers, and conductors broke new ground. In fact, many of the sexual barriers that prevented women from participating in music were weakened with FMP aid. Women composers' works were seriously considered for the first time, women conductors held the podium before male orchestras with regularity, and women musicians performed alongside men in many of the first sexually integrated orchestras. The FMP paradox, then, is that, on one hand, the project did not do enough for women musicians during the depression era, but, on the other hand, the FMP also made great strides toward the acceptance of women as musical equals.

While conventional histories have ignored the role of women in the New Deal era, Susan Ware, Winifred Wandersee, and others credit the depression era with "propel[ling] many women into new patterns of behavior that might not have occurred otherwise."[2] The economic dislocation of the era helped win the acceptance of women into society. While the government programs instituted under FDR reinforced traditional women's work, they also, according to Wandersee, "opened more doors than [they] closed."[3] While the era lacked strong and coherent feminist activity, women's roles expanded into areas previously restricted to men, including music. The depression provided an excellent opportunity for women to enter the musical field, as the lack of economic incentive made music a less desirable career for men. The undersupply of male musicians allowed for the acceptance of women into the musical realm.[4]

The prevailing attitude toward women musicians during the first third of the century held that they had neither the physical nor intellectual attributes necessary to perfect the more masculine and complicated horns and strings used in an orchestra. As Craig H. Roell, in his analysis of the social effects of the piano industry from 1890 to 1940, suggests, musical education for women, especially piano instruction, was designed not to cultivate performance virtuosi, but to aid in the feminization process. For women in the Victorian era, music was strictly within the "cult of domesticity." "Women cannot possibly play brass instruments and look pretty," opined the *Musical Standard* in 1904. This statement came in a response to the AFL-affiliated Musicians' Union of New York City when it granted women admission into its fold in 1903. While many women hoped this precedent would create more jobs for female musicians, most of the rank and file held firm to the belief that women could not withstand the rigors of musical work. Except for the harp and teaching, women supposedly lacked the proper skills to become serious musicians.[5]

This attitude prevailed well into the 1920s. When *Etude* dedicated its November 1929 issue to "Women in Music," it argued that music for women, when played on the piano or harp, was a "means of preserving hallowed life ideals . . . without which humankind could not survive." Holding to the traditional vision of women as higher principled moral guides to the nation, by playing music, women only enhanced their natural beauty. In the same *Etude* issue, an article entitled "What Great Music Owes to Women" concluded that behind every great male composer a woman contributed to his art by being his lover, friend, cook, and maid servant.[6]

While the male-dominated music field remained closed to women, some changes took place in the 1920s. The number of women musicians and teachers of music fell after a 1910 high of 84,478, or 60 percent of all workers in this occupation, to 72,678 in 1920. But three new conservatories, the Eastman School, Curtis Institute, and Juilliard, admitted women on equal status with men, and more female musicians entered the marketplace. As a result, by 1930 the percentage of women in musical fields increased by 9.5 percent from 1920. According to V. F. Calverton, in an essay on careers for women that appeared in 1929, social work was the only field that had more women members than musicians or teachers of music. Despite the high numbers, the percentage of women as part of the total work force in music actually declined by 7 percent from 1920, indicating that more men had also entered the field. By 1930, then, more women musicians faced fewer opportunities in music.[7]

The economic collapse of 1929 forced many women out of work. The Women's Bureau estimated in January 1931 that over 2,000,000 women were unemployed. The crisis exerted considerable social pressure on women not to work or develop a career. A poll from the era details that 82 percent of the American people and 75 percent of the nation's women believed that during the crisis women should stay at home and not work, perhaps making their best contribution by preserving the family. Yet, when FDR became president in 1933, he asked then-FERA administrator Harry Hopkins to hold a special conference at the White House in November 1933 to address women's issues. Here, Hopkins admitted that "women as a group have had less attention than any other unemployed group" and pledged his support "to care for the unemployed women."[8]

But early New Deal efforts fell short of meeting women's employment needs. The NRA codes enabled employers to pay women less than men for the same work performed. The PWA established no projects for women, and FERA provided work relief for only 8.8 percent, or 142,000 women, out of a total 1,600,000 cared for. The emergency Civil Works Administration became the first federal project to attempt placing professional women, such as educators and social workers, into jobs for which they had been trained. Ellen Woodward, Hopkins's assistant and director for Women's Work under CWA, emphasized that the government did not discriminate against women and always worked to "give equal work opportunity to both needy men and women." But by 1934 only 7.5 percent, or 300,000 women, received CWA jobs out of some 4,000,000 workers.[9]

When the WPA began, Hopkins recognized the need to incorporate women into the program. In his book *Spending to Save,* he argued that since one-fourth of those unemployed were female, they deserved as much attention as men. Hopkins showed his good faith by making Ellen Woodward the assistant administrator of the Women's Division; later, in July 1936, he made her assistant administrator of the WPA's Professional Projects.[10]

By the end of March 1936, 459,938 women appeared on WPA employment rolls. Twenty-two states, including California, Massachusetts, and South Carolina, had over 20 percent women WPA workers, but nationwide total female enrollment peaked at 16 percent. Among the women on the WPA rolls, 33 percent held positions in the professional-technical category and 32 percent held positions in the intermediately skilled category. On some individual projects women constituted an overwhelming majority of workers, such as the sewing project, with 96 percent, the canning project, with 72 percent, the educational project, with 62 percent, and units for housekeeping aids, librarians, and seamstresses.[11]

These units, which performed labor labeled "women's work" by contemporaries, accurately matched women's employment in the private sector during the 1930s. According to the 1940 census, women constituted over 75 percent of the total work force employed as educators, housekeepers, librarians, secretaries, nurses, laundry workers, and seamstresses. The WPA attempted to place women workers in projects where they would most likely find jobs in the private sector. While reinforcing traditional work habits and jobs, the WPA also gave those unemployed women jobs for which they were prepared. However, female employment in the WPA fell at least eight percentage points below the national unemployment rate, and, within the WPA itself, men were paid more than women, even if a woman was the sole breadwinner of the family.[12]

Roughly one-third of the WPA's women were part of the professional-technical division. Federal Project One employed 41 percent of the women in this division. Susan Ware points out that women received "unparalleled opportunity" in the arts projects. The Art Project, centered mainly in large urban areas, employed many women and allowed them to make a collective contribution to American art. In the Writers' Project, women contributed by directing the FWP state guidebooks projects and through other ventures. The Theater Project, headed by a woman, Hallie Flanagan, employed many women as actresses. In the Music Project, according to Ware, women were limited to only 2,253 out of 15,000 possible positions, and the project "displayed little interest in encouraging women musicians or composers." Ware also criticizes the FMP for not having an "impact on women's musical aspirations and creative development."[13]

A closer examination of the FMP reveals that the project incorporated some women into the American musical experience. Under the FMP banner, women conducted male or mixed orchestras on a regular basis, and in many orchestras the genders became integrated. In the private sector, the acceptance of women as musicians was slow in coming in the 1930s. The earliest women accepted into orchestras playing traditionally masculine instruments (horns and strings) came in the late 1930s with Helen Enser in New Orleans and in 1941 with Helen Kotas in Chicago, both in the horn sections. As late as 1970 some male conductors agreed with Zubin Mehta when he told the *New York Times* that he did not "think women should be in an orchestra." In popular music—jazz, swing, country, or pop—women fared little better, as they were used either as band fronts, singers, or as novelty items led by male bandleaders. Mary Lou Williams remembers that she was never permitted to be a permanent member of the many jazz and swing bands she played with in the 1920s and 1930s. Women were not considered part of the band unless they were the singers.[14] The FMP, while not a liberating force, aided many women musicians' drive to be accepted as American musicians.

The FMP understood that male musicians had an easier task in gaining WPA relief. Unemployed women faced a government system that favored male employment, as relief went to the primary breadwinner, which was presumed to be a man, and was restricted to one member of the family. Even if the man did not want to obtain relief and work, the wife was still ineligible. Under normal circumstances, given a choice between a man and a woman of equal skills, the man received federal work relief under the assumption that most women had husbands to take care of them. This, of course, was not always the case.[15]

In the FMP, the administrators decided to utilize women musicians in many capacities, but the project did not want to rock the musical boat too violently. One important reason the project held this attitude was because of the influence of the American Federation of Musicians. Unemployment of musicians during the depression reached phenomenal proportions, with the union estimating in 1933 that nearly two-thirds of the country's professional musicians were without work. The majority of these were men who were members of the AFM, and so when the FMP was created in 1935, it drew most of its participants from the union rolls. The AFM, while nominally open to women membership, did little to attract this large group, which by 1930 constituted 47 percent of those employed in the music profession. Especially during a difficult time like the 1930s, the AFM favored its male-led and male-controlled membership. As part of the larger American Federation of Labor, which in 1930 contained only 9 percent women, it should come as little surprise that the AFM did little for female musicians. As late as 1951, only twenty-nine out of over one thousand delegates to the AFM convention were women, and to this day no woman has occupied an AFM office.[16]

The FMP, therefore, decided that its employment of women would, according to an in-house report in 1938, "run parallel with their active interest and participation in music in the world at large." In the world at large, however, women musicians were limited to teaching music; they were not performing as musicians or as conductors. The FMP placed many women in its educational division; in fact, most of the 1,171 teachers on the project's rolls in 1938 were women.[17]

The private sector offered few opportunities for women as performance musicians. In New York City, for example, only 100 women held steady jobs in classical music, compared to over 17,000 men in the same profession. An editorial in the *New Republic* explained in 1938 that "most of the leading orchestras in the country refuse to employ" women, and most male musicians believe women should not be allowed to make music a career, even though most private piano teachers and schoolteachers of music were women.[18]

While private orchestras frowned on female participation, all 38 FMP orchestras included women as musicians. A young woman occupied the New York Civic Orchestra's concertmaster chair, while the privately funded New York Philharmonic Orchestra employed 106 musicians for its 1939–40 season, none of whom were female. Women also found employment in the many FMP concert orchestras, concert bands, chamber music ensembles, and represented one-half of the 1,255 persons employed for opera and choral work. Many other women gained employment in the violin, viola, and cello sections. Pittsburgh's unit had a woman as its first horn player, and many other FMP orchestras showcased their women members. The FMP Virginia orchestra employed four women, while in Oklahoma, Victor Alessandro's Federal Symphony Orchestra featured twenty-five female members out of a total of seventy-three, many of whom occupied positions of importance in the pit.[19]

The FMP also established an all-female orchestra; it was an employment venture and a publicity tool. The Commonwealth Women's Orchestra of Boston had the distinction of being the only WPA-funded orchestra composed entirely of women. Although led by a man—Solomon Braslavsky—the orchestra employed fifty women as musicians, qualifying it as one of the largest all-female organizations. Braslavsky, former conductor of the Vienna Symphony Orchestra, honed the Commonwealth Women into one of the most professional and popular of the WPA orchestras. Organized in 1936, it performed for New England audiences in concerts and during the summers at popular Massachusetts resorts until it was disbanded late in 1938.[20]

The competition for the job of conductor has always been among the strongest in the music field. There are always more qualified conductors than orchestras to conduct, and within the FMP the competition for these limited posts was keen. In an effort to allow all qualified participants to conduct, the FMP regularly featured "guest" conductors. Many women received their first opportunity to lead orchestras in this manner. By way of comparison, from 1890 to 1924, only six women led symphony or string orchestras. But, from 1924 to 1938, over twenty had the opportunity to conduct, most with the FMP.[21] Among women given guest conductorships with the FMP, Antonia Brico's name is among the most famous. A gifted pianist and conductor, she guided ten FMP performances, five with the Brooklyn Symphony in 1936 and five with the Bay Region Orchestra in Oakland and San Francisco. She also led a series of "dime" concerts that drew well over eight thousand persons. When the FMP orchestra was engaged to perform at the World's Fair in 1939, Brico received the baton for a performance. Her exposure with the FMP helped her in the private sector, and in August 1938 she became the first woman to conduct the New York Philharmonic.[22]

Not all of the women who conducted FMP orchestras achieved the fame of Brico, but they helped open the door for other women conductors. Ruth Kemper directed the Boston Women's Orchestra of the WPA in 1937, and, based upon this success, the Greenwich Symphony invited her to conduct. Leila Hanmer appeared as guest conductor for the Illinois Symphony Orchestra in 1936, and Mary Carr Moore led the Bay Area Orchestra in 1938. Prior to this exposure, Moore had conducted only three times, most recently in 1925. Ebba Sundstrom, one of the first women conductors to achieve notoriety as the leader of the successful Chicago Women's Symphony, wielded the baton for the FMP on many occasions. Her appearance in 1936 with the Philadelphia Orchestra proved so successful that the FMP scheduled another concert at Temple University. These appearances underscored her status, for Frederick Stock and Rudolf Ganz followed Sundstrom at the podium in the following weeks. Other women conductors included Henrietta Schumann at Syracuse, Elizabeth F. Woodson at Virginia, and Alicia McElroy at Portland, Oregon.[23] Assuming the leadership position with an orchestra helped crush an established tradition of the age. While Brico and Sundstrom found their way to the podium in the private sector, very few other talented women did.

In a 1936 radio interview, New York City FMP director Lee Pattison answered a query on the status of women composers before the FMP by saying that "women were supposed to make the home their chief interest; they were not supposed to express themselves." The FMP understood that few women were given the opportunity in the past to compose, and so it encouraged its orchestras to perform compositions from American women, considering their inclusion as an "integral part of the national plan." Under project auspices, twenty-eight women composers, among them Marian Bauer, Ruth Crawford, and Alda Astori, had their compositions performed and critiqued before the largest Composers' Forum Laboratory in New York City.[24]

Other successful performances of women's compositions took place before the FMP's American audiences. On the West Coast, Mary Carr Moore conducted the San Francisco FMP Symphony in a performance of her intermezzo from *David Rizzio* and an Indian tone poem *Kamiakin* before a capacity audience. She also had twelve other performances of her work by the FMP on the West Coast. Florence B. Smith Price achieved great notoriety when the WPA orchestra in Detroit performed several of her compositions in 1936, for she also broke the color barrier by being the first black female to have a work performed by the FMP.[25]

One successful prodigy promoted by the project came out of west Texas to have her works performed by the Illinois FMP Orchestra. Radie Britain, who, according to FMP publicity, "day-dreamed as [she] herded cattle on [her] snow-white cow pony" that one day she would hear her compositions played, impressed Assistant Administrator Florence Kerr and Sokoloff. They saw in her a perfect publicity tool to detail the project's effort to feature women and promote American compositions. The Britain song cycle premiere received much publicity, which proved quite a "stride for the spindle-legged little girl from the ranch," as the FMP claimed. Britain still credits the FMP with launching her career as an orchestral composer, writing that the project's Illinois Symphony Orchestra conductor Albert Goldberg "performed every book that I gave [him]." The FMP performed five different Britain compositions until 1940 in both Chicago and Los Angeles.[26]

The project's encouragement of women composers did not go unnoticed. A March 1937 issue of *Women in Music* reminded its readers that "it should not be forgotten that women were given no chance until relatively recent time to show whether they could bring forth a Bach or Beethoven."[27] The FMP gave women composers this opportunity. As part of the New York City Composers' Forum, women represented 14 percent of the compositions performed from 1935 to 1940. The project did not introduce to the world a female (or a male) Beethoven, but it did expose many Americans to the works of Ruth Ives, Barbara Coffin, Ruth Crawford, and others. Because of the FMP, many women musicians achieved some level of parity with their male counterparts. They became part of an orchestra once closed to them, conducted this same group, and even composed the score in some instances.

Why did the project encourage this musical participation when, in the private sector, women were denied access? There are perhaps several explanations, all of which deal with the political nature of government activities during the 1930s. First, and the most obvious reason, was that women in the musical professions accounted for over sixty thousand votes; and, since women were subject to losing their jobs sooner than men and the profession was shrinking as more men came into the field, assisting women in an area that was closed to them otherwise was simply smart politics. By giving them opportunities to perform, write, and conduct, the FMP was laying a foundation for itself, the WPA, and Roosevelt.[28]

A related reason was the influence women had on the FMP itself.

When the project began, one of the first organizations contacted for support was the National Federation of Music Teachers, headed by Mrs. John Jardine; the federation was invited to be a member of the FMP's advisory board. The four-hundred-thousand-member organization, composed mainly of women, called upon "every state and local president . . . to offer her services promptly to the Federal Music Project." Sokoloff also enlisted the aid of Mrs. Frederick Steinway and the New York–based National Music League, another large organization made up primarily of women.[29]

Within the WPA and FMP many women were in positions of authority. In fact, the organization that oversaw the activities of the arts project, the Division of Women's and Professional Projects, was headed by Ellen Woodward until 1938. She was also Hopkins's assistant administrator. When she left to join the Social Security Board, another woman, Florence Kerr, took her place in the WPA. The Music Project national staff included five women as administrative or special assistants, with three serving on Sokoloff's personal staff. Some state directors were women, like Harle Jervis of California, Fanny Brandeis of Kentucky, Jerome Sage of Mississippi, Ethel J. Edwards of Connecticut, and Helen Chandler Ryan of New Mexico. Most of the educational divisions in the FMP had women supervisors, and project audition boards usually included several women. Aside from the control being an audition board member gave women, many local advisory boards also featured women in positions of authority.[30]

Perhaps the closest female influence on Sokoloff was his assistant and former president of the National Federation of Music Clubs, Ruth Haller Ottaway. A staunch advocate of women's rights, this former president of the National Council of Women married Sokoloff during his FMP tenure. In 1938 she moved with him to Seattle as his project assignment was winding down. Ottaway believed that women should have the same musical rights as men in terms of performance, composition, and pay.[31]

This is not to suggest that women entered these musical realms unopposed; in fact, the final listing of American orchestral works recommended by the conductors to the scaled-down, state-controlled FMP in 1941 included only thirteen compositions by women, or about 4.8 percent of the total.[32] For the most part, the women allowed into the FMP as musical equals were the exception rather than the rule, as the majority of women on the project's payrolls were employed in the music teaching section.

Women musicians endured the crises of the depression years. Shunned by the private sector as biologically or intellectually inferior, most women found little prospect for employment as musicians. When the FMP organized in 1935, the administrators, many of whom were women, made a determined effort to include this large group into its national fold. While the FMP placed many women in traditional roles as teachers, harpists, or in choral groups, others received their first opportunity to play with a gender-integrated orchestra, to conduct it, and even to hear their own compositions. All of these advances, while not employing tens of thousands of women, played a significant role in the acceptance of women as musicians in America.

NINE

BRINGING IN ALL THE PEOPLE:
HISPANICS, GYPSIES, AND COWBOYS

The FMP did try to incorporate as many different groups of musicians into its fold as possible. Hoping to meet the needs of specific communities, the project wanted as many people involved as possible, but it did not want to upset traditional cultures or lower its own musical standards. This meant ethnic groups like the Magyars or Hispanics could retain their musical heritage while contributing to the FMP. However, this policy also restricted these musicians, whom the national office labeled "non-professionals," to performing only in narrowly defined situations.

When Paul Taylor advised in 1931 that the new migrant from Mexico was fast becoming a large minority, especially in the Southwest and in southern California, he addressed a phenomenon that was already a fact. By 1930 nearly 10 percent of Mexico's total population had migrated northward. The period of greatest movement took place during the 1920s, when, combined with European and Asian immigration restrictions, demand for cheap Mexican labor increased. During this ten-year span, nearly a half million Mexicans legally entered the United States, with untold thousands of others crossing illegally. By the time Taylor informed the American populace of this immigration in 1931, the percentage of Mexican immigration to the United States had dropped from its 1927 high of 20 percent of all immigrants to a mere 3 percent.[1]

The migration was not limited to the borderlands. Although Texas, New Mexico, and California accounted for most of the Mexican immigrants, the east and west north-central parts of the United States also drew a significant migration. Kansas, Illinois, and Michigan led the central regions in terms of population, but since most Mexican migrants to these regions traveled with the crops, their state of residence proved hard to pinpoint.[2]

This migratory status caused many Mexicans to feel isolated from

American society. This situation began to change by the early 1930s as Hispanic communities began to assert themselves in several American cities. Becoming more stationary, the new Mexican Americans sought the American dream while retaining their ethnic identity. Richard Garcia, in his study of the Mexican-American mind in San Antonio from 1929 to 1941, outlined the role traditional culture played in the formation of these communities. The San Antonio *Los Ricos*—those who believed that the best way to engrain themselves into American society was through hard work and good Mexican role models—advised their community to preserve its Mexican heritage in order to understand American culture better. They believed that by retaining strong ties to Mexico, closer ties to the United States could be made—"[these patriotic feelings toward the United States] . . . are logical extensions of the patriotism for your [country]." Much as Progressive reformers earlier in the century had used Old World cultural identification to assimilate the eastern and southern European immigrants into the American system, the *Los Ricos* advised their people to remember their former country's culture, but to transfer loyalty to their adopted home, the United States.[3]

As part of the WPA's general work relief efforts, the FMP included this ethnic minority in its operations. The national staff wanted these units to retain their traditional culture, to dress and play the music of the old homeland on traditional Mexican holidays. This helped the project meet one of its more general goals, namely, to define, retain, and synthesize a native American musical culture, which meant including the music of the old Southwest, which had been settled and governed by Spain long before the creation of the United States. The project recognized that, except for music of the indigenous peoples of North America, the "oldest folk music in America . . . came out of Spain."[4]

The bulk of this activity took place in the Southwest. In New Mexico, for example, the FMP created both a folk song collection unit and a live performance unit. Although the FMP collected some of the nation's folk music elsewhere, because of Sokoloff's lack of interest, it did not receive a high priority. Some units in the South collected spirituals, work songs, songs of the rivers and hills, but this work lasted only a short time and suffered from lack of direction. The New Mexico collection unit proved the exception. It collected, transcribed, and disseminated folk music, songs, and dances of the old Spanish West to teachers throughout the state. Five different publications came out of this effort from 1936 to 1941, including "Spanish-American Folk Songs of New Mexico."[5]

Based in Albuquerque, the FMP had nearly fifty employees who collected, transcribed, taught, and performed the folk music of the Southwest. In 1936 the city held a folk festival during which nearly one hun-

dred FMP employees and students gave presentations of Spanish or
Mexican musical folklore. Sponsored in cooperation with the University
of New Mexico's Hispanic studies department, these songs and dances
handed down through the generations attracted fifteen hundred enthusiastic listeners to the local gymnasium. Both the young and the old enjoyed the *Rancho Grande* and *La Golondrina* choruses. The dancers and
singers came under the direction of Lucia Rael, while Pedro Valles led
the FMP's ten-member Spanish string orchestra.[6]

Other regions also utilized Mexican folk music. One of San Antonio's
several Mexican units was called "Los Abajinos" and consisted of eight
singers who accompanied themselves on the fiddle, mandolin, and guitar. This group proved so successful in Texas that it was recorded for
permanent file in the Library of Congress. As far north as Wisconsin, a
project unit called the Spanish Serenaders performed traditional Southwest ballads for its audiences.[7]

While some folk collecting was done, most of the FMP's activity in
the Southwest concerned the traditional *Tipica* orchestra. The Texas final report gives excellent insight into the rationale and makeup of this
type of unit. When the FMP sent out the call for auditions in 1935, the
many Mexican musicians who tried out failed under Sokoloff's rigid classical guidelines. The Texas administrators stepped in to defend those
Mexican Americans who fell below federal standards and forced the national office to allow them to form three Tipicas. These orchestras were
made up entirely of Mexicans who were "all-American citizens," so as
not to break the project mandate of hiring United States citizens first.

The average project Tipica orchestra consisted of forty men dressed
in the traditional outfits of the Mexican musician. These colorful costumes of dark trousers, gold shirts, red ties, and white sombreros added
to the groups' attractiveness as they played traditional Spanish songs by
Barcelata, Alfonso, and Alvarado, among others. In addition to the regular strings, wood, and brass of any other orchestra, instrumentation consisted of five distinctively Spanish instruments: the *salterio,* an ancestor
of the country-western steel guitar, laid flat across the lap and plucked
by the fingers; the *bandolon,* the eighteen-stringed cousin of the mandolin, which provided deeper, thicker tones; and the *maracas, guiro,* and
clave for rhythm and texture. All of these musical instruments, nontraditional by federal standards, made the Tipica orchestras a popular FMP
attraction.[8]

While he accepted the Tipica orchestras' popularity, Sokoloff nevertheless lumped the musicians into what the national office labeled "novelty orchestras." These bands, which usually performed some type of
"popular" music, were designed to include, Sokoloff pointed out, all the

Fig. 11. San Antonio's Tipica Orchestra, 1936. Dressed in traditional garb, this orchestra was one of the most popular in all of Texas. Courtesy of the *Fort Worth Star-Telegram/* Summerville San Antonio.

different "types" of people who were musicians in the United States. The project's reasoning was more political than egalitarian, for while the New Mexico folk and Tipica units were allowed more artistic leeway, for example, it was because their "clientele . . . is definitely Spanish" and their support was needed for both the FMP and the New Deal.

These types of project organizations occurred in those areas that contained the largest percentage of Mexican Americans. Texas, with 700,000 Hispanic residents according to the 1930 census, had the largest project Tipica orchestras; the most popular were located in San Antonio. When the WPA first organized in the city, Mexican musicians did not register for the FMP because they believed they would not get work. But soon afterward, many asked for a transfer to the Music Project when they learned they could work as musicians. Overwhelmed with auditions, the Tipica was able to employ between 42 and 61 musicians over a ten-month period from October 1936 to August 1937. It gave numerous performances, 46 in public parks, 21 in schools, museums, churches, hotels, and anywhere else sponsorship could be found. The Tipica averaged an audience of 538 persons per concert, and the state administrators called it "one of the show pieces of San Antonio." The city of Dallas boasted its own federal Tipica orchestra of 35 pieces. El Paso's Tipica, directed by Manuel Licon, was also very popular: during a ten-month span in 1938 it gave 228 performances to almost 80,000 Texans.[9]

Other states with sizable Mexican populations also formed Tipica orchestras. New Mexico formed many units, including children's Tipica orchestras in Albuquerque and Las Vegas. The state also boasted the Hernandez Brothers, a popular guitar group from Bernalillo.[10] Arizona's FMP, which only employed 39 persons in its entire project, reserved five positions for its Filipino String Ensemble (Tipica) located in Phoenix. In Wisconsin, where only 2,396 persons of Mexican descent lived, the Spanish Serenaders of Milwaukee toured regularly before a total audience of 173,019 persons. Giving over 205 performances, this meant that 803 persons attended each show, compared to the 1,580 average of the Milwaukee Federal Orchestra's 702 shows over a three-year period.[11]

California, with the second-largest Mexican-American population, had only a few units. Perhaps this was due to the fact that there were so many of Sokoloff's classically trained musicians who were without work in the state, or that so many of those of Mexican heritage were migrant laborers in the agricultural valleys. Nevertheless, in Los Angeles local Hispanic music leader Jose Cantu organized two groups, the Spanish Serenaders and the Tipica Orchestra. Both played throughout the city and made frequent forays into the migrant-filled valleys for performances. The Tipica of nearly fifty Mexican musicians became, according to the *San Gabriel Eye Opener,* "one of the most popular features of the federal organization." Other Mexican units were formed in San Diego, Long Beach, and San Francisco.[12]

The FMP encouraged the Tipicas to perform on traditional Mexican holidays. The most important of these came on September 16, Mexican Independence Day. FMP Tipicas in the larger Mexican-American areas actively participated in the celebration, even though they resided in another country, with full blessing of the FMP and the Roosevelt administration. In 1937 for example, the project's Phoenix Tipica orchestra and Phoenix concert band provided musical entertainment and accompaniment for the two-day celebration. Opening-day ceremonies began with a rally at University Park, where local politicians and Mexican dignitaries gave speeches. The FMP units led a sing-a-long of the Mexican national anthem and the "Star Spangled Banner." The celebration the following year had the FMP's fourteen-piece Mexican orchestra performing for the Fiesta Queen pageant and night concerts for the two-day event. In Dallas's "Little Mexico," the 1938 celebration had the local FMP Tipica orchestra providing nightly entertainment and accompaniment for the national anthems.[13]

While the administrators believed that it was important to allow these units to retain their traditional music, costumes, and celebrations, they were also expected to perform at regular FMP-sponsored events. This meant that the Tipicas had to secure as much exposure outside their Hispanic communities as possible. Perhaps this is where Sokoloff's "novelty orchestra" label became applicable. In order to appeal to audiences outside their communities, these ethnic units had to present themselves as the popular stereotypes portrayed them—as happy, musical, and docile.

Performances for local schoolchildren, which were successful for other FMP units, became the easiest way to provide the larger community service the project demanded. The units went into the schools to emphasize, according to Texas administrators, that good music came from men and women of all classes and colors who had been saved by the federal government from the devastations of the depression. The San Antonio Tipica orchestra gave over fifteen school concerts to three thousand children in 1936–37, playing Spanish standards and the American national anthem. The schoolchildren in and around Albuquerque, New Mexico, were frequently visited by FMP units, who played various selections of folk music and Tipica music.[14]

These Mexican-American units also contributed to the project's expanded activities in the National Music Festivals. Since the festivals did not come under the direct supervision of the project, the administrators believed they had to make the FMP the most widely recognized of the participants. The songs and dances of Mexico concluded the city of San Antonio's 1937 eight-day National Music Week celebration with the FMP's Tipica orchestra providing the background music for Mexican folk dances, concertos, and poetry readings.[15]

A much simpler method for widening these units' appeal was to get them to perform anywhere the administrators could obtain sponsorship. The San Antonio Tipica played more than half of its concerts in 1936–37 in public parks and recreation centers owned by the city. These shows also brought in the largest attendance—25,510—because they were given free and usually on Friday nights or Saturday afternoons. In San Gabriel, California, Los Angeles's Spanish Serenaders and the Tipica Orchestra of the FMP had a regular engagement at the San Gabriel Mission, where the project sought to "recapture the vanishing echoes of early California musical traditions when the mission was the center of Southern [California] cultural life." The El Paso Tipica Orchestra mimicked the success of the Boston dance band by giving daily concerts in the lobby of El Paso's Union Rail Station. The El Paso unit hoped to impress the "public from all over the country" who traveled through the city.[16]

In the three-day American Music Festival, the many ethnic units played a crucial role. In the Tipica areas of Texas, the festival fully in-

corporated the Mexican units. Aside from performing their standard repertoire, the Tipica unit in El Paso also played the "Eyes of Texas" and
"America." One hundred and forty Mexican-American children sang
"Yankee Doodle" and "Dixie" to the accompaniment of the Tipica orchestra before over seven hundred people at El Paso's Liberty Hall. The
highlight of the evening came when the Mexican unit gave an electrifying Spanish version of Sousa's "Stars and Stripes Forever." The San Antonio unit dedicated its time in the festival to promoting Mexican-American compositions, giving two concerts featuring the Tipica orchestra.[17]

These units participated in other patriotic activities. San Antonio's
Tipica helped celebrate the Texas centennial in 1936 by giving "a series
of semiweekly concerts which . . . typify San Antonio's traditional Spanish atmosphere." The forty-four-piece band traveled to Fort Worth as
San Antonio's contribution to the centennial celebration. When the FMP
began to collect distinctive American musical recordings for the Library
of Congress in 1936, the first groups recorded were San Antonio's Tipica
and Los Abajinos. The FMP also encouraged the Mexican musicians to
compose new songs that combined the traditional Mexican sound with
the new American outlook. San Antonio's listing of materials performed
included twenty new compositions written by members of the Tipica that
were given regular performances amidst the traditional songs and folk
songs.[18]

When Sokoloff reviewed the project's activities in 1936, he alluded
to the eighty-one dance, theater, and novelty orchestras under federal
guidance. The Tipicas were under this "novelty" umbrella, as were other
regional and ethnic musical groups like the Gypsy, Hungarian, Hawaiian, and Cowboy groups. Why the FMP only brought these few into its
fold is unclear. Perhaps it had to do with who applied for project work
and who did not, or who was able to pass the audition.[19]

Regardless, some ethnic groups received surprising representation in
the FMP, including some Eastern European ethnic groups. In Detroit,
two small bands—one made up of seven Serbs and Croats in a band called
the Tamburitzans and the second an eight-member Hungarian Gypsy
band called the Detroit Gypsy Orchestra—gave concerts throughout the
city. Most of their shows took place in the area's hospitals, bringing "cheer
to many who sorely need such a pleasant change of atmosphere," as the
Detroit Federation of Musicians periodical said. The units also brought
their ethnic music and folk instruments into the classrooms for discussion. The Detroit FMP sent notices to local schools that outlined the
educational value of bringing these unusual groups to the schools, sug-
gesting that these units be invited into the classroom to detail the culture not only of another people, but of the diverse culture of America.
Other cities in the industrial Midwest with large numbers of Eastern

Fig. 12. Detroit Tamburitzans. Part of the FMP's novelty orchestras, groups like these were created to meet specific local demands. Courtesy of the Detroit Public Library.

Europeans also had ethnic project units. Pittsburgh had a Gypsy orchestra composed of twenty-two musicians who played native Hungarian tunes throughout the city. Cleveland had a Gypsy band, and Chicago boasted a large Hungarian concert orchestra. Even Los Angeles had a Hungarian unit, called the Hungarian Symphonette No. 7, which one local newspaper labeled "one of the most popular units" of the FMP.[20]

Out West the FMP tended more toward Hawaiian and Cowboy bands. In California, the members of a Hawaiian unit gave concerts dressed in their native attire. Organized as the Long Beach Hawaiian Orchestra, they gave regular performances in and around the Los Angeles area and utilized the songs and dances from the islands. And, for some reason, there was a Hawaiian trio as part of the Oklahoma FMP. By all accounts, this group proved very popular.[21] More linked to the popular image of the West is the cowboy. What better way to document the project's commitment to America then by utilizing the mythic cowboy and his songs? During the 1930s, Hollywood movies helped the cowboy image become intertwined with hillbilly or country music and achieve widespread acceptance among American audiences. The project, hoping to cash in on this phenomenon, created several of these bands throughout the Southwest. The groups included the Arbuckle Buckaroos, a seven-piece cowboy band, the Red River Hill Billies, a small bluegrass unit, Devil Dan's Trio, which played contemporary cowboy tunes, and Bang Crosby's Caddo Creek Jug Blowers, composed of thirty bottles. Dallas's cowboy group, the Sizzlers, specialized in the traditional cowboy songs of the Southwest, which utilized the guitar and harmonica. Out in California, the cowboy bands achieved popularity with elementary schoolchildren in Orange County and gave regular shows at the schools. The success of the unit forced the project administrators to extend their contract in order to play throughout the summer of 1936. These bands performed in full cowboy regalia and sang both traditional and modern Western tunes.[22]

The project made little attempt to incorporate the other mythic character, the Native American, into its musical American picture. Instead, the FMP collected recordings of some of the songs and dance lines of the American Indians. The Oklahoma project collected over three hundred recordings from the tribes in the state. Under the direction of Chippewa Bee M. Barry, also known as Pe-ahm-e-squeet, the unit recorded and secured some songs that had never before been saved, including music from the Cheyenne, Kiowa, Sac and Fox, Apache, Pawnee, Ottawa, and Osage tribes. The rationale was that since the "full-blooded Indian population is speedily declining . . . it will be only a matter of a brief number of years before all the older Indians on 'God's Drum' are memories." Other states also collected Native American music, including a Mississippi unit, which recorded a Choctaw tribe, and Pennsylvania, which recorded the Corn Planter Festival (which was also captured on film), to name a few.[23]

The FMP utilized these regional groups both to entertain the specific audiences they attracted and to entertain the general population. The United States, as its citizens knew, contained many different groups, each with distinct attributes. The FMP sought to detail the similarities in these distinctions through music. The message that the FMP wanted to present to all of America was that all citizens—poor, rich, black, woman, immigrant, or native—had a place in the larger society.

Yet, within this message the project also segregated these units from its more "serious" and larger performing units through the audition process. While talented, these ethnic musicians were often looked down on as "popular" or folk musicians because they could not pass the European designed and taught musical audition. So, while it was open to other races and ethnicities, the project put these groups into its "novelty" division and reserved the bulk of its economic resources for those orchestras and symphonies that the administrators believed were better for the people of the country.

TEN

AN END OF IT ALL

The difficulties that plagued the WPA prior to 1939 intensified and signaled the end of the federally directed arts projects. These problems, ranging from the continuing war fever abroad and red-baiting at home, forced the Federal Arts Projects to accept cutbacks and, in some cases, total elimination. By the end of August 1939 two of the original arts projects were gone and the other two had been transferred to the states and redirected in terms of emphasis and influence. An analysis of the role of the FMP as a federal activity ends in mid-1939, when control from Washington was transferred to each state, which now assumed their own music projects.

Initially, 1939 began much as the previous years of the FMP's existence. Orchestras performed, people attended, and, in keeping with their tradition of reaching into America's communities, from January until June FMP units performed before over three million persons. However, administrative problems within the WPA and FMP indicated an uncertain future. Top administrators began to leave the WPA in 1938 to take new posts within the Roosevelt administration. The most prominent of these departures was WPA chief Harry Hopkins. His tenure as WPA head had begun winding down in 1937, for both personal and political reasons. The death of his wife in October 1937 and his subsequent battle with cancer kept him from actively dealing with the growing resentment that the WPA had to face in the post-1936 period. By the time he was able to return to full duty in the spring of 1938, he had already lost much of his earlier political support because of his and the WPA's involvement in the 1936 election campaigns, which were designed to defeat New Deal opponents in Congress. As Richard McKinzie writes, "The more Hopkins practiced politics the more he lost interest in the details" of the WPA. He left the WPA in December 1938 to assume the role of secretary of commerce. He was replaced by a nonpolitical army officer, Colonel F. C. Harrington, from the secretary of war's office. Ellen Woodward, Hopkins's assistant, soon followed Hopkins out of the WPA and was transferred to the Social Security Board. Harrington recommended Florence Kerr to take her place. By early 1939, four of the other five top WPA directors also resigned.[1]

Sokoloff had also decided to resign in 1938. With his many years in conducting music, he grew tired of his administrative duties and wanted to return to his profession. During the summer of 1938 he took a temporary leave to conduct the Seattle Symphony, and when the season ended he tendered his official resignation to the federal government. There were, of course, other reasons for his leaving. His leadership abilities, which had always been suspect, were under increased scrutiny. Attacks from musicians and professional groups had grown in both number and intensity. Many of these critiques, like the one sent to President Roosevelt in 1937 from a group calling itself the "Taxpayers of New York City Professional Artists Group," pointed out that Sokoloff's leadership was weak and that he had done little for American music. In fact, the irate "Taxpayers" questioned whether his position was simply "honorary." Internal divisions had also surfaced within the FMP concerning Sokoloff's commitment to classical music over other more vernacular music. He was challenged to emphasize less symphonic music and more folk- and popular-oriented music. Sokoloff felt the pressure and wanted out. He agreed to remain as the national director until May 19, 1939, in order to assure a smooth transition of authority. William Mayfarth, an assistant to Sokoloff for three years, was named interim director until he was replaced later that year by Earl Moore.[2]

These administrative uncertainties only highlighted the precarious nature of the arts projects and of the FMP. Charges of scandal, corruption, and boondoggling made the whole WPA a political football, which even FDR distanced himself from by 1939. The cutbacks of 1937 set the stage for future restraints, and when the Dies Committee found un-American tendencies among some Project One employees, many supporters vanished. In early January of 1939, Roosevelt asked Congress for an $875,000,000 special relief allocation for the WPA. This money was designed to get the work-relief project through until a new budget for 1939 took effect in July. While recognizing congressional opposition, the president pointed out that any cutbacks "before the expansion of private industry is ready to take up the slack" would lead to human misery and a decline in purchasing power. Congress ignored FDR's plea and cut $150,000,000 from the package. When Roosevelt asked that the monies be reinstated, Congress responded by calling for an investigation of the

WPA. The cuts remained and affected the white-collar workers, especially those involved in the arts projects.[3]

Some opponents wondered whether the time had come to end the WPA. After four years and billions of dollars, critics challenged Roosevelt's plan for recovery as boondoggling and political patronage. But, by 1939, the WPA had become a major employer, and many feared that those on its employment rolls would never find adequate private employment, especially those involved in white-collar projects. These fears generally fell on deaf ears. For example, when the president of the Columbus AFM local wrote to his Congressman to complain of proposed budget cuts, John M. Vorys replied that "if a musician . . . after a temporary period of help . . . finds that he still can't find a private job in his chosen field, I think he will have to enter some other field of work."[4] Furthermore, Oregon Senator Charles McNary feared that the admitted patronage of the WPA had encouraged spending to escalate out of control. During its first full year of operation, WPA expenditures totaled $1,270,235,065, a sum surpassed in both 1937 and 1938. Although spending had been cut in 1938 by some $400,000,000, estimated expenditures for 1939 were over $2,250,000,000. McNary questioned whether the WPA was able to "stimulate private employment" and asked for the "outright abolition of the WPA and the return to the States and localities the responsibility of administering relief."[5]

The WPA and the arts projects still had some supporters. On behalf of a hundred American mayors, New York Mayor Fiorello LaGuardia testified before Congress for continued project activity. Nelson Rockefeller, in a letter to Edward T. Taylor, chair of the congressional subcommittee investigating the WPA, wrote that to suspend the Federal Arts Projects would be "extremely unfortunate from the human and cultural point of view." Rockefeller sent a copy of the letter to Roosevelt, who thanked him and blandly replied, "We need all the help we can get to educate the Congress and the nation" about the benefits of the WPA and its arts projects. Heywood Broun also wrote to Roosevelt in support of the WPA and its arts projects. The president's response was cool, as he indicated that the WPA needs "some projects of the non-construction type." Missouri Congressman John Cochran introduced into the *Congressional Record* a telegram from the St. Louis local AFM president Samuel Meyers that detailed the patriotic virtues of the WPA and FMP and called upon "every worker—and every thinking citizen" to lobby their representatives for the creation of a permanent civil service modeled after the WPA.[6] At the AFM's national convention in 1939, the union drafted a letter to be sent to all Congressmen in protest of the cuts. President Weber asked all members to wire their representatives to support the FMP. Seventeen locals joined together to petition the AFM to send a special representative to Washington to lobby for the protection of the FMP from cuts. Local 802 complained that "the very lives of thousands of our fellow members and their families now employed on Federal Music Projects are being menaced by threatened emasculation of the WPA through drastic reduction in emergency relief appropriations and cuts in present personnel." In the end, the June convention passed five separate resolutions asking Congress to spare the FMP.[7]

But it was too little too late. Before the federal fiscal year's budget came to an end on June 30, 1939, new appropriations passed. June 17 forever altered the WPA and the arts projects. The budget for 1940's Emergency Relief Administration, from which the WPA and the arts projects received their monies, was cut drastically, and the WPA's operations were thus altered. On June 30 the Federal Theater Project was completely abolished and the House ordered the other projects to significantly cut their budgets. The WPA's total allocation was cut, and the new guidelines for the remaining arts projects issued at the end of July called for the transfer of control to the states. After August 31, 1939, all WPA projects had to have state or local sponsorship and administration or they would be phased out. The president and his advisors, while not in support of the cutbacks, did little to oppose them. By 1939 FDR's congressional support had weakened considerably, and, in light of the pro-Red accusations leveled at some projects and the political patronage charge linked to the 1936 and 1938 elections, the administration felt it had no choice but to sign the 1939 budget bill. The cut was recognized by many within FDR's circle and by opponents as punishment for the president's perceived leftist turn; it was a clear victory for the anti–New Deal, conservative forces gathering momentum in Washington.[8]

With the transfer to state control complete by late summer, the *Federal* Music Project came to an end. The individual state projects continued the patriotic aspect of the 1935–39 years, as international affairs accentuated the sentiment. In 1942 some state music projects performed for the nation's soldiers and sailors preparing for action overseas, as well as for American citizen in need of a distraction from the grim toll of war. The state music projects, still partially funded by the federal government, came to an end without fanfare on June 30, 1943.

What did the FMP accomplish during its federal years? From October 1935 to August 1939, project musical organizations gave 224,698 performances before 148,159,699 American citizens. During this time, over 6,772 American compositions were played, with over 60 percent coming from contemporary composers.[9] Even in sophisticated New York City, many people heard their first cultivated musical performance at

FMP-sponsored free or low-cost concerts. As project administrator Florence Kerr pointed out, "There is abundant evidence that [the FMP] has become a force of vast cultural implications . . . in the future of our country." New Hampshire's administrators called the FMP "the most constructive force ever effected in the educational and cultural life of the country." Noted musicologist John Tasker Howard credited the FMP with the expansion of musical activities and interest during the depression era; composer Virgil Thomson believed that the project was primarily responsible for establishing the credibility of symphonic music in America.[10] A 1937 *Musical America* editorial best outlined the value of the project: "[Its] ramifications are so many, the quality and worth of what has been undertaken and its manner of achievement so diverse . . . it is inconceivable that so much should be going on without its playing some constructive part in the country's musical progress, no matter how transient and ephemeral, or inferior in quality, the great bulk of this welter of accomplishment may be."[11]

Many have pointed to the 1930s as the time when American composers better defined their art music. Nicholas Tawa writes in *Serenading the Reluctant Eagle* that the era of the thirties and early forties deserves the label as the "golden age of American music." During this time America's composers produced "vital" works for their newfound audience. Alan Levy views the thirties as the end of an era when American composers "slavishly" followed European models and concentrated instead on the "emergence of a unique and mature American musical character." The FMP's effect in this birthright cannot be ignored. This is not to say that the project alone was responsible for the musical awakening Sokoloff proclaimed in the 1930s, for much of the groundwork was laid earlier. But the project's emphasis on American works did much to help spread cultivated music, especially American works, to the public. Before the FMP, for example, the Chicago Symphony was alone in its reputation as a place where American compositions could be heard. After 1935 the symphonies in Los Angeles, San Francisco, Cleveland, and elsewhere became showplaces for the American composer. The percentage of American works performed by the country's private orchestras more than doubled by 1943, from 9.7 percent during 1939–40 to nearly 21 percent three years later.[12]

Many composers also dovetailed their rediscovery of the American audience with the FMP. Aaron Copland completed his *El Salon Mexico* in 1936, and followed soon after with *Billy the Kid* in 1938. Other composers also wrote for the new American audience: Virgil Thomson composed *The Plow That Broke the Plains* (1936) and *The River* (1938); Roy Harris wrote *When Johnny Comes Marching Home* (1935); Elie Siegmeister composed *Song of Democracy* (1938) and *Western Suite* (1938); William

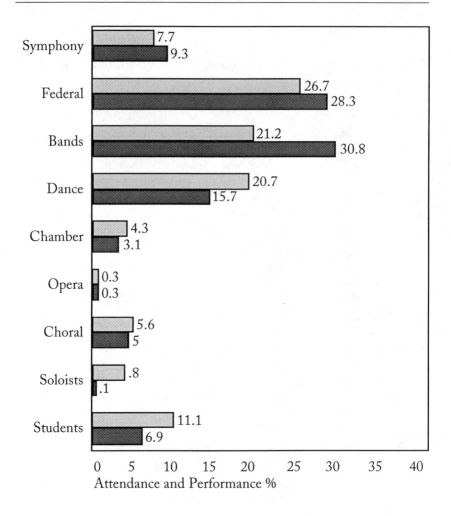

Fig. 13. FMP activity and attendance percentages, 1935–1939.

Legend
 Performance %

Attendance %

Source: Memo from Hewes to Fredenhagen, Feb. 12, 1940, Box 32, FMP.

Schuman wrote *American Festival Overture* (1939); and Randall Thompson composed *The Peaceable Kingdom* (1936), to name but a few. It was at FMP-sponsored composer forums that many of these new scores had their first hearing, and before project audiences they had their full premiere. Howard Hanson told America's music educators in 1939 that "at last [America] is taking her place not only in the field of performance but in the field of creation."[13]

The tendencies toward Americanism in cultivated music not only came from the FMP, but also were tied into the whole Americanism revival that marked the depression decade. When FDR was first elected, he told the people that the reaffirmation of the American spirit was needed to save the country, and a kind of nationalism spread across the country. But this patriotism differed from the chauvinism commonly associated with nationalism because the failure manifested in the economic collapse was seen not as just the failure of capitalism but of America. If the national ideal, which by the 1930s had come to include the basic tenets of capitalism, was flawed, then perhaps democracy too had failed. And with the Soviet model to compare itself to, America's understanding of its ideology was suffering from an identification crisis. If there was no such thing as the American Dream, then the country as a whole had no collective past or common bonds on which to draw, which inevitably put the future into direct question.

The economic failure challenged American ideals, the national aim, the collective body. Many began to search for proof of the American Dream, or perhaps of its death. Alfred Kazin's *On Native Grounds* is the most often cited of these introspections, but many others searched the American countryside for proof that the ideal—the American spirit FDR said was needed to solve the country's problems—was still alive. Kazin set the tone for the whole cultural awakening of the era when, in analyzing Archibald MacLeish's poem "The American Cause," he defined the rediscovery: "there was suddenly a whole world of marvels on the continent to possess—a whole world of rivers and scenes, of folklore and regional culture, of a heroic tradition to reclaim and of forgotten heroes to follow. America was here, now."[14]

Scholars have begun to analyze the popular culture of the era and its connection to the national consciousness. Characters created or brought to life in the 1930s, like Batman or Superman, cartoon movies from Disney, movies by Capra and Ford, stars like Fonda, Stewart, Gable, Davis, Hayworth, and Leigh, all reinforced the traditional values of family, community, and the work ethic. Hollywood churned out profitable movies extolling the virtues of the American Dream. Many detailed a classless society where hard work still won the day and the government reflected the needs of the people over big business. Movies like *Mr. Smith Goes to Washington, The Grapes of Wrath, Gone with the Wind,* and even *The Wizard of Oz* focused on how, by working together as Americans, any problem could be solved. Even the gangster and B-grade Westerns catered to this theme. Many of the gangster films, like *I Am a Fugitive,* were less about crime than about social injustice and the survival of the defiant, independent American. Other films, like *Scarface, The Petrified Forest,* or *Public Enemy,* portrayed the gangster as a relic of a bygone era or as a victim of his own tactics. In the end, good did triumph over evil, and money in and of itself did not mean acceptance. In the cowboy pictures of the era, the action reinforced the traditional American concepts of individualism and hard work. What better characterization of America was there than a Gene Autry or a Roy Rogers, both of whom played characters who brought justice, peace, and unity to a fragmented America. Even the openings of Hollywood's films became Americanist spectacles, as "small town" premieres combined the best Hollywood glitz with the country's smaller communities. A new, democratic Hollywood shared its gala openings with the whole country.[15]

Other popular culture items mirrored Hollywood's profitable tactic. The popularity of pinball and the board game Monopoly document the dominance of traditional middle-class values. Even the activities of Disney's Mickey Mouse tied into the 1930s national sentiment. No matter how terrible things were, by following the rules and working hard, Mickey and his pals eventually returned home. The repeal of the Eighteenth Amendment brought nightclubs back into vogue across the country, along with a new democratic nightlife. In popular music, 1935 saw the beginnings of a swing revolution that would employ thousands of musicians and revive a nearly dead music industry. Swing was created and performed by regular Americans, white and black, many from middle to lower economic backgrounds. They were of many ethnicities and religions, and, in keeping with its melting-pot sound, swing became the first truly integrated popular music. Country music also came of age during the thirties, riding on the coattail of the Western movies. Songs by Gene Autry, Roy Rogers, the Sons of the Pioneers, Bob Wills, and many others painted a picture of a mythic cowboy in his individual quest for truth, peace, and unity. Even the musical theater discovered Americana, as *Oklahoma* and *Porgy and Bess* attest.[16]

The intellectual movement of the 1930s tended toward an interesting form of cultural nationalism. As Warren Susman has argued, during the depression decade, American intellectuals and the people tried to find a national culture rooted in the ordinary, or folk, idea. Much of this quest led to a romantic attachment to a mythic agrarian past, as evidenced by the popularity of historical fiction and movies in which the machine had not yet replaced human virtues and initiative. It was as though America was redefining itself in response to the fundamental changes wrought by the rise of the machine age and the relativistic ideas of modernism. Within this search for a usable past, history and culture intersected, as art and thought found themselves faced with an identity crisis of their own. Referring back to William James's notion concerning consciousness and thought, ideas without use were useless, and so art without social purpose or theories without application had little individual or social value. Both the intellectual revolt against formalism and the art for art's sake movement that sprang up within the modernist ideology were shaken in the depression decade and were forever transformed from modernism's avant-garde experimentation to liberal agenda development. This change was not limited to the intelligentsia; as Charles Alexander has observed, ordinary people recognized that their nation had "reached a turning point" in its history and that they were now involved in its redefinition. Kazin's recollection that "never before did a nation seem so hungry for news of itself" fits exactly into this nationalistic milieu. By mid-decade, the American definition took on more and more of a middle-class tone, as the radicalism enunciated earlier in the era evaporated and was replaced by the more acceptable American Dream, in which hard work and individual sacrifice brought reward to both the individual and the nation. Joan Shelley Rubin's interesting analysis of the rise of middlebrow culture captures this mood nicely, arguing that within the 1930s the image of the middle class as intelligent, practical, and conservative dominated American fiction and criticism. This meant that, among many other things, while citizens may not have liked the manner in which Martin Dies went about his investigation of and attack upon the government, public opinion polls held him in high esteem as a patriot. The contradiction inherent in 1930s culture and thought was exemplified by the mere existence of the Federal Arts Projects, which were designed to provide work relief to unemployed artists while at the same time reinforcing the ideals of the American dream.[17]

Roosevelt understood the people's sentiments toward Americanism and used them to his political advantage. He urged the country's middle-class citizenry to sing the praises of America by advising them to go out and see the real America: "Take a second-hand car, put on a flannel shirt, drive out to the Coast by the northern route and come back by the southern route. Don't stop anywhere where you have to pay more than $2.00 for your room and bath. Don't talk to your banking friends or your Chamber of Commerce friends, but specialize on the gasoline station man, the small restaurant keeper and the farmers you meet by the wayside and your fellow automobile travellers."[18] The policies of his administration tried to tap into this sentiment, as pluralistic, middle-class reform ideals dominated FDR's legislation, from the CCC, WPA, Social Security, to the Wagner Act. Ellen Woodward wrote to the president in 1937 that his actions "will have justified all of our struggles as a nation, to survive the depression." The New Deal functioned as the shaper of the new American consciousness; it succeeded by introducing its consensus into small towns and big cities, largely because Roosevelt was able to convince the people that they were their programs and that they should feel proud of the WPA and other government activities. Many of the work-relief projects, like the CCC morning flag raising, reinforced the Americanness of the government. The activities of the Farm Security Administration's photographic section, which gave the American people movies like *The River* and photographs from Walker Evans, Dorothea Lange, and Margaret Bourke-White, helped prove that the American Dream still existed in the hearts and minds of the American people. The arts projects also relied to a large degree on patriotic exercises, with only the FTP not being able to display its Americanness to the satisfaction of the politicians and the people. America's painters copied the Diego Rivera mural style and displayed the beauty of the ordinary life of America's people in post offices and government buildings. With similar motives, Federal Writers' Project employees wrote guidebooks to the states.[19]

The Federal Music Project tied easily into the cultural nationalism so evident during the era. The project focused many of its activities on reaching the ordinary citizen outside the large urban areas. Within this goal, the FMP also sought to uplift these same people to an appreciation of cultivated music, considered by its administrators as quality music. Much in the same way contemporary fiction was concerned with the middle-class consciousness, so to was the FMP, for its cultivated selections and use of patriotism and nationalism rarely dealt with the issues and controversies within classical music. Rather, simply by providing the masses with recognizable quality music, the cultivated musicians involved with the project would create, Sokoloff announced in 1936, something "very beautiful and significant."[20] The project did not pay composers to write workers' marches or radical music, but instead relied on patriotic classics by Sousa, Foster, and Gershwin, and even attempted to promote the American opera *Gettysburg*. The FMP was not experimental; it was conservative, headed by conservative leaders, and very much in line with American middle-class ideals. The FMP wanted to bring its music to the American people, to give them every opportunity to hear cultivated music, so that they could participate and help unify a country fragmented because of the depression. As an editorial in the *Musician* put it, the ac-

tivity of the FMP would lead to a single voice that would give "utterance
to a spiritual idealism that can make a conglomerate assemblage of
peoples a composite unity—a Nation."[21] More than a music project, the
FMP sought to unify Americans through patriotic rhetoric and festivals,
through its support of American composers and conductors, by showing
musicians who worked hard to earn their relief money, and by trying to
prove not only the FMP's community worth but also the value of democracy and the American Dream.

Herein lies the fundamental contradiction of the pluralistic vision
enunciated by FDR and the FMP. As it mirrored middle-class views concerning community involvement, Americanness, and quality music, the
project distanced itself from those musical activities it deemed unworthy
or common. The emphasis on cultivated music, while noble and within
the middle-class vision of both the New Deal and American consciousness, meant that the FMP could ignore the bulk of unemployed musicians who neither had the training nor the skill to perform classical compositions. Moreover, as AFM president Weber had pointed out to Sokoloff in
1935, before the depression there had been little support for classical orchestras outside of the large urban areas, and therefore few musicians
could count on working in this realm after the FMP tenure. If the project
were to rehabilitate and employ musicians, as it was charged to do, then
the emphasis had to favor the popular musician over the classical one.
Yet, ideologically, Sokoloff and the FMP saw little value in performing
popular music, regardless of the economic reality or the popular taste.
The project encouraged cultivated music because it believed it to be better music than any other. The fact that the people preferred other vernacular musics simply meant that they were ignorant to the beauty of
cultivated music and needed to be educated, uplifted, and brought within
the realm of middle-class ideals. This tendency is evident throughout
this work, but especially in chapter 7, where the role of African American music is discussed. In effect, by focusing on how well black FMP
units could play classical music, even if at times audition standards were
lowered to allow these musicians onto the rolls, the project wanted to
prove that all people could be trained to appreciate and enjoy good, safe
music. This ideology was replayed time and time again throughout the
life of the project, as it sought to justify itself by bloating its attendance
numbers, increasing its performances, and churning out pro-FMP, cultivated music press releases. "The American people—all of them—loved
and could appreciate good music" was the unwritten refrain of the FMP-
produced propaganda. As project supporter Redfern Mason wrote in 1937
about an FMP choral performance, "There was a wistful beauty about
this WPA cohort" made up of nearly all racial groups, "Jews and Gen-

tile, Catholic and Protestant, Negro and White, Nordic and Latin." The chorus, according to the reviewer, melded into one and represented the American people.[22] The project, like the New Deal itself, was part of a greater social movement toward homogenization in American society. Bound closely to consumer capitalism, advertising, and the idea of the American Dream, the foundation of the post–World War II consensus was laid during the 1930s through the FMP, WPA, CCC, and other New Deal programs. The country is in this together, went the depression-era rhetoric, and, while this rhetoric enabled the government to resist any substantial changes in the power structure and still deal with issues of economic and social crisis, it also effectively muted the diversity of the American mosaic and attempted to meld the country into one vision. The FMP is a clear example of this activity and forms the core of the paradox of the 1930s, when individualism was held in high esteem, but conformity was rewarded.

NOTES

Preface

1. Rhonda F. Levine, *Class Struggle and the New Deal: Industrial Labor, Industrial Capital, and the State* (Lawrence, Kans.: Univ. of Kansas Press, 1988), especially 5–19. The idea that the New Deal had to balance the conservative with the liberal is, of course, not new, as this tightrope forms the basis of most New Deal historiography. Levine's is one of the first, however, to place this debate within the context of class-state relations.

2. Still the best sources to discuss the totality of Roosevelt and the New Deal are Arthur Schlesinger Jr., *The Coming of the New Deal*, vols. 1–3 (Boston: Houghton Mifflin, 1959–60); William E. Leuchtenberg, *FDR and the New Deal, 1932–1940* (New York: Harper and Row, 1963); and, from a more cultural perspective, Richard Pells, *Radical Visions and American Dreams* (Middletown, Conn.: Wesleyan Univ. Press, 1974).

3. "Unemployed Arts," *Fortune* 15 (May 1937): 110; Leuchtenberg, *FDR*, 120–22; *Final Report on the WPA Program, 1935–1943* (Washington, D.C.: Government Printing Office [hereafter referred to as GPO], 1946), 2–5.

4. Roosevelt, as quoted in Robert Dallek, *FDR and American Foreign Policy* (New York: Oxford Univ. Press, 1979), 160.

5. Paul Conkin, *The New Deal* (New York: Crowell, 1967), 52–54; Donald S. Howard, *The WPA and Federal Relief Policy* (New York: Russell Sage, 1943), 108; *Final Report on the WPA Program*, 7; Robert E. Sherwood, *Roosevelt and Hopkins: An Intimate History* (New York: Harper, 1958), 69; Schlesinger, *The Politics of Upheaval*, 343–61.

6. Harry Hopkins, *The Realities of Unemployment* (Washington: GPO, n.d.), n.p.; Harry Hopkins, speech before unified neighborhoods, Mar. 14, 1936; CBS speech, June 4, 1936, both in *Principal Speeches of Harry L. Hopkins* (Washington: GPO, 1938), n.p.

7. Harry Hopkins, *Spending to Save: The Complete Story of Relief* (New York: Norton, 1936), 174–75; Sherwood, *Roosevelt and Hopkins*, 3–4; Ellen Woodward, *Testimony Before the House Committee on Patents, 1938*, no. 1, pt. 1, 88; letter, Jacob Baker, assistant administrator, to all state WPA directors, Authorization of the Federal Arts Projects, August 2, 1935, Papers of Harry L. Hopkins, no. 24, WPA

miscellaneous, 1935–1938, FDR Library; Richard D. McKinzie, *The New Deal for Artists* (Princeton, N.J.: Princeton Univ. Press, 1973), x–xi, 22–25; *Final Report on the WPA Program,* 253–54; press release for Sept. 8, 1935, "President Approves Allotment for Cultural Programs," WPA Papers, Raymond P. Chase Papers, Minnesota Historical Society (hereafter referred to as MinnHistSoc); "Music Given Place in Vast Federal Art Project," *Musical America* 56 (Aug. 1935): 3–4.

8.   Harry Hopkins, speech to WPA field representatives, Dec. 28, 1935, *Principal Speeches*; Warren Susman, *Culture and Commitment* (New York: Braziller, 1973), 188–91; David M. Potter, "The Historians' Use of Nationalism and Vice Versa," *American Historical Review* 67 (July 1962): 924–50; Warren Susman, "The Thirties," in *The Development of an American Culture,* Stanley Coben and Lormar Ratner, eds. (Englewood Cliffs, N.J. : Prentice Hall, 1983), 221; William W. Bremer, "Along the 'American Way': The New Deal's Work Relief Programs for the Unemployed," *Journal of American History* 62 (Dec. 1975): 636.

9.   Typescript of proceedings of WPA luncheon meeting, Dec. 28, 1935, 32–33, Papers of Harry L. Hopkins, no. 25, FDR Library.

10. This dialectic lay at the core of each of the projects and, in a larger sense, of the entirety of the New Deal. Jerre Mangione discusses this dilemma in relation to the Writers' Project in *The Dream and the Deal: The Federal Writers' Project, 1935–1943* (Boston: Little, Brown, 1972), 42.

11. Monty Noam Penkower, *The Federal Writers' Project: A Study in Government Patronage of the Arts* (Chicago: Univ. of Illinois Press, 1977), especially 25–51, 89–116; Mangione, *The Dream and the Deal,* 249–53.

12. Matthew Baigell, *The American Scene: American Painting of the 1930s* (New York: Praeger, 1974), 13; Belisario R. Contreras, *Tradition and Innovation in New Deal Art* (Lewisburg, Pa.: Bucknell Univ. Press, 1983), 18–21, 169–195, Cahill as quoted on 150.

13. McKinzie, *The New Deal for Artists,* 110–50; Contreras, *Tradition and Innovation,* 155; Ralph Purcell, *Government Art: A Study of American Experience* (Washington, D.C.: Public Affairs Press, 1956), 56–57; Landgren in Francis V. O'Connor, ed., *The New Deal Art Projects: An Anthology of Memoirs* (Washington, D.C.: Smithsonian Institution Press, 1972), 317. See also O'Connor's *Art for the Millions: Essays from the 1930s by Artists and Administrators of the WPA Federal Art Project* (Greewich, Conn.: New York Graphic Society, 1973); and Marlene Park and Gerald E. Markowitz, *Democratic Vistas: Post Office and Public Art in the New Deal* (Philadelphia: Temple Univ. Press, 1984).

14. Jane DeHart Mathews, *The Federal Theater, 1935–1939: Plays, Relief, and Politics* (Princeton, N.J.: Princeton Univ. Press, 1967), vii–x, chapters 1–3; John O'Connor and Lorraine Brown, eds., *Free, Adult, Uncensored: The Living History of the Federal Theatre Project* (Washington, D.C.: New Republic Books, 1978),1–30; Tony Buttitta and Barry Witham, *Uncle Sam Presents: A Memoir of the Federal Theatre, 1935–1939* (Philadelphia: Univ. of Pennsylvania Press, 1982), 1–5. For a contemporary look, see Willson Whitman, *Bread and Circuses: A Study of Federal Theatre* (Freeport, N.Y.: 1937; reprint, Books for Libraries Press, 1972), and memoirs by Hallie Flanagan, *Arena* (New York: Blom, 1940), and John Houseman, *Run Through: A Memoir* (New York: Simon and Schuster, 1972).

15. Flanagan quote from Whitman, *Bread and Circuses,* 172. For an excellent overview of many of the FTP productions, see Buttitta and Witham, *Uncle Sam Pre-*

sents, and for an overview of African-American participation, see Evelyn Q. Craig, *Black Drama of the Federal Theatre Era* (Amherst: Univ. of Massachusetts Press, 1980).

16. Nikolai Sokoloff, *The Federal Music Project* (Washington D.C.: GPO, 1936), frontispiece.

The Contradictions of Creation

1. Sokoloff, *The Federal Music Project,* 9–10.

2. William F. McDonald, *Federal Relief Administration and the Arts* (Columbus: Ohio State Univ. Press, 1969), 586; "Effects of Technological Change upon Employment in the Motion-Picture Theaters of Washington, D.C.," *Monthly Labor Review* 33 (Nov. 1931): 2; Grace Overmeyer, "The Musician Starves," *American Mercury* 32 (June 1934): 224–31; Daniel Mason Gregory, "The Radio v. The Virtuoso," *American Mercury* 20 (Aug. 1930): 454–60; "Chicago Local no. 10 Curtails Recordings," *The International Musician* (Jan. 1937): 4; Russell Sanjek, *American Popular Music and Its Business, The First Four Hundred Years,* vol. III (New York: Oxford Univ. Press, 1989).

3. Ray Allan Billington, "Government and the Arts: The WPA Experiment," *American Quarterly* 13 (Winter 1962): 468; John Tasker Howard, "Better Days for Music," *Harper's* 74 (1937): 485; McDonald, *Federal Relief Administration and the Arts,* 587.

4. McDonald, *Federal Relief Administration and the Arts,* 586–91; Overmeyer, "The Musician Starves," 226.

5. Joseph N. Weber, "The Present Status of Relief for Unemployed Musicians," *The International Musician* (July 1935): 1.

6. McDonald, *Federal Relief Administration and the Arts,* 592–601; Cornelius B. Canon, "The Federal Music Project of the WPA: Music in a Democracy," (Ph.D. diss., Univ. of Minnesota, 1963), 20–33.

7. "Music Clubs in Relief Plan for Jobless Musicians," *Musician* 39 (Feb. 1934): 17; McDonald, *Federal Relief Administration and the Arts,* 598–99.

8. *Government Aid During the Depression to Professional, Technical, and other Service Workers* (Washington, n.d.), 19; report of George Foster, folder no. 1, Library of Congress (hereafter referred to as Foster, file, folder number, LibofCong).

9. "WPA Music Project's Gains Seen As Lasting," *St. Paul Pioneer Press,* June 13, 1937, Minnesota clippings, box 88, Federal Music Project, National Archives, Washington D.C., WPA files 211.1 and Record Group 69 (FMP clippings hereafter referred to by state name, box number, FMP).

10. "Musicians Have Full Week in Prospect," *Syracuse Herald,* Oct. 18, 1936, New York state clippings, box 88, FMP; Jannelle Jedd Warren Findley, "Of Tears and Need: The Federal Music Project, 1935–1939." (Ph.D. diss., George Washington Univ., 1973), 39.

11. "Dr. Sokoloff, Clubs Hear 1,000 Children," *Richmond Times-Dispatch,* Apr. 22, 1937, Virginia clippings, box 88, FMP.

12. Mrs. Henry Morganthau to Hopkins, Aug. 22, 1935, letters, correspondence, box 375, WPA files 211.1, Record Group 69; record of program operation and accomplishment, California, Federal Theater Project, George Mason Univ., 4 (various records of the FTP in this collection are hereafter referred to by state name,

FTP, GMasUniv); Sokoloff to regional directors, June 22, 1938, Foster, no. 4, LibofCong.

13. "Regional Music Directors Appointed," *Musical America* 56 (Oct. 25, 1935): 3.

14. "WPA Enlists Advice of Noted Musicians," *Musical America* 56 (Nov. 10, 1935): 4; "NFMC Head Issues Call," *Musical America* 56 (Nov. 25, 1935): 4.

15. "Resolution no. 12, proposed by Peter Kleinkauf, Official Proceedings," *The International Musician* (June 1936): 17; "Hopkins' New Work Order Aids Unions," *The International Musician* (Sept. 1935): 6.

16. H. Wiley Hitchcock, *Music in the United States: A Historical Introduction,* 2d ed. (Englewood Cliffs, N.J.: Prentice-Hall, 1974), chapters 3–6, is one of the best sources to describe the rise and development of these two musical camps. Quotes are taken from pages 51, 55. Other musical histories outline similar patterns. See Charles Hamm, *Music in the New World* (New York: Norton, 1983), especially chapters 7, 8, 11–14; and Gilbert Chase, *America's Music: From the Pilgrims to the Present,* 3d ed. (Urbana: Univ. of Illinois Press, 1987), especially part three. Lawrence Levine, *Highbrow/Lowbrow: The Emergence of Cultural Hierarchy in America* (Cambridge: Harvard Univ. Press, 1988), is one of the best sources that describe how this division occurs throughout American culture in the late nineteenth century. Also see Russell Sanjek, *American Popular Music and Its Business,* for a discussion of the importance of marketing, sales, and consumption on the music business from the very start of the country.

17. "President's Report to the Detroit Convention: Federal Relief to Unemployed," *The International Musician* (June 1936): 22–24; Freddie Williams, Chicago AFM local, to FDR, Nov. 11, 1936, President's official file, 104, music, 1935–36, box 1, FDR Library.

18. Sokoloff to Baker, interoffice memo, Nov. 13, 1935, correspondence, box 375, WPA files 211.1; *Federal Project One: The WPA in Ohio, 1936* (Washington, D.C.: GPO, 1936), 3–21; "WPA Music Projects Achieve Results," *Salt Lake City Desert-News,* June 20, 1936, Utah clippings, box 80, FMP.

19. Carol Wilmoth, "Heavenly Harmony: The WPA Symphony Orchestra, 1937–1942," *The Chronicles of Oklahoma* 64 (Summer 1986): 36; "Music in Chicago," typescript, FWP, 99–100, IllHistSoc; report on activity of civic symphony, Jan. 1936–Sept. 1937, box 15, FMP; Wisconsin Final Report, 1–2, Wisconsin Historical Society (hereafter referred to as WiscHistSoc); William Arvold, Wisconsin state director, to Sokoloff, Mar. 5, 1937, WiscHistSoc; *Government Aid During the Depression to Professional, Technical, and Service Workers,* 19, Foster no. 1, LibofCong.

20. California clippings, Mar.–June 1936, box 46, FMP; "Street Dance on June 25 Will Be Free," *Cuyahoga Falls News,* June 19, 1936, Ohio clippings, box 72, FMP; Sokoloff, *The Federal Music Project,* cover page; regional meeting, June 24, 1936, Foster no. 4, LibofCong; Purcell, *Government Art,* 54–55.

21. McFarland to Sokoloff, NYC educational report for Dec. 1935, box 14, FMP; Sokoloff, *The Federal Music Project,* cover page.

22. "WPA Symphony," *Detroit News,* July 4, 1936, Michigan clippings, box 65, FMP; office correspondence, Hewes to Durham, June 9, 1938, p. 2, box 32, FMP; memo from Franklin to Hewes, Feb. 19, 1937, p. 23, box 32, FMP; "Native Music Given Praise," *Los Angeles Times,* May 17, 1936, California clippings, box 46, FMP.

23. Sokoloff, *The Federal Music Project,* 22–23.

24. Untitled article, *The Keynote,* Oct. 1936, FMP files, Detroit Public Library (hereafter referred to as DetPubLib).

25. Jervis to Dean, Aug. 13, 1937, California miscellaneous, 1936–37, box 26, FMP; Sokoloff testifying before House Committee on Patents, 75th Congress, 1938, no. 1, pt. 1, 126–27.

26. Clifton to Sokoloff, Oct. 16, 1935; Sokoloff to Clifton, Oct. 26, 1935, analysis, box 370, WPA files, 211.1; Sokoloff before FMP regional meeting, 1938, 10, Foster no. 4, LibofCong.

27. "Federal Music Project," *Current History* 49 (Sept. 1938): 42–44; Hewes to Bliven, Sept. 22, 1936, box 32, FMP; office correspondence, Hewes to Collier for packet to Bliven, June 1, 1936, box 32, FMP.

28. "WPA Units Give N.Y. Demonstration List," *Musical America* 57 (Apr. 10, 1936): 39.

29. Andre Polsh, *International Musician,* Dec. 1936, magazine stories, Hopkins file, and editorials and articles sent to Harold Stein, Jan. 1937, box 23, FMP.

30. "Sokoloff Arrives to Conduct Seattle Symphony Orchestra," *Seattle Post-Intelligencer,* Nov. 1, 1938, 1938 files, box 88, FMP.

31. "President's Report," 24.

32. "Statement of Lee Pattison with regard to the Aims of the FMP as requested by the New York Guide," 1936, box 23, the Papers of Lee Pattison, Claremont Graduate School, Claremont, California (hereafter referred to by file year, box number, Pattison Papers).

33. Record of program operations, Kentucky, 1–5, Kentucky State Archives; Maier to Hewes, Apr. 24, 1936, analysis, box 365, WPA files, 211.1.

The People's Music, 1935–1936

1. *San Francisco News,* Aug. 31, 1938; Ira Welborn, *Cleveland Press,* July 10, 1937; both cited in Canon, "The Federal Music Project," 111.

2. Edwin Hughes, "Forum: The Effect of WPA Projects on the Work of the Private Piano Teacher," *MTNA Proceedings 1936* (Oberlin: MTNA, 1937): 144–46; Lloyd Goodrich, "The Federal Government and Art," *Magazine of Art* 41 (Oct. 1948): 236–38.

3. "WPA Melody for Twenty Millions," *The Literary Digest* 122 (Sept. 19, 1936): 22; Eduard C. Lindeman, "Farewell to Bohemia," *Survey Graphic* (Apr. 1937): 207–8.

4. "Federal Survey Shows Michigan's Music Needs," *Musical America* 57 (Dec. 25, 1937): 17; Guy Maier, "Federal Music Project's Contribution to American Music," *MTNA Volume of Proceedings, 1936* (Oberlin: MTNA, 1937): 97.

5. Nikolai Sokoloff, "What the FMP is doing in Education," *Music Educators National Conference Yearbook, 1936* (Chicago: MENC, 1937): 379–80; "Unemployed Arts," 177.

6. WPA of Louisiana, record of program operation and accomplishment, music, Jan. 31, 1943, FTP, GMasUniv, 4–5; WPA of Virginia, program of operation and accomplishments, 1941, FTP, GMasUniv, 3; Sokoloff quoted in "A Right to Music," editorial, *Chico (Calif.) Record,* Jan. 7, 1937, 1937 Hopkins, box 23, FMP.

7. Julia Aynes, "All-Grieg Concert By WPA Orchestra Arranged," *Huntington Herald-Advertiser,* June 27, 1937, West Virginia clippings, box 80, FMP; "County WPA Orchestra Disbands; Fine Record," *Shamokin,* June 1937, Pennsylvania clip-

pings, box 76, FMP; "WPA Orchestra Has Given 248 Concerts in Two Years' Time," *Pueblo Star-Journal,* Feb. 20, 1938, Colorado clippings, box 55, FMP; Utah State Sinfonietta, summary of operations, 1936–37, Utah files, box 45, FMP.

8. Record of operation and accomplishments for Iowa Music Project, FTP, GMasUniv, 4.

9. Excerpts from letters, July 1935, New York City, department reports, box 14, FMP; J. W. Beach to FMP, letters sent to Stein, Jan. 7, 11, 1937, box 23, FMP; Robert Veatch to FMP, letters sent to Stein, Jan. 7, 11, 1937, box 23, FMP.

10. "WPA Orchestra Gives Program for Exchangites," *Toledo Signal,* Dec. 19, 1936, Ohio clippings, box 87, FMP; "Federal Music Project Completes First Year," *Omaha True Voice,* May 28, 1937, Nebraska clippings, box 67, FMP; "U.S. Project Bands Play 177 Concerts," *Indianapolis Star,* July 31, 1938, clippings, Indiana State Library (hereafter referred to as IndStLib); "Federal Music Project Hopes for a Song Conscious Nation," *Wilmington Star,* Jan. 3, 1937, Delaware clippings, box 59, FMP.

11. Record of program and operation, Kansas Music Project, FTP, GMasUniv, 5; approved testimony for FMP, Hopkins 1937, box 23, FMP.

12. Kansas record of program and operation, music, FTP, GMasUniv, 5; record of programs and accomplishments, Wisconsin Music Project, FTP, GMasUniv, 8.

13. "The State Puts on a Concert," editorial, *Minneapolis Star,* May 1936, Hopkins 1937, box 23, FMP; letter excerpt, Exhibit B sent to National Education Council, Dec. 5, 1936, box 23, FMP.

14. *Miami Herald,* Jan. 15, 1939, in William J. Dahlenburg, "Music in the Culture of Miami, 1920–1966," (Ph.D. diss., Florida State Univ., 1967), 80–81.

15. 20, Foster no. 1, LibofCong.

16. J. Fred MacDonald, *Don't Touch That Dial: Radio Programming in American Life from 1920–1960* (Chicago: Nelson-Hall, 1974), 25–62; David Nye, *Electrifying America: Social Meaning of a New Technology, 1880–1940* (Cambridge: MIT Press, 1991), 22–156; Susman, "The Thirties," 228.

17. Frank Biocca, "Media and Perceptual Shifts: Early Radio and the Clash of Musical Cultures," *Journal of Popular Culture* 24 (Fall 1986): 1–15. *The Etude* is quoted on 11.

18. Richard W. Steele, *Propaganda in an Open Society: The Roosevelt Administration and the Media, 1933–1941* (Westport, Conn.: Greenwood Press, 1985), 16–25; Charles Alexander, *Nationalism in American Thought, 1930–1945* (Chicago: Rand McNally, 1969), 93–99.

19. Findley, "Of Tears and Need," 120–26; MacDonald, *Don't Touch That Dial,* 626–27; FMP in Indiana, 1936–37, Indiana clippings file, IndStLib, 6; Oregon record of program and operations, FMP, FTP, GMasUniv, 4.

20. Kenneth E. Hendrickson Jr., "A Case Study in the Politics of Culture: The Federal Arts Projects in Iowa," *Upper Midwest History* 4 (1984): 36; chart listing from Canon, "The Federal Music Project," 166–69.

21. Rhode Island record of program and operation, FMP, GMasUniv, 5; Ohio record of program and accomplishments, FMP, GMasUniv, 10; Michigan record of program and accomplishments, FMP, GMasUniv, 6–8.

22. "State Symphony Concert Tonight," *Richmond Newsleader,* May 27, 1936, Virginia clippings, box 80, FMP; "WPA Music Projects Achieve Results," *Salt Lake City Desert News,* June 20, 1936, Utah clippings, box 80, FMP; "State Music Di-

rector Praises WPA Band Under Direction of Professor McCennan in Eunice," *Eunice Review* Mar. 11, 1937, New Mexico clippings, box 69, FMP.

23. Roscoe Wright, "WPA: A Community Appraisal," *Current History and Forum* 49 (Feb. 1939): 42–44; "Music from the Mountains," *Asheville (N.C.) Citizen*, Nov. 16, 1938, Hopkins, box 23, FMP; editorial, *Williamsport Sun*, n.d.; exhibit sent to National Education Council, Dec. 5, 1936, box 23, FMP; "Florida Symphony Orchestra," editorial, *Jacksonville Times-Union*, Dec. 16, 1937, Florida clippings, box 60, FMP.

24. Craig H. Roell, *The Piano in America, 1890–1940* (Chapel Hill, N.C.: Univ. of North Carolina Press, 1989), especially chapters 4–6.

25. "FMP Hoping for a 'Song Conscious' Nation," *Wilmington Star*, Jan. 3, 1937, Delaware clippings, box 59, FMP; George Albee to FMP, Jan. 21, 1938; Sokoloff to Albee, Jan. 25, 1938, Hewes, box 32, FMP.

Expansion, Curtailment, and Attack, 1937–1938

1. Franklin Roosevelt as quoted in Dallek, *FDR and American Foreign Policy*, 122, see also 148–61, 172; Franklin D. Roosevelt, "Quarantine the Aggressors" speech, Chicago, Illinois, Oct. 5, 1937, in *The Public Papers and Addresses of FDR*, Samuel I. Roseman, comp. (New York: Russell and Russell, 1941), 7: 406–11; Leuchtenberg, *FDR*, 284.

2. David Shannon, *Between the Wars: America, 1919–1941* (Boston: Houghton Mifflin, 1965): 178–79.

3. Dallek, *FDR and American Foreign Policy*, 147, 158–59; *Final Report on the WPA Program*, 29; Richard Polenberg, "The Decline of the New Deal, 1937–1940," in John Braeman, et al., eds., *The New Deal: The National Level* (Columbus: Ohio State Univ. Press, 1975), 246–48; Pells, *Radical Visions*, 310.

4. Memo sent to department heads, Apr. 13, 1937, *The Public Papers and Addresses of FDR*, 6: 156; Work Relief Appropriations for 1938, *The Public Papers and Addresses of FDR*, 6: 164; Four Hundredth Press Conference, Oct. 6, 1937, in *The Public Papers and Addresses of FDR*, 7: 419.

5. Letter, Roosevelt to Hopkins, July 1, 1936, WPA box 444c, file no. 7 July–Sept. 1936, FDR Library; MacDonald, *Don't Touch That Dial*, 337; "No Drastic Cuts in Relief Rolls, President Says," *The International Musician* (Jan. 1937): 1.

6. Aliens were sometimes released from the WPA even when no American citizen could be found for a job. See letter, Hopkins to New York Representative Caroline O'Day, Aug. 5, 1937, WPA box 444c, file no. 13 miscellaneous, FDR Library; *New York Times*, June 13, 1937, 1; O'Connor, *The New Deal Art Projects*, 1, foreword.

7. David J. Maurer, "Public Relief Programs and Policies in Ohio, 1929–39," (Ph.D. diss., Ohio State Univ., 1962), 113–17; Harry Hopkins, "Speech Before U.S. Conference of Mayors," Nov. 19, 1935, *Principal Speeches of Harry Hopkins*, typescript, n.d., 3; Harry Hopkins, "Speech over CBS Radio," June 4, 1936, *Principal Speeches of Harry Hopkins*, 4.

8. Series of letters between Roosevelt, Hopkins, and Bell, Nov. 19–Dec. 15, 1937, WPA, box 444c, file no. 8, Nov.–Dec., 1937, FDR Library; letter, Roosevelt to New York Representative Charles A. Buckley, May 21, 1938, WPA, box 444c, file no. 14, miscellaneous, FDR Library; Howard, "Better Days for Music," 107; "Regular Meeting of the International Executive Board, June 9, 1938," *The Inter-*

national Musician (July 1938): 14; Barbara Tischler, *An American Music: The Search for an American Musical Identity* (New York: Oxford Univ. Press, 1986), 141; "Special Supplement," *The International Musician* (June 1939): 14–15.

9. James R. Floyd, "The Federal Muse: A Study of Executive Initiative in Federal Participation on the Arts, 1933–1943," (Ph.D. diss., Kent State Univ., 1975), 247–50.

10. Robert Goldberg, *Grassroots Resistance: Social Movements in Twentieth-Century America* (Belmont, Calif.: Wadsworth, 1991), 101–7.

11. Ellen Woodward to Harry Hopkins, Dec. 5, 1936, response to Combs, box 23, FMP.

12. John P. Loomis, "Reds and Rackets in Work Relief," *Saturday Evening Post* 209 (June 5, 1937): 103; telegram, Historical Survey employee no. 372202 to Roosevelt (copies to Hopkins and Secret Service), Oct. 23, 1937, WPA, 444c, file no. 14, miscellaneous, FDR Library; letter, Hopkins to Marvin McIntyre, assistant secretary to the president, Mar. 20, 1936, WPA, 444c, file no. 7, Mar.–June, 1936, FDR Library.

13. Hearings before Special Committee on Un-American Activities, House of Representatives, 75th Congress, vol. 1, 1938; O'Connor and Brown, *Free, Adult, Uncensored*, 31–32; Martin Dies, *The Trojan Horse* (New York: Ayer, 1940), 298.

14. Martin Dies, *Martin Dies' Story* (New York: Bookmailer, 1963), 50.

15. Ralph Easley to FDR, July 16, 1937, as reprinted in Joan B. Werthman, "The New Deal Federal Art Programs, 1935–1939," (Ph.D. diss., St. John's Univ., 1971), 104–6.

16. Testimony of Wallace Stark, Hearings before a Special Committee, vol. 1, 1938: 928–31 (hereafter referred to by name, Hearings, and page number); Francis Verdi, Hearings, 833; William Humphrey, Hearings, 829–30; Leo Dawson, Hearings, 934; Foster report, 31, LibofCong; O'Connor and Brown, *Free, Adult, Uncensored*, 32–33; Mangione, *The Dream and the Deal*, 187–88.

17. Mathews, *The Federal Theater*, 198–235, quote from 116; Stark, Hearings, 5763, 5772; Report of the Special Committee, Jan. 3, 1939, 4.

18. Penkower, *The Federal Writers' Project*, 181–91.

19. Testimony of White before the House Subcommittee on Appropriations, 1939, pt. 1: 1104.

20. Arthur Ekirch, *Ideologies and Utopias* (Chicago: Quadrangle, 1969), 165; Neal Canon, "Art for Whose Sake: The Federal Music Project of the WPA," in *Challenges in American Culture*, Ray Brown et al., eds. (Bowling Green: Popular Press, 1970), 85–100; Investigation of the WPA Activities, Hearings before the House Subcommittee on Appropriations, 1940, pt. 3: 27.

21. Rhonda Levine, *Class Struggle*, 132–36; "Reds Seek Party Control," *The International Musician* (Sept. 15, 1935): 15.

22. "Resolution no. 10, introduced by Raymond J. Meurer," resolutions, 1935 convention, *The International Musician* (July 1935): 17; "Congratulatory Correspondence, 1937 Convention," *The International Musician* (Aug. 1937): 16.

23. Chalmers Clifton to Sokoloff, Oct. 16, 1935, 211.1 analysis, box 370, FMP; Findley, "Of Tears and Need," 272–73; Warren Susman, *Culture as History: The Transformation of American Society in the Twentieth Century* (New York: Pantheon, 1984), 192; Pells, *Radical Visions*, 194–368; Arthur Ekirch, *Ideologies and Utopias*, 166.

24. Howard, "Better Days for Music," 484; Nicholas E. Tawa, *Serenading the Reluctant Eagle: American Musical Life, 1925–1945* (New York: Schirmer Books, 1984), 114–18.

25. Sokoloff to Woodward, Dec. 17, 1936, 1936–37, Woodward/Hewes, box 32, FMP.

26. Performance and attendance reports, 1937–38, boxes 21–22, FMP; "Philadelphia WPA Music Heard by Nearly 700,000 since January," *Philadelphia L'Osservatore,* Sept. 19, 1937, Pennsylvania clippings, box 76, FMP; press release, Nov. 1938, Department of Information, New York state files, box 44, FMP.

27. Federal Music Project in Indiana, Oct. 1, 1936–July 31, 1937, clippings file, IndStLib; West Virginia two-week report, box 45, FMP.

28. Press release, June 13, 1936, Hewes to Durham for approval, Collier/Hewes 1936, box 32, FMP; 1936 performance reports, FMP files, box 20, FMP; Sokoloff to Harold Stein, Jan. 9, 11, 1937, box 23, FMP; Federal Music Project in Indiana, Oct. 1, 1936–July 31, 1937, clippings file, IndStLib; West Virginia two-week report, box 45, FMP.

29. Edwyn Pfister, "WPA Music a Benefit to All Classes," *Milwaukee Leader,* Apr. 12, 1938; Wisconsin clippings, FMP; Gail Martin, Utah, "U.S. Compositions Well Received," Feb. 24, 1938, "Rendition of Haydn Piece Thrills Patrons," Oct. 5, 1937, both *Desert City News,* Utah clipping file, box 80, FMP.

30. *San Francisco News,* Aug. 31, 1938, as cited in Canon, "Art for Whose Sake," 112–13.

31. Harris Pine, "Federal Music Project Should Be Continued," *The International Musician* (June 1937): 19.

The Only Response: Expanded Exposure

1. "Right To Music," editorial, *Chico Record,* Jan. 7, 1937, 1937 Hopkins M341 file, 11E4 clippings, box 23, FMP.

2. Canon, "Art for Whose Sake," 90; "Philadelphia WPA Music Heard by Nearly 700,000," *Philadelphia L'Osservatore,* Sept. 19, 1937, Pennsylvania clippings, box 76, FMP; "Music Heard by 100,000," *Kansas City Star,* Sept. 18, 1938, Kansas clippings, box 62, FMP; two-week report, Aug. 15–27, 1938, West Virginia reports, box 45, FMP; "Federal Project Musicians Play 3,186 Concerts in State," *Madison Capitol Times,* Sept. 18, 1938, Wisconsin clippings, WiscHistSoc.

3. "Estimate 12,000 Throng Streets," *Grand Island Morning Bulletin,* Oct. 21, 1938, Nebraska clippings, box 67, FMP; "Local Girls on Band Concert Program Here," *Ames Tribune-Times,* July 26, 1938, Iowa clippings, box 62, FMP; "WPA Concert Makes Hit in All-American Program," Lewiston, Apr. 11, 1937, Maine clippings, box 62, FMP.

4. "Victor Alessandro Brings Famous Federal Orchestra Here Tuesday," *Southwestern,* Apr. 1938, Oklahoma clippings, box 75, FMP; "Symphony Comes to All of Virginia," *Richmond Times-Dispatch,* Apr. 3, 1938, Virginia clippings, box 80, FMP; narrative reports, California, Jan. 1938, as cited in Canon, "Art for Whose Sake," 108; Frances Wayne, "Notes on Music," *Denver Post,* Sept. 1938, Colorado clippings, box 55, FMP.

5. Lee Pattison to ———, Jan. 15, 1937, B1, no. 22, Pattison Papers; booklet, *Theater of Music,* B1, no. 19, Pattison Papers; "WPA Music Theater opened in New York City," *The International Musician* (Feb. 4, 1937): 4.

6. MacDonald, *Don't Touch That Dial,* 634; "Eleven Girls, Wearing Costumes of Mother Countries, Pledge Peace," *Baltimore Sun,* June 4, 1937, Maryland clippings, box 62, FMP; "Music for the Mountains," editorial, *North Carolina Citizen,* Nov. 16, 1938, in report on the FMP, 1935–1939, box 25, FMP; "Another Singin' Day Is Drawing Near," *Kentucky Progress Magazine* (Spring 1936), in Kentucky Folk Music, box 34, FMP.

7. Findley, "Of Tears and Need," 140; MacDonald, *Don't Touch That Dial,* 634; "Song Festival To Be June 14," *Louisville Daily Independent,* June 6, 1936; "Hill Folks To Play, Sing in Song Festival," *Louisville Daily Independent,* June 14, 1936, Kentucky clippings, box 62, FMP; Sokoloff to the Ashland Folk Festival, Hewes to Edmunds, July 9, 1937, Kentucky Folk Music file, box 34, FMP.

8. Music Shrines Department, letter from Jessie MacBride, Apr. 14, 1936, MacBride, box 38, FMP.

9. "Wins over Handicap," *Detroit News,* Apr. 16, 1936, FMP files, DetPubLib; press release, 1936, Hewes, 1936–38; press release, 1939, New York state files, box 44, FMP.

10. Salomon to Hewes, Feb. 26, 1936, 1935–37 analysis, box 367, WPA 211.1.

11. Notes for the Play Bureau, memo from Reyher to Mayfarth, June 5, 1937, Reyher/ Hewes, box 32, FMP.

12. Story for FMP written at Jacob's Band Journal's request, Foster no. 12, LibofCong.

13. Roell, *The Piano in America,* 193–99; "May Festival of Music," Bureau of Cooperating Agencies, Helen Kaufman to Lilian Jackson, Apr. 1936, 1936 Music Week Festival, box 35, FMP; "6,000 on WPA to Join Music Week Fetes," *New York Times,* Apr. 24, 1938.

14. Office correspondence, Hewes to Collier, May 14, 1938, Collier/Hewes, box 32, FMP; MacDonald, *Don't Touch That Dial,* 635–36; "Local Music Week Observance Opens With Splendid Concert Auspices WPA Music Project," Lewiston, May 9, 1937, Maine clippings, box 62, FMP.

15. Press release, May 1938, New York City, box 13, FMP; "Native Music Fete is Opened by WPA," *Musical America* 58 (May 10, 1938): 34; Program, "An All-American Concert," May 7, 1938, GMasUniv.

16. "WPA Pageant Attended by 3,200 People," *Hannibal Courier-Post Journal,* July 9, 1937; "Music Program," *St. Louis Dispatch,* July 3, 1937, Missouri clippings, box 66, FMP.

17. "Memphis Will Honor Those Killed in War," *Memphis Commercial Appeal,* May 30, 1937, Tennessee clippings, box 79, FMP; "Impressive Rites Are Held on War Anniversary Here," Huntington, Nov. 11, 1938, West Virginia clippings, box 80, FMP; "Patriotic Fraternal Groups Join in Navy Day Observance," *Phoenix Gazette,* Oct. 27, 1938, Arizona clippings, box 46, FMP.

18. Press release, Sept. 1937, Pennsylvania state files, box 45, FMP; John O. Chequer, *White Plains Argus,* Sept. 24, 1937, New York clippings 1936–37, box 44, FMP; "Constitution Day Program Is Announced," *Phoenix Gazette,* Sept. 18, 1937; "Constitution Program Will Be Held Tonight," *Phoenix Republican,* Sept. 17, 1937, Arizona clippings, box 46, FMP.

19. *Dover (N.H.) Daily Democrat,* Feb. 21, 1938; *Manchester Union-Leader,* Feb. 21, 1938, New Hampshire clippings, box 67, FMP; MacDonald, *Don't Touch That Dial,* 635; Findley, "Of Tears and Need," 230.

20. Ralph Lewando, "WPA Musical Group Offers Fine Program," *Pittsburgh Press,*

Feb. 22, 1938, Pennsylvania clippings, box 77, FMP; "Designation of February as American Music Month, Bill Passed Over," (S1443), statement by Mr. Clark, Mar. 1938, *Congressional Record* 83: 4097.

21. Martin L. Davey, governor of the state of Ohio, "Proclamation," January 20, 1938, Foster no. 10, LibofCong; Frank Murphy, governor of the state of Michigan, "Proclamation to the People of Michigan," Feb. 1938, Foster no. 10, LibofCong; "Proclamation to the People of New Jersey," New Jersey miscellaneous, 1936–40, box 27, FMP.

22. "National Music Week Proclamation," *Long Island Independent,* Feb. 17, 1938, New York clippings, box 69, FMP; "WPA Plans Three Day Music Festival," *Manchester Union-Leader,* Feb. 21, 1938, New Hampshire clippings, box 67, FMP; "Proclamation Asking Music Event Urged," *Manitowoc Herald,* Jan. 11, 1938; "Proclamation," Wausau, Feb. 21, 1938, Wisconsin FMP files, WiscHistSoc; Cecil F. Bates, mayor of Mobile, Alabama, "Proclamation," and Daniel W. Hoan, mayor of Milwaukee, Wisconsin, "Proclamation," Foster no. 10, LibofCong.

23. "American Music Programs," *Meridian Star,* Feb. 20, 1938; "Adult Music Classes Give Two Recitals," *McComb Daily Enterprise,* Feb. 22, 1938, Mississippi clippings, box 66, FMP; "America Makes Music," Charleston, Feb. 26, 1938, West Virginia clippings, box 80, FMP; "Oregon Set to Music," *Portland Oregonian,* Feb. 1938, Oregon clippings, box 75, FMP; "Patriotic Program of Women's Club Open to Public," *Wilmington Press,* Feb. 13, 1938, California clippings, box 46, FMP.

24. "Patriotic Program by Local WPA Group," *Lewiston Evening Journal,* Feb. 23, 1938, Maine clippings, box 62, FMP; "First President Theme," *Portland Oregonian,* Feb. 1938, Oregon clippings, box 75, FMP; "Capacity Crowd Turn Out for Public Concert," *Niagara Falls Gazette,* Feb. 23, 1938, New York clippings, box 69, FMP; "Concert Well Attended," *Williamsport Sun,* Feb. 22, 1938; "WPA Musical Program Given," *Erie Dispatch,* Feb. 22, 1938, Pennsylvania clippings, box 75, FMP; "American Music is Well Received by Wheelingites," Wheeling, Feb. 24, 1938, West Virginia clippings, box 80, FMP; "WPA FMP Sponsoring American Music Program," *Clarksdale Daily Register,* Feb. 22, 1938, Mississippi clippings, box 66, FMP; "Made-In America Music Featured by Civic Orchestra," *Omaha World-Herald,* Feb. 20, 1938, Nebraska clippings, box 67, FMP; "Celebrate Music Week with FMP," *Fox Valley Free Press,* FMP Wisconsin files, WiscHistSoc.

25. "Two Arkansas Composers to Have Premieres," *Arkansas Democrat,* Feb. 20, 1938; "WPA Concert Scheduled Today," *Arkansas Gazette,* Feb. 20, 1938, Arkansas clippings, box 46, FMP; "Fete Washington," *Cleveland Press,* Feb. 19, 1938, Ohio clippings, box 75, FMP; "Work of Two Local Composers Will Be Heard on Program," *Grand Rapids Press,* Feb. 20, 1938, Michigan clippings, box 65, FMP; "Handy Masterpiece Scores at Concert," *Memphis Press,* Feb. 21, 1938, Tennessee clippings, box 79, FMP.

26. "3 Day Festival of Music Scheduled to Begin Tomorrow," *Phoenix Republic,* Feb. 20, 1938, Arizona clippings, box 46, FMP; "WPA Band Concert Features American Composers Music," *Memphis Commercial Appeal,* Feb. 21, 1938, Tennessee clippings, box 79, FMP; "Band Gives Third Concert in Legion Hall," Superior, FMP Wisconsin files, WiscHistSoc; "Program Presented at Carolina Home," South Carolina, Feb. 1938, South Carolina clippings, box 79, FMP.

27. Cole to Hewes, Feb. 1938, box 31, FMP.

Gettysburg: An Opera for the People

1. "Confederates Make Ready to Meet Their Former Foes," and "Throngs Flock to Gettysburg," *Los Angeles Times,* June 27, 1938. "President Dedicates Eternal Peace Light at Gettysburg," *Los Angeles Times,* July 4, 1938, 1; "Gettysburg Farewell," *Newsweek* 12 (July 11, 1938): 12; "Text of President's Address at Shrine of Patriotism," *Los Angeles Times,* July 4, 1938.

2. Gail Martin, "Fanfare," *Salt Lake City Desert News,* June 18, 1938, Utah clippings, box 80, FMP.

3. Barbara Zuck, *A History of Musical Americanism* (Ann Arbor: UMI Research Press, 1980), 161; Ray Allen Billington, "Government and the Arts: The WPA Experience," *American Quarterly* 13 (Winter 1961): 466–79.

4. John Dizikes, *Opera in American: A Cultural History* (New Haven: Yale Univ. Press, 1993), 311–443; Eduard Lindeman, "Farewell to Bohemia," *Survey Graphic* (Apr. 1937): 207–8; Herbert Gans, "American Popular Culture and High Culture in a Changing Class Structure," *Prospects* 10 (1985): 17–21.

5. On the similarities of the FMP opera technology and the FTP *Living Newspaper,* see O'Connor, *The New Deal Art Projects,* 10–15, and Whitman, *Bread and Circuses,* 85–89; "Considering the Vast Panorama of Federal Music Activity," *Musical America* 57 (May 25, 1937): 16; Frederich Warren, "Needed: A New Deal for Singers," *Musician* 39 (Mar. 1934): 17; editorial, *Musician* 42 (Jan. 1937):14; McDonald, *Federal Relief Administration and the Arts,* 621–23.

6. Memo to Dorothy Fredenhagen from Hewes, Feb. 12, 1940, box 32, FMP; Nikolai Sokoloff, "America's Vast Musical Awakening," *Etude* 55 (Apr. 1937): 221; Peter Mehren, "San Diego's Opera Unit of the WPA Federal Music Project," *Journal of San Diego History* 18 (Summer 1972): 12–21.

7. "Don't Pity the American Composer," *The Baton,* Jan. 1937, box 12, FMP.

8. Press release, FMP, for Sept. 26, 1936, R. P. Chase Papers, MinnHistSoc; "The Federal Music Project Takes Inventory," *Musical America* 58 (Feb. 10, 1938): 179.

9. Press release, *Wilderness Stone,* May, 1936; *Wilderness Stone,* program, May 24, 1936, Manhattan Theatre, boxes 1 and 2, folders 6 and 12, Pattison Papers.

10. Nikolai Sokoloff, *The Federal Music Project Manual,* n.d., 14–19; *The Romance of Robot,* music by Frederick Hart, libretto by Tillman Breiseth (Washington, D.C.: WPA, 1937), box 1, 1937, folder 27, Pattison Papers, quotes from pp. 6–14; Olin Downes, "Chamber Operas Are Given by WPA," *New York Times,* Apr. 13, 1937, amusement section, 3; program for *Romance of Robot,* GMasUniv; letter, Lee Pattison, director of New York City FMP, to supporter, Jan. 15, 1937, box 1, folder 27, Pattison Papers; letter, Mrs. Preston Edwards of the Taxpayers of New York City Professional Artists Group to President Roosevelt, July 16, 1937, president's official file, box 444c, file no. 13, WPA miscellaneous, FDR Library. For a more complex overview of the ideas of the machine age, modernism, and its critics, see Peter Wollen, "Cineman/Americanism? the Robot," in *Modernity and Mass Culture,* James Naremore and Patrick Brantlinger, eds. (Bloomington: Indiana Univ. Press, 1991), 42–69.

11. Marjory N. Fisher, *San Francisco News,* Dec. 3, 1936; *Oakland Post-Enquirer,* Dec. 4, 1936; John Hobart, *San Francisco Chronicle,* Dec. 4, 1936; program and musical score from *Take Your Choice,* GMasUniv.

12. *Gettysburg* program, GMasUniv; Isabela Morse Jones, "New American Opera Gets Pacific Premiere," *Los Angeles Times* California clippings, FMP; Neil Butterworth,

A Dictionary of American Composers (New York: Garland Publishers, 1984), 397; "Concert and Opera . . . 'Gettysburg' for Stage," *New York Times,* May 29, 1938.

13. "American Compositions," in 1937 Hopkins, box 23, FMP; Gilbert Seldes, "Jazz, Opera, or Ballet?" *Modern Music* 16 (Mar. 1939):15–16; Pearl Brown Brands, "Music Written About Abraham Lincoln," *Etude* 56 (Feb. 1938): 77–78.

14. Lawrence W. Levine, "Hollywood's Washington: Film Images of National Politics During the Great Depression," *Prospects* 10 (1985): 181; Charles Alexander, *Here the Country Lies: Nationalism and the Arts in the 20th Century* (Bloomington: Univ. of Indiana Press, 1980), 194.

15. "Concert and Opera . . . 'Gettysburg' for Stage"; "New Opera 'Gettysburg' To Be Broadcast by Federal Unit," *San Diego Sun,* July 4, 1938, 4; Jones, "New American Opera Gets Pacific Premiere."

16. "Federals Will Present New American Opera," *Los Angeles Times,* May 1, 1938, California clippings, box 50, FMP; "American Opera Set for May 10," May 1, 1938; "Address Set to Music," May 8, 1938; "'Gettysburg' Tonight," May 10, 1938, all from *Los Angeles Examiner,* box 50, FMP; "'Gettysburg' Opera Americana, sara' presentata dal Teatro Federale,"*La Parola Degli Italiani,* May 5, 1938; "Federal Music Project Majusi Musora," *Magyarsag,* May 6, 1938, box 50, FMP.

17. "'Gettysburg' in Local Opera Production," *Variety* May 7, 1938, box 50, FMP; "Ralph Bellamy Backstage Helper," *Los Angeles Evening News,* May 9, 1938, box 50, FMP.

18. Harle Jervis to Sokoloff, May 16, 1938, in California miscellaneous reports, 1938, box 27, FMP; "Concert and Opera . . . 'Gettysburg' for Stage"; Jervis to Sokoloff, box 27, FMP; "Address Set to Music," *Los Angeles Examiner,* May 8, 1938, box 50, FMP.

19. Frank Mittauer, "The Federals Present a New Opera in Outline," *Los Angeles Evening News,* May 11, 1938, box 50, FMP.

20. Carl Bronson, "Music of 'Gettysburg' Enthuses Audience," *Los Angeles Herald and Express,* May 11, 1938, box 50, FMP.

21. "4 'Gettysburg' Episodes Given," *Los Angeles Examiner,* May 11, 1938, box 50, FMP; Bronson, "Music of 'Gettysburg,'"; Gail Martin, "Fanfare," *Salt Lake City Desert News,* June 18, 1938, Utah clippings, box 80, FMP.

22. Sara Boynoff, "New Opera Premiered by Federals," *Los Angeles Daily News,* May 11, 1938; Frank Mittauer, "The Federals Present a New Opera"; Fay M. Jackson, "Hollywood," *California Eagle,* May 19, 1938, box 50, FMP.

23. Newsletter, Los Angeles FMP, "*Gettysburg* Tops Music Month," May 13, 1938, WPA, box 444c, file no. 14, miscellaneous, FDR Library; "Gettysburg Will be Celebrated in Concert," *Los Angeles Times,* July 3, 1938.

24. "'Gettysburg' War on Program," *Los Angeles Daily News,* July 4, 1938; "'Gettysburg' Opera at Park Tonight," *Los Angeles Examiner,* July 4, 1938; "'Gettysburg' Concert Scheduled in Park," *Los Angeles Times,* July 4, 1938, box 50, FMP; Arthur Johnson, director of Public Relations, Los Angles FMP, to Charles Marsh, FMP district supervisor, July 5, 1938, in California miscellaneous 1938–40, box 26, FMP; "New Opera 'Gettysburg' To Be Broadcast by Federal Unit," 4; announcement, Balboa Park, San Diego, July 1, 1938, California clippings, box 51, FMP.

25. "New Opera 'Gettysburg' To Be Broadcast by Federal Unit," 4; "Gettysburg Concert Scheduled in Park"; at no time did the *Times* advise its readers of the time the broadcast was to take place or the station the opera was to be broadcast over.

Johnson to Marsh, July 5, 1938, in California miscellaneous, 1938–40, box 26, FMP; "New Opera 'Gettysburg' To Be Broadcast by Federal Unit," 4; Dedication to *Gettysburg* as quoted in Canon, "Federal Music Project," 260.

26. Gastone Usigli in the *Gettysburg* program, Sept. 23, 1938, in 1938 California miscellaneous, box 39, FMP; "Hear America First," *Los Angeles Times*, editorial, May 9, 1938; "Musicians Enthused By New Opera," *Los Angeles Times*. California clippings, FMP.

27. Program, box 39, FMP; southern California project annual report, 1938, in 1937–38 California annual reports, box 12, FMP.

28. "Support for an Opera," *Los Angeles Evening News*, Sept. 3, 1938, box 51, FMP.

29. Hewes to John Selby, Sept. 9, 1938, 1935–37, box 369, WPA, 211.1.

30. "All-American Cast to Sing in 'Gettysburg,'" *Los Angeles Daily News*, Sept. 17, 1938, box 51, FMP; "Chamber Foundation Backs 'Gettysburg,'" *Hollywood Citizen News*, Sept. 17, 1938; "Premiere Is Arranged," *Pasadena Star News*, Sept. 17, 1938; "'Gettysburg' Given in Bowl," *Riverside Press*, Sept. 17, 1938; "Foundation to Give 'Gettysburg' Opera," *Los Angeles Examiner*, Sept. 18, 1938, box 51, all FMP.

31. "'Gettysburg' Premiere at Bowl Tonight," *Los Angeles Examiner*, Sept. 23, 1938, box 51, FMP; Edwin Schallert, "Gettysburg Premiere Brilliant as Production," *Los Angeles Times*; program, box 39, FMP; program, box 39; program, GMasUniv; Jones, "Bowl Premiere Offers New American Opera," *Los Angeles Times* California clippings, FMP; Southern California annual report, 1938, box 12, FMP.

32. Program, GMasUniv; press release, Sept. 17, 1938, box 51, FMP; "'Gettysburg' To Be Given at Bowl," *Riverside Press*, Sept. 17, 1938, box 51, FMP; Carl Bronson, "'Gettysburg' in Premiere Rehearsals," *Los Angeles Herald and Examiner*, Sept. 17, 1938, box 51, FMP.

33. Jones, "New American Opera Gets Pacific Premiere" *Los Angeles Times*; "Opera and Concert," *New York Times*, Sept. 18, 1938; "New Opera 'Gettysburg' To Be Broadcast by Federal Unit," 4; Schallert, "Gettysburg Premiere Brilliant as Production."

34. "New Opera to Open at Bowl," *Santa Monica Outlook*, Sept. 17, 1938, box 51, FMP.

35. Press release, Sept. 17, 1938; "'Gettysburg' to Have Premiere at Hollywood Bowl Tonight," *Los Angeles Examiner*, Sept. 23, 1938, box 51, FMP; "Folk Play Takes Vacation," *Los Angeles Times*, Sept. 18, 1939.

36. *Gettysburg* Program, GMasUniv.

37. "Mrs. Carter Lauds Opera 'Gettysburg,'" *Los Angeles Examiner*, Sept. 19, 1938, box 51, FMP; Carl Bronson, "'Gettysburg' in Triumph," *Los Angeles Herald and Express*, Sept. 24, 1938, box 51, FMP; "'Gettysburg' Makes Debut," *Los Angeles Evening News*, Sept. 24, 1938, box 51, FMP; "'Gettysburg' Premiere Held at Bowl," *Hollywood Citizen-News*, Sept. 24, 1938; "'Gettysburg' American Opera, in Big Bow," *Variety*, Sept. 24, 1938, box 51, FMP; Alfred Price Quinn, "Music," *B'nai B'rith Messenger*, Sept. 30, 1938, box 51, FMP; Hal B. Crain, "Hollywood Hears New Native Opera," *Musical America* 57 (Oct. 1938): 10.

38. Press release, Sept. 17, 1938, box 51, FMP; letter from Hewes to Clifton, Sept. 16, 1938, box 369, WPA, 211.1, FMP; "'Gettysburg,' American Opera, in Big Bow"; "Premiere for 'Gettysburg,'" *Los Angeles Evening News*, Sept. 23, 1938, box 51, FMP; "Concert and Opera . . . 'Gettysburg' for Stage."

39. Hewes to Tindall, Oct. 20, 1938, 1935–39, box 369, WPA, 211.1; Tindall to Hewes, Nov. 10, 1938, box 369, WPA, 211.1.
40. Hal B. Crain, "LA WPA Effort Criticized," *Musical America* 56 (Aug. 1937): 23.

Evaluation and Participation: American Composers and the FMP

1. Alan Howard Levy, *Musical Nationalism: American Composers Search for Identity* (Westport, Conn.: Greenwood, 1983), 14–29; Canon, "Federal Music Project," 119, 174.
2. Malcolm Cowley, *Exile's Return: A Literary Odyssey of the 1920s* (New York: Viking, 1951); Stearns quote from Raymond H. Geselbracht, "Evolution and the New World Vision in the Music of Charles Ives," *Journal of American Studies* 8 (Aug. 1974): 211; Virgil Thompson, "America's Musical Maturity: A 20th Century Story," *Yale Review* 51 (1961): 66–71; Levy, *Musical Nationalism*, i–x, chapters 3–6; Charles Hamm, *Music in the New World* (New York: Norton, 1983), chapters 18–20; H. Wiley Hitchcock, *Music in the United States: A Historical Introduction* (Englewood Cliffs, N.J.: Prentice-Hall, 1974), 173–205; Gilbert Chase, *America's Music: From the Pilgrims to the Present* (Urbana: Univ. of Illinois Press, 1987), chapters 25–27; Glenn Watkins, *Soundings: Music in the Twentieth Century* (New York: Schirmer, 1988), 235–462.
3. Zuck, *A History of Musical Americanism*, 171, 272.
4. David King Dunaway, "Unsung Songs of Protest: The Composers Collective of New York," *New York Folklore* 5 (Summer 1979): 2.
5. Robbie Lieberman, *"My Song Is My Weapon": People's Songs, American Communism, and the Politics of Culture, 1930–1950* (Urbana: Univ. of Illinois Press, 1988): 25–31.
6. Roy Harris, "American Music Enters a New Phase," *Scribner's* 96 (Oct. 1934): 218–21; John Tasker Howard, "Better Days for Music," *Harper's* 174 (Apr. 1937): 483–91; Roy Harris, "Does Music Have to Be European," *Scribner's* 91 (Apr. 1932): 208–9.
7. Oscar Levant, as quoted in Zuck, *A History of Musical Americanism*, 95; Aaron Copland, as quoted in Tawa, *Serenading the Reluctant Eagle*, 31; Virgil Thompson, as quoted in Tawa, *Serenading the Reluctant Eagle*, 34.
8. Dunaway, "Unsung Songs Of Protest," 7–13; Levy, *Musical Nationalism*, 135.
9. Charles Seeger, "Grass Roots for American Composers," *Modern Music* 15 (Mar.–Apr. 1931): 143–49; Charles Seeger, "On Proletarian Music," *Modern Music* 11 (Mar. 1934): 121–27; Hanns Eisler, "Reflections on the Future of the Composer," *Modern Music* 12 (May 1935): 180–86.
10. *Index of American Composers*, as quoted in Canon, "Federal Music Project," 134; "Don't Pity the American Composer," *FMP Baton*, Jan. 1937, California file, box 12, FMP; release, June 4, 1938, Hewes/Collier file, box 32, FMP.
11. Tischler, *An American Music*, 139–41; regional meeting, June 22–24, 1936, minutes, 7, Foster no. 4, LibofCong.
12. Frances Boardman, "American Music Culture Dawn is Seen," *St. Paul Universal Weekly*, July 31, 1938, Minnesota clippings, box 66, FMP; Howard Hanson to Sokoloff, June 27, 1936, letters file H, box 32, FMP; both quotes found in *Inventory: An Appraisal of Results of the FMP*, (Washington, D.C.: GPO, 1938), 4; Samuel Chotzinoff, "Composers' Forum Series Ends Tomorrow Night," *New York Post*, June 23, 1936, New York education music file, box 14, FMP; Agate quote in

Ashley Pettis, "The WPA and the American Composer," *Musical Quarterly* 26 (Jan. 1940): 101.

13. Sokoloff to Harold Stein, Jan. 9–11, 1937, box 23, FMP; Sokoloff, *The Federal Music Project,* 23.

14. "WPA Plans a Composers' Laboratory in New York," *Musical America* 55 (Oct. 10, 1935): 32; "Wide WPA Activity in New York City," *Musical America* 55 (Nov. 10, 1935): 34; Ashley Pettis, Composers' Forum transcripts, as quoted in Canon, "Federal Music Project," 124; Frances McFarland, "The FMP in New York City," *Music Educators National Conference Yearbook, 1936* (Chicago: MENC, 1936), 386.

15. Press release, n.d. [1936], R. P. Chase Papers, MinnHistSoc; press release, Mar. 7, 1937; FMP of New York City, 1936–38, New York state file, box 44, FMP; MacDonald, *Don't Touch That Dial,* 625–26.

16. Sokoloff, *The Federal Music Project,* 23–24; press release, Mar. 7, 1937, New York state file, 1936–38, box 44, FMP.

17. Harris and Schumann, comments before composers' forum, June 15, 1938, and Oct. 11, 1938, as quoted in Canon, "Federal Music Project," 257–58; Harold Morris to the FMP, Dec. 1935, New York City Educational Division, 1935, box 14, FMP; Marion Bauer to the FMP, Jan. 28, 1936, New York City Educational, box 14, FMP; William Schuman, as quoted in Canon, "Federal Music Project," 127–30.

18. Frank Colby, "The Salvation of American Composers," *FMP Baton,* Dec. 1936, California clippings, box 12, FMP; "New Phase of Musicians' Aid Is Planned by WPA," *Musical America* 56 (Jan. 25, 1936): 20; "American Works Have Prominent Place in New York Relief Symphony Lists," *Musical America* 55 (July 1935): 26; press release, June 4, 1936, Hewes to Collier, 1936 office correspondence, box 32, FMP; "Head of WPA Music Issues Compilation," *Musical America* 59 (Apr. 10, 1939): 23.

19. "Head of WPA Music Issues Compilation," 23.

20. Canon, "Federal Music Project," 114–40; "Block Score Given in San Francisco," *Musical America* 57 (Apr. 25, 1937): 23; Marjory Fisher, "Search Work Given in San Francisco," *Musical America* 58 (Oct. 10, 1937): 16; *Congressional Quarterly* 79 (Aug. 1935): 12473; Sokoloff report on FMP to Sirovich Committee, Dec. 1, 1937, box 25, FMP; memo to WPA administrator, May 29, 1937, WPA box 444c, file no. 8, May, July 1937, FDR Library.

21. Report on purposes and activities, Philadelphia, 1937, box 15, FMP.

22. Oklahoma FMP report, box 15, FMP; "Indian Music and Dance Revue Exposition Feature," *Tulsa Tribune,* Oklahoma clippings, box 74, FMP; Frederick W. Goodrich, report on FMP in Oregon, 1935–1942, original handwritten copy, 11, Oregon Historical Society; Cecil Betron, "Detroiter's Composition in First Performance Here," *Detroit News,* Mar. 15, 1939, FMP files, DetPubLib.

23. "American Conductors," *The International Musician* (Apr. 1937): 12; Canon, "Federal Music Project," 83.

24. Oklahoma FMP report, Aug. 16, 1940, Victor Alessandro, box 15, FMP; Carol Wilmoth, "Heavenly Harmony: The WPA Symphony Orchestra, 1937–1942," *The Chronicles of Oklahoma* 64 (Summer 1986): 35–52; "Police Marksman's Gun Stays Home Nights as Maestro Roth Wields Baton," *Toledo Bee,* Apr. 2, 1936, Ohio clippings, box 72, FMP; "Conductor for WPA Is Young American," *Detroit News,* Nov. 11, 1936, FMP files, DetPubLib; Vicki L. Eaklor, "The Illinois Symphony

Orchestra, 1936–1942: Microcosm of a Cultural New Deal," in *Selected Papers in Illinois History, 1980* (Illinois Historical Society, 1982), 69–77.

25. Sokoloff testimony before House Committee on Patents, no. 1, pt. 1, 1938: 126–27.

26. Performance and attendance chart, June 1939, FMP; McDonald, *Federal Relief Administration and the Arts,* 643; letter, Roosevelt to Vernon Leftwich, California Society of Composers, Jan. 28, 1937, president's personal file, file no. 100, music miscellaneous, FDR Library. Roosevelt's response, while typically noncommittal, represents one of his few responses to any FMP activity. The president, so far as can be found, never attended a project concert and rarely spoke in either public or private about the FMP's activities.

27. Alfred Frankenstein, *San Francisco Chronicle,* Mar. 20, 1936, excerpts in interoffice memo, Dec. 7, 1936, box 23, FMP; "Music Outside of New York," FMP Newsletter, New York City, July 1936, New York City clippings, box 15, FMP; Jacob Weinberg to Sokoloff, n.d., excerpts from letters, July 1935, department reports file, box 14, FMP; Charles Wakefield Cadman, comment relating to FMP by distinguished persons, excerpts, 1937 report to Hopkins, box 23, FMP; William Grant Still, "The American Composer," *FMP Baton,* Mar. 1937, California clippings, box 12, FMP.

Exposure, Not Equality: Black Musicians and the FMP

1. Maya Angelou, *I Know Why the Caged Bird Sings* (New York: Random House, 1969), 41.

2. "Unemployment Among Negroes," *The World Tomorrow* 14 (May 1931): 135–36; John B. Kirby, *Black Americans in the Roosevelt Era: Liberalism and Race* (Knoxville: Univ. of Tennessee Press, 1980), 97–110; Charles S. Johnson, "Incidence upon the Negroes," *American Journal of Sociology* 40 (May 1935): 737–45; Harvard Sitkoff, *A New Deal for Blacks* (New York: Oxford Univ. Press, 1978), 34–39.

3. C. Vann Woodward, *The Strange Career of Jim Crow* (New York: Oxford Univ. Press, 1974), 118; Norma L. Daoust, "Building the Democratic Party: Black Voting in Providence in the 1930s," *Rhode Island History* 44 (Aug. 1985): 80–88; John Hope Franklin, *From Slavery to Freedom: A History of Negro Americans* (New York: Knopf, 1974): 398–99; Raymond Wolters, "The New Deal and the Negro," in Braemen, et al., *The New Deal,* 206–8.

4. Leslie H. Fishel Jr., "The Negro and The New Deal," 178–81; Ronald Heinemann, "Blue Eagle or Black Buzzard? The NRA in Virginia," *Virginia Magazine of History and Biography* 89 (1981): 90–100; John P. Davis, "Blue Eagles and Black Workers," *New Republic* 81 (Nov. 14, 1934): 7–9; Langston Hughes, "Ballad of Roosevelt," in Davis, "Blue Eagles," 9.

5. Nancy L. Grant, *TVA and Black Americans* (Philadelphia: Temple Univ. Press, 1989); Sitkoff, *A New Deal for Blacks,* 40–55; Fishel, "The Negro and The New Deal," 181.

6. Kirby, *Black Americans in the Roosevelt Era,* 76–96.

7. Sitkoff, *A New Deal for Blacks,* 59–83; Fishel, "The Negro and the New Deal," 182–83; Wolters, "The New Deal and the Negro," 193; FDR address at the dedication of the new chemistry building, Howard Univ., Oct. 26, 1936, in *The Public Papers and Addresses of FDR,* vol. 5, 1936: 538.

8. Franklin D. Roosevelt, "A Greeting to the NAACP," June 25, 1938, in *The Pub-*

lic Papers and Addresses of FDR, vol. 7, 1938: 401; Harry Hopkins, *Spending to Save: The Complete Story of Relief* (New York: W. W. Norton, 1936), 160–61; Harry Hopkins, "Speech at Teachers' College," Columbia Univ., May 15, 1937, *Principal Speeches of Harry Hopkins,* n.p.

9. Larry Whatley, "The WPA in Mississippi," *Journal of Mississippi History* 30 (Feb. 1968): 35–50; Terkel as cited in Sitkoff, *A New Deal for Blacks,* 69–71; Franklin, *From Slavery to Freedom,* 407.

10. "The New Deal and the Negro," speech of Honorable Arthur W. Mitchell, Illinois, in the House of Representatives, Oct. 14, 1942 (Washington, D.C.: 1942), 3–16.

11. "The New Deal and the Negro," 4, 16; *Workers on Relief in the U.S., March 1935* (Washington: GPO, 1937), 8; Penkower, *The Federal Writers' Project,* 66–67. For a discussion of the problems faced by African Americans participating in the FTP, see E. Quinta Craig, *Black Drama of the Federal Theater Project: Beyond the Formal Horizons* (Amherst: Univ. of Massachusetts Press, 1980).

12. MacDonald, *Federal Relief Administration and the Arts,* 614; state of Wisconsin, performance and attendance chart, FMP files, WiscHistSoc.

13. Swing as a name developed as an outgrowth of the need to de-emphasize the blackness of jazz. The BBC substituted the word swing for jazz so as not to offend its listeners. Leslie B. Rout, "Economics and Race in Jazz," in *Frontiers of American Culture*; Alexander, *Nationalism in American Thought,* 82–83; Gunther Schuller, *The Swing Era* (Oxford: Oxford Univ. Press, 1989); James Lincoln Collier, *Benny Goodman and the Swing Era* (Oxford: Oxford Univ. Press, 1989); Kenneth J. Bindas, "Race, Class, and Ethnicity Among Swing Era Musicians," in *America's Musical Pulse: Popular Music in Twentieth-Century Society,* Kenneth J. Bindas, ed. (Westport, Conn.: Greenwood Press, 1992), 73–82.

14. Carl R. Diton, "The Present Status of Negro-American Musical Endeavor," *Musician* 20 (Nov. 1915): 689; White, "The Musical Genius of the American Negro," 306; Georgia Ryder, "Another Look at Some American Cantatas," *The Black Perspective in Music* 3 (May 1975): 136–37.

15. Leonard Goines, "Black Musicians and Composers," *Allegro* 73 (June 1973): 6, 22; "The Anderson Case," *Musical America* 59 (Mar. 12, 1939): 16.

16. "Negroes in the Professions," *Literary Digest* 117 (May 12, 1934): 41.

17. Gail Martin, "Federal Project Chief High in Praise of Sinfonetta," *Salt Lake City Desert News* Apr. 6, 1937, Utah clippings, box 88, FMP.

18. Release from Hewes to Thomas Parker to Professor Alain Locke of Howard Univ., Nov. 3, 1938, Hewes, box 30, FMP; Sokoloff to Foster, March 4, 1938, Foster no. 31, LibofCong.

19. "American Folk Singers Heard in Jordan Hall," *Boston Transcript,* Nov. 29, 1937, Massachusetts clippings, box 64, FMP; "WPA Music Project Presents Original Works of Negroes," *Eagle,* May 1, 1936, California clippings, FMP; report from NYC Educational Division, Mar. 1936, performance reports, box 34, FMP.

20. "High Praise Given Negro Orchestra," *Richmond Newsletter,* Oct. 14, 1937, Virginia clippings, box 80, FMP; "Negro Singers Are Praised by O. J. Jones and Others," Princeton, Kent, Kentucky clippings, box 62, FMP; "Negroes Will Give Concert," *Charlotte Observer,* Nov. 30, 1936, North Carolina clippings, box 72, FMP.

21. Cooper Holsworth, "Works Progress in Music," *Chicago Music News,* June 16, 1938, Illinois clippings, box 87, FMP; "Joseph Cole, Soloist, Slated for Local Premiere March 20," *Michigan Chronicle,* Mar. 19, 1938; "Two Soloists Will Appear

With Civic Orchestra Sunday," *Detroit Tribune,* Mar. 19, 1938; "Detroit Civic Orchestra Will Present Symphony Composed by Noted Colored Musician," *Detroit Tribune,* Feb. 11, 1939, all from the FMP in Detroit files, DetPubLib.

22. "First Harvest of Harmony Big Success," *Grand Island Daily Independent,* Oct. 21, 1938; "Estimated 12,000 Throng Streets," *Grand Island Morning Bulletin,* Oct. 21, 1938, Nebraska clippings, box 67, FMP; "Negro Choirs Draw Throng," *Omaha World-Herald,* Apr. 25, 1938, Nebraska clippings, box 67, FMP; "Large Crowd Enjoys Cantata at W. High," Parsons, Kansas, clippings, box 62, FMP.

23. W. L. Dean to Sokoloff, California miscellaneous files, 1936–39, box 26, FMP; "WPA Music Project Achieves Results," *Salt Lake City Desert News,* Utah clippings, box 80, FMP; Southern California annual report, 1938, California annual report, box 12, FMP; "An All-Negro Cast," *California Evening News,* June 28, 1938, California clippings, box 50, FMP; "Project Programs in San Francisco," *Musical America* 58 (Sept. 1937): 20.

24. "Musical Program on Mother's Day," *Hope Star,* May 11, 1937, Arkansas clippings, box 46, FMP; E. Stapleton, FMP North Carolina director, to William Mayfarth, Apr. 24, 1939, miscellaneous reports, New York, 1936–39, box 28, FMP; "FMP Here Given High Compliments by National Inspector," *Kansas City Kansan,* Oct. 5, 1938, Kansas clippings, box 62, FMP; Rene Salomon to Hewes, June 9, 1936, 1936–40 miscellaneous reports, box 27, FMP; "Negro WPA Orchestra Gives Concert Friday," *Richmond News-Leader,* Oct. 13, 1936, Virginia clippings, box 80, FMP; "WPA Negro Choir Will Sing Sunday," *Savannah News,* Nov. 26, 1936, Georgia clippings, box 61, FMP; "Music Class for Negroes," *Duncan Banner,* Feb. 20, 1938, Oklahoma clippings, box 74, FMP; "WPA Music Project in Detroit," *The Keynote,* Oct.–Nov., 1938, Michigan clippings, box 87, FMP; "WPA Orchestra to Play in Parks," *Akron Sun Times,* Ohio clippings, box 72, FMP.

25. Educational reports, Florida, 1938, box 16, FMP; "Negro Glee Club to Give Program at VA Hospital," *Albuquerque News Journal,* Mar. 31, 1937; "Sick Veterans to Hear Program by Choristers," *Albuquerque Journal,* Dec. 13, 1937, New Mexico clippings, box 69, FMP.

26. George Seltzer, *Music Matters: The Performer and the American Federation of Musicians* (Metuchen, N.J.: Scarecrow Press, 1989), 108–17; Donald Spivey, *Union and the Black Musician: The Narrative of William Everett Samuels of Chicago Local 208* (New York, 1984); Application for recognition, Tampa Colored Local 721, AFM convention 1937, *The International Musician* (Aug. 1937): 14.

27. Frances Boardman, "Civic Jubilee Singers Give Charming Concert," *St. Paul Pioneer Press,* May 14, 1936, Minnesota clippings, box 66, FMP; "Week of Garden Tours Featured by Negro Chorus," *Vicksburg Democrat,* Mississippi clippings, box 66, FMP; Sokoloff, *The Federal Music Project,* 26–27, GMasUniv.

28. "American Folk Singers on WPA Program," *Woburn Times,* Feb. 23, 1938, Massachusetts clippings, box 64, FMP; Mississippi Folk Music, June 1936, B34; Helene G. Alfond to Jerome Sage, Sept. 11, 1936, Mississippi miscellaneous, 1936–40, box 27, FMP.

29. "Swan Song of Colored Chorus Last Night," *Las Cruces Sun,* Aug. 16, 1938, New Mexico clippings, box 659, FMP; "Negro WPA Orchestra Gives Concert Friday," *Richmond News-Leader,* Oct. 31, 1936, Virginia clippings, box 80, FMP; "Blues Get Dignity in Rewriting," *Oklahoma City Times,* June 24, 1938, Okla-

homa clippings, box 74, FMP; Louisiana narrative reports, June 1936, as quoted in Findley, "Of Tears and Need," 144.

30. "Protest Made on WPA Group," *Boston Chronicle*, Sept. 19, 1936; performance reports, Massachusetts, 1936, box 63, FMP; Arnold to Sokoloff, Apr. 26, 1938, FMP files, WiscHistSoc; performance reports, New York, box 44, FMP.

31. "A Survey of Music Ed Facilities in the Separate Schools of Oklahoma," 1939, Foster no. 38, LibofCong; Audition Boards, box 375, WPA, 211.1; Florida ed. reports, black narrative, 1936–39, boxes 16–17, FMP; Tennessee record of operation, GMasUniv; Kansas record of operation, n.p., n.d., 1939, GMasUniv.

32. "Combined Negro Chorus to Give Program Here," *Tampa Tribune*, May 5, 1937, Florida clippings, box 60, FMP; "Audience Thrilled by Negro Spirituals at Music Festival Here," *Asheville (N.C.) Citizen*, Sept. 24, 1937, North Carolina clippings, box 72, FMP; "Colored Citizens Invited to Become Members of Orchestral Association," *Norfolk Journal-Guide*, Oct. 17, 1936; "WPA Negro Group Gives Concert Friday," *Richmond News-Leader*, Oct. 28, 1936, Virginia clippings, box 80, FMP; "WPA FMP, Roswell, Fine Stringed Instruments, Negro Spirituals," *Roswell Record*, June 13, 1938, New Mexico clippings, box 69, FMP.

33. "Total and Negro Population by State and Per Cent of Negro Population in Each State in 1930," *The Missionary Review of the World* 59 (June 1936): 288–89.

34. Spivey, *Union and the Black Musician*, 48.

Stepdaughters of Orpheus: Women Musicians and the FMP

1. Gail Martin, "Federal Project Chief High in Praise of Utah Sinfonietta," *Salt Lake City Desert News*, Apr. 6, 1937, Utah clippings, box 88, FMP.

2. Susan Ware, *Holding Their Own: American Women in the 1930s* (Boston: Twayne, 1982), 17.

3. Winifred Wandersee, "A New Deal for Women: Government Programs, 1933–1940," in *The Roosevelt New Deal*, Wilbur J. Cohen, ed. (Austin: LBJ Library, 1986), 185–86; Alice Kessler-Harris, *Out to Work: A History of Wage Earning Women in the United States* (New York: Oxford Univ. Press, 1982), 250–72.

4. Raymond M. Panzer, "Stepdaughters of Orpheus," *Independent Woman* 15 (Feb. 1936): 39. For an excellent examination of the social changes among women during the period, see Elaine Tyler May, *Homeward Bound: American Families in the Cold War Era* (New York: Basic Books, 1988), 37–57.

5. Roell, *The Piano in America*, 13–22; Frederique Petrides, "Women in Orchestras," *Etude* 56 (July 1938), 430; Judith Tick, "Passed Away Is the Piano Girl," in *Women Making Music*, Jane Bowers and Judith Tick, eds. (Urbana, Ill.: Univ. of Illinois Press, 1986), 332–33.

6. "Women in Music: Twin Souls of Civilization," *Etude* 48 (Nov. 1929): 793; Carl Engel, "What Great Music Owes to Women," *Etude* 48 (Nov. 1929): 797.

7. Carol Neuls-Bates, "Women's Orchestras in the U.S., 1925–45," in *Women Making Music*, 349–50; Janet M. Hooks, *Women's Occupations Through Seven Decades* (Washington, D.C.: GPO, 1947), 27, 65, 167; V. F. Calverton, "Carriers for Women," *Current History* 29 (Jan. 1929): 634; Robyn Muncy, *Creating a Female Dominion in American Reform, 1890–1935* (New York: Oxford Univ. Press, 1991).

8. "Unemployment Among Women in the Early Years of the Depression," *Monthly Labor Review* 38 (Apr. 1934): 790–95; Kessler-Harris, *Out to Work*, 254–55. Polling information taken from Hadley Cantril, ed., *Public Opinion, 1935–1946*

(Princeton, N.J.: Princeton Univ. Press, 1951), 1044, as cited in Kessler-Harris, *Out to Work*, 375; Helen Hill Weed, "The New Deal that Women Want," *Current History* 41 (Nov. 1939): 183; Proceedings, Conference on Emergency Needs of Women, FERA, Monday, Nov. 20, 1933, The White House, Harry Hopkins Papers, box 25, file no. 12, FDR Library.

9. Weed, "The New Deal Women Want," 180–83; Ellen S. Woodward, "The New Federal Relief," *Independent Woman* 13 (Apr. 1934): 104–5.

10. Hopkins, *Spending to Save*, 161; press release, July 3, 1936, *Principal Speeches of Harry Hopkins*.

11. "An Analysis of Employment of Women on WPA Projects, December 1935 through May 1936," typescript, report to Hopkins, 1–72, LibofCong.

12. Hooks, *Women's Occupations*, 30; "Women and the WPA," *Woman Worker* 18 (Sept. 1938): 8; Winifred D. Wandersee, "A New Deal for Women," 190; Kessler-Harris, *Out to Work*, 263.

13. Ware, *Holding Their Own*, 142–52. Ware's critique, based entirely upon employment statistics of the FMP, does not judge the other projects on employment statistics alone; yet, in another essay, she considers the 12 to 19 percentile of women employed in the whole WPA as respectable. During its tenure, the FMP employed an average of at least 15 percent women. See Susan Ware, "Women and the New Deal," in *Fifty Years Later: The New Deal Evaluated*, Harvard Sitkoff, ed. (New York: Knopf, 1985), 124.

14. Seltzer, *Music Matters*, 214–18; Linda Dahl, *Stormy Weather* (New York: Limelight, 1981); Hazel V. Carby, "'It Jus' Be's Dat Way Sometime': The Sexual Politics of Women's Blues," *Radical America* 20 (1986): 9–22; Karen A. Saucier, "Women and Country Music," in Kenneth J. Bindas, ed. *America's Musical Pulse: Popular Music in Twentieth-Century American Society*, 213–20; Virginia W. Cooper, "Women in Popular Music: A Quantitative Analysis of Feminine Images over Time," *Sex Roles* 13 (1985): 499–505; Burton W. Peretti, *The Creation of Jazz: Music, Race and Culture in Urban America* (Urbana: Univ. of Illinois Press, 1992), 123.

15. Susan Ware, "Women and the New Deal," 124. Alice Kessler-Harris points out that this tendency was not unique to the WPA. The 1932 Federal Economy Act allowed for over sixteen hundred women to lose their jobs, and across the country school systems refused to hire married women teachers. Also, the New Deal relief and employment programs to that point all had discriminatory hiring practices. Kessler-Harris, *Out to Work*, 257–60.

16. McDonald, *Federal Relief Administration and the Arts*, 586; Grace Overmeyer, "The Musician Starves," *American Mercury* 32 (June 1934): 224–31; Seltzer, *Music Matters*, 268–69.

17. "Women in the FMP," 4; Virginia Price to Hewes, Nov. 22, 1938, box 30, FMP.

18. Ware, *Holding Their Own*, 164; "Women as Musicians," editorial, *New Republic* 95 (July 13, 1938): 263; Roell, *The Piano in America*, 225–65.

19. William G. King, *The Philharmonic Symphony Orchestra of New York, Season 1939–40* (New York: New York Symphony, 1940); "Women in the FMP," 3; Evelyn Gilhagen, "Up the Musical Scale," *Independent Woman* 17 (Mar. 1938): 83–84; Oklahoma Federal Symphony Orchestra, program booklet, 1939, DetPubLib.

20. Address, Nikolai Sokoloff to Conference of State Directors of the Division of Women's and Professional Projects, Washington, D.C., May 5, 1936, 117, Harry Hopkins Papers, file no. 26, FDR Library; "Women's Orchestra," *Boston City-*

News, Aug. 27, 1937; "Second Concert by Women's Orchestra," *Falmouth Enterprise,* Aug. 27, 1937; "Jordan Hall," *Boston Globe,* Dec. 29, 1937, all Massachusetts clippings, box 64, FMP files.

21. *Women in Music,* Sept. 1938, box 87, FMP.

22. "Women in the FMP," 2; Tawa, *Serenading the Reluctant Eagle,* 111; Christine Ammer, *Unsung: A History of Women in American Music* (Westport, Conn.: Greenwood Press, 1980), 111–14; "Antonia Brico's Triumph," *Newsweek* 8 (Aug. 1, 1938): 21.

23. *Women in Music,* Sept. 1938, box 87, FMP; Hewes to Joel Lay, Illinois State director, Aug. 13, 1938, 1935–37 analysis, box 365, WPA, 211.1; Marjory Fisher, "Coast WPA Men Led by Many Women," *Musical America* 58 (May 25, 1938): 4; Catherine Parsons Smith and Cynthia Richardson, *Mary Carr Moore: American Composer* (Ann Arbor: Univ. of Michigan Press, 1987), 165; Hewes to Mayfarth, Apr. 17, 1936, 1935–37 analysis, box 367, WPA 211.1; "Famous Conductor Arrives Tomorrow," *Washington Herald,* May 3, 1936; "2 Lady Conductors Discuss U.S. Music Potentialities," *Washington Daily-News,* May 5, 1936, box 59, FMP; "Women in the FMP," 2.

24. Radio text, May 5, 1936, New York state file, box 44, FMP; "Women in the FMP," 3.

25. Marjory Fisher, "Coast WPA Men Led by Mary Moore," *Musical America* 58 (May 25, 1938): 29; Smith and Richardson, *Mary Carr Moore,* 165; Ammer, *Unsung,* 152–53.

26. Press release, Feb. 4, 1939, 1–4, Jan. 1939 Cole/Hewes, box 31, FMP; Radie Britain to author, Feb. 22, 1990, author's files; brochure for Radie Britain, sent to author Sept. 8, 1988, author's files.

27. "The Truth of the Matter," *Women in Music* (Mar. 1937), New York clippings, box 87, FMP.

28. Hooks, *Women's Occupations,* 167.

29. "NFMC Issues Call," *Musical America* 56 (Nov. 25, 1935): 9; "WPA Enlists Advice of Noted Musicians," *Musical America* 56 (Nov. 10, 1935): 6.

30. Ellen Woodward kept in constant contact with Mrs. Roosevelt concerning the Women's Division, as Eleanor Roosevelt's papers contain several files of memos, notes, and letters from Woodward on this project. Mrs. Roosevelt also held a number of informal "teas" for the Women's Division and other women's groups. See correspondence with government departments, box 672, file[s] Ellen Woodward, Eleanor Roosevelt Papers, FDR Library; letter, Woodward to Eleanor Roosevelt, Apr. 30, 1936, Re Mrs. Roosevelt's Tea for wives of WPA administrators and members of the Women's Division for May 4, 1936, Office of Social Entertainment, box 9, file no. 34, FDR Library; "State Music Director Praises WPA Band Under Direction of Professor McLennan in Eunice," *Eunice Review,* Mar. 11, 1937, New Mexico clippings, box 69; Mary Barnum Bush Hauck to Harry Hewes, Apr. 20, 1936, 211.1, 1935–37 analysis, box 367; Southwest Regions advisory boards, January 25, 1936, 211.1, box 375; Tennessee report, n.d., Tennessee, box 45, all FMP; minutes of regional meeting, FMP, June 22–24, 1936, Foster no. 4, LibofCong; *The Federal Music Project* (Washington, D.C.: GPO, 1936), GMasUniv; "Some WPA Administrators," *Pickaxe and Pencil: References for the Study of the WPA,* Marguerite D. Bloxom, comp. (Washington, D.C.: GPO, 1982), 77–82.

31. "Kid Arrives to Conduct Seattle Symphony Orchestra," *Seattle Post-Intelligencer,* Nov. 1, 1938, 1938 file, box 88, FMP.

32. *List of American Orchestral Works Recommended by the WPA Music Conductors, July 1941* (Washington, D.C.: WPA, GPO, 1941).

Bringing in All the People: Hispanics, Gypsies, and Cowboys

1. Paul S. Taylor, "Mexicans North of the Rio Grande," *Survey Graphic* 56 (May 1, 1931): 135–40, 197; Emory Bogardus, *The Mexican in the United States* (Los Angeles: USC School of Research Studies, 1934; reprint, New York: Arno, 1970), 1–16; Carey McWilliams, *North from Mexico* (Philadelphia: Lippincott, 1948), 162–88.

2. "Increase in Mexican Population in the United States, 1920–1930," *Monthly Labor Review* 37 (July 1933): 45–48.

3. Richard A. Garcia, "The Making of a Mexican-American Mind, San Antonio, Texas, 1929–1941: A Social and Intellectual History of an Ethnic Community." (Ph.D. diss., Univ. of California, Irvine, 1980), 538–48.

4. Press release, 1937, New Mexico folk music file, box 34, FMP.

5. Charles R. Cutter, "The WPA Federal Music Project in New Mexico." *New Mexico Historical Review* 61 (July, 1986): 203–16.

6. "Folk Festival to be Held Thursday," "Folk Songs, Dances, Will be Presented by WPA Artists," *Albuquerque Tribune*, June 1, 1936; "WPA Music Project Classes Perform Publicly Thursday," "Big Crowd Attend Folk Song Program," *Albuquerque Journal*, June 4, 5, 1936, New Mexico clippings, box 69, FMP; McDonald, *Federal Relief Administration and the Arts*, 638–39; Harriet Monk, "Society," *Albuquerque Journal*, Sept. 8, 1937, New Mexico clippings, box 69, FMP.

7. Record of operation, Texas FMP, 1, GMasUniv.

8. Texas FMP, Oct. 1936–Aug. 1937, Texas, box 45, FMP; record of operations, Texas FMP, 1–9, GMasUniv.

9. Sokoloff, *The Federal Music Project*, 7; Sokoloff to Paul Felton, Apr. 6, 1938, Vermont miscellaneous reports, 1936–1939, box 28, FMP; Texas FMP, Oct. 1936–Aug. 1937, box 45, FMP; record of program operational accomplishments, Texas, 3, GMasUniv; "Government Music Project Here Has Varied Activities"; and "Concert to Be Given by Tipica Orchestra as United States Music Project," both *Dallas News*, Apr. 10, 1936, Texas clippings, box 79, FMP; "Children of Mexican Descent Sing Famous American Songs," *El Paso Times*, Feb. 22, 1938, Texas clippings, box 79, FMP.

10. Cutter, "WPA Federal Music Project in New Mexico," 208.

11. "Performance and Attendance Chart," Wisconsin FMP program of operation, WiscHistSoc.

12. "Jose Cantu Will Direct Sunday's Concert in Mission Patio," *San Gabriel Eye Opener*, July 16, 1936; "Two Concerts Slated Sunday," *San Pedro News Pilot*, July 16, 1936, California clippings, box 96, FMP.

13. "Phoenix Valley Mexicans to Celebrate Independence," *Phoenix Republic*, Sept. 15, 1937, Arizona clippings, box 46, FMP; "Mexican Junta Plans for Independence Fiesta to be Held," *South Side Progress*, Aug. 8, 1938, Arizona clippings, box 46, FMP; "Little Mexico and Its Residents Dress Up for Two Day Independence Event," *Dallas Dispatch-Journal*, Sept. 16, 1938, Texas clippings, box 79, FMP.

14. Texas FMP, 8, Oct. 1936–Aug. 1937, box 45, FMP; "WPA Music at Los Cunas," *Albuquerque Journal*, May 2, 1937; "Tularosa WPA Music Program Given Here May 9," *Tularosa Paper*, May 1937, New Mexico clippings, box 69, FMP.

15. "Mexican Program Ends Music Week," *San Antonio Express,* May 8, 1937, Texas clippings, box 79, FMP.
16. Texas FMP, 8, Oct. 1936–Aug. 1937, box 45, FMP; *San Gabriel Eye Opener,* July 16, 1936, California clippings, box 46, FMP; record of operation, Texas, 8, GMasUniv.
17. "Children of Mexican Descent Sing Famous American Songs," "Final Concert Tonight," both *El Paso Times,* Feb. 22–23, 1938; "Federal Symphony Presents 2 Concerts," *San Antonio Light,* Feb. 20, 1938, Texas clippings, box 79, FMP.
18. "Spanish Music and Dances to be Given as Centennial Summer Programs in Plazas," *San Antonio Light,* June 1936; "San Antonio Brings Touch of Old Mexico to Show," *San Antonio Star-Telegram,* Sept. 8, 1936, both Texas clippings, box 79, FMP; New Mexico Folk Music, 2, box 34, FMP; Texas FMP, Oct. 1936–Aug. 1937, 12, box 45, FMP.
19. Sokoloff, *The Federal Music Project,* 7.
20. "The WPA Music Project in Detroit," *The Keynote,* Oct.–Nov. 1938, Michigan clippings, box 87, FMP; record of operation, Michigan, GMasUniv; memorandum from the Council of Social Agencies, Oct. 20, 1938, FMP files, DetPubLib; Sokoloff, *The Federal Music Project,* 14; New Mexico Folk Music, box 34; "Hungarian Orchestra to Play at Leuzinger," *Inglewood,* May 4, 1936, California clippings, 1936, box 46, FMP.
21. "Two Concerts Slated Sunday," *San Pedro News Pilot,* July 16, 1936; "Hawaiian Music Will be Played," *Outlook,* Apr. 4, 1936, both California clippings, box 46, FMP; "First Anniversary Federal Project to be Observed," *Ardmore Armorite,* Mar. 1, 1937, Oklahoma clippings, box 74, FMP.
22. "Government Music Project Has Varied Activities," *Dallas News,* Apr. 10, 1936; "Concert to be Given by Tipica Orchestra as United States Music Project," *Dallas News,* Mar. 3, 1936, Texas clippings, box 79, FMP; "Cowboy Bands at Schools in Area," *Bulletin,* Mar. 16, 1936; "Cowboy Band Will Appear in Van Nuys," *Van Nuys News,* July 27, 1936, California clippings, box 46, FMP.
23. McDonald, *Federal Relief Administration and the Arts,* 639; "Folk Music Research by FMP in Oklahoma," Oklahoma files, box 15, FMP; FMP to Mrs. Paul Ellison, Georgia Southwestern College, Nov. 25, 1936, New York City Folk Music; Mississippi Folk file, box 34, FMP.

An End of It All

1. Performance and attendance report, Jan.–June 1939, reports, box 33, FMP; letter, Harry L. Hopkins to FDR, letter of resignation, Dec. 23, 1938, WPA miscellaneous, file 444c, FDR Library; letter, FDR to Harrington, Dec. 24, 1938, WPA miscellaneous, file 444c, FDR Library; memorandum, Harrington to Marvin McIntyre, secretary to the president, Dec. 30, 1938, WPA miscellaneous, file 444c, FDR Library; Canon, "Federal Music Project," 67; McKinzie, *The New Deal for Artists,* 150–51; Mathews, *The Federal Theater,* 135.
2. Findley, "Of Tears and Need," 278–79; McDonald, *Federal Relief Administration and the Arts,* 605; "Sokoloff Arrives to Conduct Seattle Symphony Orchestra," *Seattle Post-Intelligencer,* Nov. 1, 1938, 1938 file, box 31, FMP; letter, Taxpayers of New York City Professional Artists Group to FDR, July 16, 1937, WPA miscellaneous, 444c, no. 13, FDR Library.

3. "Relief Cuts Would Be Serious, Says President," *The International Musician* (Jan. 1939): 14; "WPA," editorial, *The International Musician* (Feb. 1939): 12.
4. Vorys to Arthur E. Strong, Jan. 27, 1939, as quoted in Jeffery Livingston, "John M. Vorys," (Ph.D. diss., Univ. of Toledo, 1989).
5. Charles McNary, "Shall We Return Relief to the States?" *Vital Speeches of the Day* 5 (May 1, 1939): 432-34.
6. Letter, FDR to Nelson A. Rockefeller, June 6, 1939, with copy of June 1, 1939, letter from Rockefeller to Congressman Edward Taylor also sent to FDR, president's personal files, no. 6035, Rockefeller, Nelson, FDR Library; letter, FDR to Heywood Broun, May 6, 1939, 444c, no. 14, WPA miscellaneous, FDR Library; "Relief Situation," editorial, *The International Musician* (Jan. 1939): 12. This exchange of letters brings into question the president's commitment to the arts projects, and particularly the FMP. During the FMP's tenure, according to the Office of the Chief of Social Entertainments, White House functions, records, and correspondence, 1935-1939 (boxes 24-45, FDR Library), no project band ever played at an official function at the White House. In fact, Roosevelt's papers reveal that he said little or nothing concerning the FMP. A number of times he was invited to hear project concerts, but he graciously refused. This seems to indicate that the FMP was not high on the president's list of priorities, and, while he had much to say about the other arts projects, suggests again that the music project was not as politically or aesthetically important as its sister projects. For invitations from the FMP, see letter, Ellen Woodward to FDR, Sept. 14, 1936, and response, McIntyre to Woodward, Sept. 21, 1936, POF 200, no. 29, ii, June 10-Nov. 3, 1936, FDR Library; letter, Regis Luke (project supervisor, New York State) to FDR, Sept. 15, 1936, and response, McIntyre to Luke, Sept. 19, 1936, POF 200, no. 29, ii, Sept. 15-28, 1936, FDR Library.
7. "Minutes of 1939 Convention," 39; "Official Proceedings and Recommendations," 31; "Resolution[s] 80, 87, 38, 18, 83," 14, 34, 39, 42, all *The International Musician* (Sept. 1939).
8. Memorandum, Harrington to FDR, June 30, 1939, liquidation of the arts projects, 444c, no. 14, miscellaneous, FDR Library; extension of remarks made by Hon. John J. Cochran, Missouri, June 15, 1939, *Congressional Record* 84 (1939): 2634; Arthur McMahon, John Millet, and Gladys Ogden, *The Administration of Federal Work Relief* (Chicago: Committee on Public Administration, 1941), 256-57; Werthman, "The New Deal Federal Art Programs," 62-124.
9. This figure does not include the many composer forum laboratories across the country. Press release, Aug. 18, 1939, Cole/Hewes, Aug. 1939, FMP.
10. Barbara Blumberg, *The New Deal and the Unemployed: A View from New York City* (Lewisburg, Pa.: Bucknell Univ. Press, 1979), 184; memo to Virginia Price from Hewes, July 29, 1939, Price, Aug. 1939, FMP; New Hampshire final report, LibofCong, 5; Zuck, *A History of Musical Americanism*, 181.
11. "Considering the Vast Panorama of Musical Activity," *Musical America* 57 (May 25, 1937): 16.
12. Roell, *The Piano in America*, 248-49; Tawa, *Serenading the Reluctant Eagle*, 136; Levy, *Musical Nationalism*, 136; John H. Mueller, *The American Symphony Orchestra: A Social History of Musical Taste* (Bloomington: Univ. of Indiana Press, 1951), 279; Tischler, *An American Music*, 151; Zuck, *A History of Musical Americanism*.

13. Howard Hanson, "Music in American Life Today," *Music Educators National Conference Yearbook, 1939–1940* (Chicago: MENC, 1940), 11.

14. Alfred Kazin, *On Native Grounds* (New York: Reynal and Hitchcock, 1942), 503.

15. Lawrence W. Levine, "American Culture and the Great Depression," *Yale Review* 74 (Winter 1985): 220–21; Robert Sklar, *Movie-Made America: A Social History of American Movies* (New York: Vintage, 1975); Andrew Bergman, *We're in the Money: Depression America and Its Films* (New York: New York Univ. Press, 1971); P. H. Melling, "The Mind of the Mob: Hollywood and Popular Culture in the 1930s," in *Cinema, Politics, and Society in America,* Philip Davies and Brian Neve, eds. (New York: St. Martin's, 1981), 19–41; Will Wright, *Six Guns and Society: A Structural Study of the Western* (Berkeley: Univ. of California Press, 1975); Todd McCarthy and Charles Flynn, eds., *Kings of the B's* (New York: Dutton, 1975); Joseph J. Waldmeir, "The Cowboy, the Knight and Popular Taste," *Southern Folklore Quarterly* 22 (Sept. 1958): 113–20; David Karnes, "The Glamorous Crowd: Hollywood Movies Premieres Between the Wars," *American Quarterly* 38 (Fall 1986): 536–72.

16. Susman, *Culture as History,* 197–98; Lewis A. Erenberg, "From New York to Middletown: Repeal and the Legitimization of Nightlife in the Great Depression," *American Quarterly* 38 (Winter 1986): 761–78; Edward Pessen, "The Kingdom of Swing: New York City in the Late 1930s," *New York History* LXX (July 1989): 277–308; Bindas, "Race, Class, and Ethnicity Among Swing Era Musicians," 73–82; Sanjek, *American Popular Music and Its Business, Vol. III, 1900–1984;* Bill C. Malone, *Country Music USA: A Fifty Year History* (Austin: Univ. of Texas Press, 1968); Kenneth J. Bindas, "Western Mystic: Bob Nolan and His Songs," *Western Historical Quarterly* XVII (Oct. 1986): 439–56; J. E. Vacha, "Posterity Was Just Around the Corner: The Influence of the Depression on the Development of the American Musical Theater in the Thirties," *South Atlantic Quarterly* 67 (Aug. 1968): 573–90.

17. Susman, *Culture as History,* 188–191; Alexander, *Nationalism in American Thought,* 1; Kazin, *On Native Grounds,* 486–87; Pells, *Radical Visions,* 150–51; Susman, "The Thirties," 235; Joan Shelley Rubin, *The Making of Middle Brow Culture* (Chapel Hill: Univ. of North Carolina Press, 1991); Mangione, *The Dream and the Deal,* 5; Yesohua Arieli, *Individualism and Nationalism in American Ideology* (Cambridge: Harvard Univ. Press, 1954); Louis Synder, *The Meaning of Nationalism* (New Brunswick: Rutgers Univ. Press, 1954); Hans Kohn, *Nationalism: Its Meaning and History* (Princeton, N.J.: Van Nostrand, 1957).

18. FDR "Radio Address to the Forum on Current Affairs," Oct. 5, 1937, *Public Papers and Addresses,* vol. 6: 412–13.

19. Letter, Ellen Woodward to FDR, Sept. 29, 1937, 444c, no. 8, WPA, Aug.–Oct. 1937, FDR Library; Dale E. Soder, "The New Deal Comes To Shawnee," *The Chronicles of Oklahoma* 63 (Summer 1985): 116–28; John A. Garraty, "New Deal, National Socialism, and the Great Depression," in Alonzo L. Hamby, ed., *The New Deal: Analysis and Interpretation* (New York: Longman, 1981), 219–47; Roy Emerson Stryker and Nancy Wood, *In This Proud Land: America 1935–1943 as Seen in the FSA Photographs* (Greenwich, Conn.: New York Graphic Society, 1973); see also a number of state photo books that have come out recently, such as Robert L. Reid, *Picturing Minnesota, 1936–1943: Photographs from the FSA* (St. Paul,

Minn.: Minnesota Historical Society Press, 1989). For a comprehensive bibliography concerning the activities of the arts projects, see Bloxom, *Pickaxe and Pencil*.

20. Address, Sokoloff to WPA Conference of State Directors of the Division of Women's and Professional Projects, May 5, 1936, p. 115, Papers of Harry Hopkins, no. 26, principal addresses, FDR Library.

21. Editorial, *The Musician* (Jan. 1939): 14.

22. Redfern Mason, writing in the *Boston Globe* as reproduced in *The Baton*, June 1937, California clippings, box 12, FMP.

BIBLIOGRAPHY

Archives

Claremont Graduate School, Claremont, California, the Papers of Lee Pattison. Abbreviated as file, number, Pattison Papers.

Detroit Public Library, Detroit, Michigan, clippings, letters, photos. Abbreviated as DetPubLib.

Franklin D. Roosevelt Presidential Library, Hyde Park, New York, WPA files, the Papers of Harry Hopkins, the Papers of Eleanor Roosevelt. Abbreviated as file, number, and papers, FDR Library.

George Mason Univ., Fairfax, Virginia, Federal Theater Archives and selected state reports, programs and letters. Abbreviated as file, number, GMasUniv.

Illinois Historical Library, Springfield, Illinois, typescript, "Music in Chicago," clippings, and photos. Abbreviated as file, number, IllHistSoc.

Indiana State Library, Indianapolis, Indiana, clippings, reports, programs. Abbreviated as IndStLib.

Kentucky State Archives, Lexington, Kentucky, Kentucky record of operation.

Library of Congress, Washington D.C., report of George Foster and final reports. Abbreviated as file, folder no., LibofCong.

Lousiana State Univ. Archives, Baton Rouge, Lousiana, programs, report. Abbreviated as LSU.

Minnesota Historical Society, St. Paul, Minnesota, Raymond Chase Papers. Abbreviated as R. P. Chase Papers, MinnHistSoc.

National Archives, Washington, D.C., WPA files 211.1 and Record Group 69, Federal Music Project files. Abbreviated in notes as file title, box number, and location (FMP or WPA).

Oregon Historical Society, Portland, Oregon.

Wisconsin Historical Society, Madison, Wisconsin, clippings, letters, and final report. Abbreviated as file, WiscHistSoc.

Dissertations

Canon, Cornelius Baird. "The Federal Music Project of the WPA: Music in a Democracy." Ph.D. diss., Univ. of Minnesota, 1963.

Dahlenberg, William J. "Music in the Culture of Miami: 1920–1966." Ed.D. diss., Florida State Univ., 1967.

Findley, Jannelle Jedd Warren. "Of Tears and Need: The Federal Music Project, 1935–1939." Ph.D. diss., George Washington Univ., 1973.

Floyd, James Ralph. "The Federal Muse: A Study of Executive Initiative in Federal Participation in the Arts, 1933–1943." Ph.D. diss., Kent State Univ., 1975.

Garcia, Richard Amado. "The Making of a Mexican-American Mind, San Antonio, Texas, 1929–1941: A Social and Intellectual History of an Ethnic Community." Ph.D. diss., Univ. of California, Irvine, 1980.

Maurer, David J. "Public Relief Programs and Policies in Ohio, 1929–1939." Ph.D. diss., Ohio State Univ., 1962.

Werthman, Joan B. "The New Deal Federal Art Programs, 1935–1939." Ph.D. diss., St. John's Univ., 1971.

Woodworth, William Henry. "The Federal Music Project of the WPA in New Jersey." Ed.D. diss., Univ. of Michigan, 1970.

Government Publications

"An Analysis of Women in the WPA." Washington: Government Printing Office (GPO), 1936.

Assigned Occupations of Persons Employed on the WPA Projects, 1937. Washington: GPO, 1939.

Federal Project One: WPA Art Projects in Ohio, 1936. Columbus: GPO, 1937.

Final Report on the WPA Programs, 1935–1943. Washington: GPO, 1946.

Hopkins, Harry. "Activities of the WPA." Washington: GPO, 1936.

Hopkins, Harry L. *Principal Speeches of Harry L. Hopkins.* Washington: GPO, 1938.

Hopkins, Harry L. *The Realities of Unemployment.* Washington: GPO, n.d.

House Committee on Appropriations, Hearings, 1938. Washington: GPO, 1938.

House Committee on Patents, Hearings, 1935. Washington: GPO, 1935.

House Committee on Patents, Hearings, 1935. No. 2, pt. 1. Washington: GPO, 1935.

House Committee on Patents, Hearings, 1935. No. 2, pt. 2, Washington: GPO, 1935.

House Committee on Patents, Hearings, 1938. No. 1, pt. 1. Washington: GPO, 1938.

House Special Committee on Un-American Activities, Hearings, 1938. Washington: GPO, 1939.

House Subcommittee of Appropriations, Investigation of WPA Activities. Pts. 1 and 3, 1939, 1940. Washington: GPO, 1939–40.

Inventory: An Appraisal of Results of the WPA. Washington: GPO, 1938.

Report on the Progress of the WPA. Washington: GPO, 1942.

Sokoloff, Nikolai. *The Federal Music Project.* Washington: GPO, 1935.

"Summary of Work and Relief Statistics, 1933–1940." Washington: GPO, 1941.

Usual Occupations of Persons Eligible for WPA Employment, 1936. Washington: GPO, 1937.

Workers on Relief in the U.S., Mar. 1935. Washington: GPO, 1935.

Books

Acuna, Rodolfo. *Occupied America: The Chicano's Struggle toward Liberation.* San Francisco: Canfield Press, 1972.

Alexander, Charles. *Nationalism in American Thought, 1930–1945.* Chicago: Rand McNally, 1969.

————. *Here the Country Lies: Nationalism and the Arts in the 20th Century.* Bloomington: Univ. of Indiana Press, 1980.

Ammer, Christine. *Unsung: A History of Women in America.* Westport, Conn.: Greenwood Press, 1980.

Angelou, Maya. *I Know Why the Caged Bird Sings.* New York: Random House, 1969.

Arieli, Yehoshua. *Individualism and Nationalism in American Ideology.* Cambridge: Harvard Univ. Press, 1964.

Baigell, Matthew. *The American Scene: American Painting of the 1930s.* New York: Praeger, 1974.

Bergman, Andrew. *We're in the Money: Depression America and Its Films.* New York: 1971.

Bindas, Kenneth J., ed. *America's Musical Pulse: Popular Music in Twentieth-Century Society.* Westport, Conn.: Greenwood Press, 1992.

Blakey, George T. *Hard Times and the New Deal in Kentucky 1929–1939.* Lexington: Univ. Press of Kentucky, 1986.

Bloxom, Marguerite D., comp. *Pickaxe and Pencil: References for the Study of the WPA.* Washington, D.C.: GPO, 1982.

Blumberg, Barbara. *The New Deal and the Unemployed: The View from NYC.* Lewisburg, Pa.: Bucknell Univ. Press, 1979.

Bogardus, Emory S. *The Mexican in the United States.* Los Angeles: USC School for Research Studies, 1934. Reprint, New York: Arno Press, 1970.

Bowers, Jane, and Judith Tick, eds. *Women Making Music: The Western Art Tradition, 1150–1950.* Urbana: Univ. of Illinois Press, 1986.

Butterworth, Neil. *A Dictionary of American Composers.* New York: Garland, 1984.

Buttita, Tony, and Barry Witham. *Uncle Sam Presents: A Memoir of the Federal Theater Project, 1935–1939.* Philadelphia: Univ. of Pennsylvania, 1982.

Chase, Gilbert. *America's Music: From the Pilgrims to the Present.* 3d ed. Urbana: Univ. of Illinois Press, 1987.

Coben, Stanley, and Lorman Ratner. *The Development of American Culture.* Englewood Cliffs, N.J.: Prentice-Hall, 1970.

Collier, James Lincoln. *Benny Goodman and the Swing Era.* New York: Oxford Univ. Press, 1989

Conkin, Paul K. *The New Deal.* New York: Crowell, 1967.

Contreras, Belisario R. *Tradition and Innovation in New Deal Art.* Lewisburg: Cornell Univ. Press, 1983.

Copland, Aaron. *Our New Music.* New York: Whittlesey House, McGraw Hill, 1941.

Cowell, Henry, ed. *American Composers on American Music.* Stanford: Stanford Univ. Press, 1933.

Cowley, Malcolm. *Exile's Return: A Literary Odyssey of the 1920s.* New York, Viking, 1931.

Craig, Evelyn Q. *Black Drama of the Federal Theatre Era: Beyond the Formal Horizons.* Amherst: Univ. of Massachusetts Press, 1980.

Dahl, Linda. *Stormy Weather.* New York: Limelight, 1981.

Dallek, Robert. *FDR and American Foreign Policy, 1932–1945.* New York: Oxford Univ. Press, 1979.

Davies, Philip, and Brian Neve, eds. *Cinema, Politics, and Society in America.* New York: St. Martin's, 1981.

Dies, Martin. *The Trojan Horse.* New York: Ayer, 1940.

————. *Martin Dies' Story.* New York: Bookmailer, 1963.

Dizikes, John. *Opera in America: A Cultural History.* New Haven, Conn.: Yale Univ. Press, 1993.

Ekirch, Arthur A. *Ideologies and Utopias: The Impact of the New Deal on American Thought.* Chicago: Quadrangle Books, 1969.

Erskine, John. *Philharmonic-Symphony Society of New York: First Hundred Years.* New York: Da Capo Press, 1943.

Flanagan, Hallie. *Arena: The History of the Federal Theater.* New York: Blom, 1940.

Franklin, John Hope. *From Slavery to Freedom: A History of Negro Americans.* New York: Knopf, 1974.

Goldberg, Robert. *Grassroots Resistance: Social Movements in Twentieth-Century America.* Belmont, Calif.: Wadsworth, 1991.

Glone, Harry F. "The New Alphabet Challenges Our Cities," in *Music Educators National Yearbook,* vol. 27. Chicago, 1936.

Grant, Nancy L. *TVA and Black Americans.* Philadelphia: Temple Univ. Press, 1989.

Hamby, Alonzo L., ed. *The New Deal: Analysis and Interpretation.* New York: Longman, 1981.

Hamm, Charles. *Music in the New World.* New York: Norton, 1983.

Hare, Maud Cuney. *Negro Musicians and Their Music.* Washington D.C.: The Associated Publishers, 1936.

Hearns, Charles R. *The American Dream and the Great Depression.* Westport, Conn.: Greenwood Press, 1977.

Heinemann, Ronald, L. *Depression and New Deal in Virginia: The Enduring Dominion.* Charlottesville: Univ. Press of Virginia, 1983.

Hitchcock, H. Wiley. *Music in the United States: A Historical Introduction.* 2d ed. Englewood Cliffs, N.J.: Prentice-Hall, 1974.

Hofstadter, Richard. *The Age of Reform: From Bryant to FDR.* New York: Knopf, 1955.

Hooks, Janet M. *Women's Occupations Through Seven Decades.* Washington D.C.: GPO, 1947.

Hopkins, Harry. *Spending to Save: The Complete Story of Relief.* New York: W. W. Norton and Company, 1936.

Houseman, John. *Run-Through: A Memoir.* New York: Simon and Schuster, 1972.

Howard, Donald S. *The WPA and Federal Relief Policy.* New York: Russell Sage Foundation, 1943.

Kazin, Alfred. *On Native Grounds.* New York: Reynal and Hitchcock, 1942.

Kessler-Harris, Alice. *Out to Work: A History of Wage Earning Women in the United States.* New York: Oxford Univ. Press, 1982.

Kirby, John B. *Black Americans in the Roosevelt Era: Liberalism and Race.* Knoxville: Univ. of Tennessee Press, 1980.

Kohn, Hans. *American Nationalism.* New York: Macmillan, 1957.

———. *The Idea of Nationalism.* New York: Macmillan, 1944.

Kohn, Hans, and Daniel Walden. *Readings in American Nationalism.* New York: Van Nostrand Reinhold, 1970.

Leonard, Neil. *Jazz and the White Americans.* Chicago: Univ. of Chicago Press, 1962.

Leuchtenburg, William E. *FDR and the New Deal 1932–1940.* New York: Harper and Row, 1963.

Levine, Lawrence W. *Highbrow/Lowbrow: The Emergence of Cultural Hierarchy in America.* Cambridge: Harvard Univ. Press, 1988.

Levine, Rhonda F. *Class Struggle and the New Deal: Industrial Labor, Industrial Capital, and the State.* Lawrence, Kans.: Univ. of Kansas Press, 1988.

Levy, Alan Howard. *Musical Nationalism: American Composers' Search for Identity.* Westport, Conn.: Greenwood Press, 1984.

Lieberman, Robbie. *"My Song Is My Weapon": People's Songs, American Communism, and the Politics of Culture, 1930–1950.* Urbana: Univ. of Illinois Press, 1988.

Malone, Bill C. *Country Music USA: A Fifty Year History.* Austin, Tex.: Univ. of Texas Press, 1968.

Mangione, Jerre. *The Dream and the Deal: The Federal Writers' Project, 1935–1943.* Boston: Little, Brown, 1972

Mathews, Jane DeHart. *The Federal Theater Project, 1935–1939.* Princeton: Princeton Univ. Press, 1967.

May, Elaine Tyler. *Homeward Bound: American Families in the Cold War Era.* New York: Basic Books, 1988.

McCarthy, Toss, and Charles Flynn, eds. *King of the B's.* New York: Dutton, 1975.

McDonald, J. Fred. *Don't Touch That Dial: Radio Programming in American Life.* Chicago: Nelson-Hall, 1979.

McDonald, William F. *Federal Relief Administration and the Arts.* Columbus: Ohio State Univ. Press, 1969.

McFarland, Frances. "The FMP in New York City," in *Music Educators National Conference,* vol. 27. Chicago, 1936.

McKinzie, Richard D. *The New Deal for Artists.* Princeton, N.J.: Princeton Univ. Press, 1973.

McMahon, Arthur W., John Millet, and Gladys Ogden. *The Administration of Federal Work Relief.* Chicago: Pub. for the Committee on Public Administration of the Social Sciences Research Council by Public Administration Service, 1941.

McWilliams, Carey. *North from Mexico: The Spanish Speaking People of the U.S.* Philadelphia: J. B. Lippincott Co., 1948.

Meltzer, Milton. *Violins and Shovels: The WPA Arts Project.* New York: Delacorte Press, 1976.

Millett, John. *The WPA in New York City.* New York: Arno Press, 1938.

Mueller, John H. *The American Symphony Orchestra.* Bloomington: Indiana Univ. Press, 1951.

Nash, Gerald D. *The Crucial Era: The Great Depression and World War II, 1929–1945.* New York: St. Martin's Press, 1979.

Netzer, Dick. *The Subsidized Muse: Public Support for the Arts in the United States.* Cambridge: Cambridge Univ. Press, 1978.

Nye, David. *Electrifying America: Social Meaning of a New Technology, 1880–1940.* Cambridge, Mass.: MIT Press, 1991.

O'Connor, Francis V. *Art for the Millions: Essays from the 1930s by Artists and Administrators of the WPA Federal Art Project.* New York: New York Graphic Society, 1973.

———, ed. *The New Deal Art Projects: An Anthology of Memoirs.* Washington, D.C.: Smithsonian Institution Press, 1972.

O'Connor, John, and Lorraine Brown, eds. *Free, Adult, Uncensored: The Living History of the Federal Theatre Project.* Washington D.C.: New Republic Books, 1978.

Ogden, August R. *The Dies Committee: A Study of the Special House Committee for the Investigation of UnAmerican Activities, 1938–1944.* Washington: The Catholic Univ. of America Press, 1945.

Overmyer, Grace. *Government and the Arts.* New York: W. W. Norton and Company, 1939.

Park, Marlene, and Gerald E. Markowitz. *Democratic Vistas: Post Office and Public Art in the New Deal.* Philadelphia: Temple Univ. Press, 1984.

Patterson, James T.. *Congressional Conservatism and the New Deal: The Growth of the Conservative Coalition in Congress, 1933–1939.* Lexington: Univ. Press of Kentucky, 1967.

Pells, Richard. *Radical Visions and American Dreams.* Middletown, Conn.: Wesleyan Press, 1974.

Penkower, Monty Noam. *The Federal Writers' Project: A Study in Government Patronage of the Arts.* Chicago: Univ. of Chicago Press, 1977.

Peretti, Burton W. *The Creation of Jazz: Music, Race and Culture in Urban America.* Urbana: Univ. of Illinois Press, 1992.

Purcell, Ralph. *Government and Art: A Study of the American Experience.* Washington: Public Affairs Office, 1956.

Roell, Craig. *The Piano in America, 1890–1940.* Chapel Hill: Univ. of North Carolina Press, 1989.

Roosevelt, Elliot. *FDR: His Personal Letters, 1928–1945.* New York: Duell, Sloan and Pearce, 1950.

Roosevelt, Franklin D. *The Complete Presidential Press Conferences of FDR,* 25 vols. New York: Da Capo Press, 1972.

Roseman, Samuel I. *The Public Papers and Address of FDR,* vols. IV–VIII. New York: Random House, 1950.

Sanjek, Russell. *American Popular Music and Its Business: The First Four Hundred Years,* vols. 1–3. New York: Oxford Univ. Press, 1988.

Schlesinger, Arthur, Jr. *The Coming of the New Deal,* vols. I, II, III. Boston: Houghton Mifflin, 1959.

Schuller, Gunther. *The Swing Era.* New York: Oxford Univ. Press, 1989.

Seltzer, George. *Music Matters: The Performer and the American Federation of Musicians.* Metuchen, N.J.: Scarecrow, 1989.

Shafer, Boyd C. *Nationalism, Myth and Reality.* New York: Harcourt Brace, 1955.

———. *Faces of Nationalism.* New York: Harcourt Brace Jovanovich, 1970.

Shannon, David. *Between the Wars: America 1919–1941.* Boston: Houghton Mifflin, 1965.

Sherwood, Robert E. *Roosevelt and Hopkins: An Intimate History.* New York: Harper, 1948.

Simon, Rita James. *As We Saw the Thirties.* Urbana: Univ. of Illinois Press, 1967.

Sitkoff, Harvard. *A New Deal for Blacks.* New York: Oxford Univ. Press, 1978.

Sklar, Robert. *Movie-Made America: A Social History of American Movies.* New York: Vintage Books, 1977.

Skowrouski, JoAnn. *Women in American Music.* Metuchen, N.J.: Scarecrow Press, 1978.

Smith, Catherine Parsons, and Cynthia Richardson. *Mary Carr Moore: American Composer.* Ann Arbor: UMI, 1987.

Snyder Louis L. *The Meaning of Nationalism.* New Brunswick, N.J.: Rutgers Univ. Press, 1954. Reprint, Westport, Conn.: Greenwood Press, 1968, 1972.

Sochen, June. *The Unbridgeable Gap: Blacks and Their Quest for the American Dream, 1900–1930.* Chicago: Rand McNally, 1972.

Spivey, Donald. *Union and the Black Musician: The Narrative of William Everett Samuels of Chicago Local 208.* Lanham, Md.: Univ. Press of America, 1984.

Steele, Richard W. *Propaganda in an Open Society: The Roosevelt Administration and the Media, 1933–1941.* Westport, Conn.: Greenwood Press, 1985.

Susman, Warren. *Culture as History: The Transformation of American Society in the Twentieth Century.* New York: Pantheon, 1984.

———. *Culture and Commitment.* New York: G. Braziller, 1973.

Tawa, Nicholas E. *Serenading the Reluctant Eagle: American Musical Life, 1925–1945.* New York: Schirmer Books, 1984.

Terkel, Studs. *Hard Times.* New York: Pantheon Books, 1986.

Thomas, Jean. *Ballad Makin' in the Mountains of Kentucky.* New York: H. Holt and Company, 1939.

Tischler, Barbara L. *An American Music: The Search for an American Musical Identification.* New York: Oxford Univ. Press, 1986.

Ware, Susan. *Beyond Suffrage: Women in the New Deal.* Cambridge: Harvard Univ. Press, 1981.

———. *Holding Our Own: American Women in the 1930s.* Boston: Twayne, 1982.

Watkins, Glenn. *Soundings: Music in the Twentieth Century.* New York: Schirmer, 1988.

White, Graham J. *FDR and the Press.* Chicago: Univ. Of Chicago Press, 1979.

Whitman, Wilson. *Bread and Circuses.* 1937. Reprint, New York: Books for Libraries, 1972.

Woodward, C. Vann. *The Strange Career of Jim Crow.* New York: Oxford Univ. Press, 1974.

Wright, Will. *Six Guns and Society: A Structural Study of the Western.* Berkeley: Univ. of California Press, 1975.

Zuck, Barbara. *A History of Musical Americanism.* Ann Arbor: UMI Research Press, 1980.

Articles

"America, Conductor Maker." Editorial. *Musical America* 59 (Jan. 10, 1939): 16.

"American Music in Oklahoma." *Musician* 43 (Aug. 1938): 143.

"American Scene: Final Analysis of the Unemployment Census." *Living Age* 355 (Nov. 1938): 268.

"The Anderson Case." Editorial. *Musical America* 59 (Mar. 10, 1939): 16.

"Antonio Brico Waves . . ." *Newsweek* 5 (Mar. 2, 1935): 22.

"Antonio Brico's Triumph." *Newsweek* 12 (Aug. 1, 1938): 21.

Arvey, Verna. "Worthwhile Music in the Movies." *Etude* 57 (Mar. 1939): 152, 205.

Blair, E. N. "First Aides to Uncle Sam." *Independent Woman* 17 (Sept. 1938): 276–78.

Barrell, E. A. "Notable Musical Women." *Etude* 47 (Nov. 1929), 805–6, 897.

Bauer, Harold. "Growing Demand for Music." *Musician* 40 (January 1935): 4.

Bauer, Marion. "Have We an American Music." *Musical America* 10 (Feb. 1940): 22, 271–72.

Billington, Ray Allen. "Government and the Arts: The WPA Experience." *American Quarterly* 13 (Winter 1962): 466–79.

Bindas, Kenneth J. "Western Mystic: Bob Nolan and His Songs." *Western Historical Quarterly* XVII (Oct. 1986): 439–56.

Biocca, Frank. "Media and Perceptual Shifts: Early Radio and the Clash of Musical Cultures." *Journal of Popular Culture* 24 (Fall 1986): 1–15.

Blakey, George T. "The New Deal in Rural Kentucky, 1931–1941." *Register of the Kentucky Historical Society* 84 (Spring 1986): 146–91.

"Block Score Given in San Francisco." *Musical America* 58 (Apr. 5, 1938): 32.

Borroff, Edith. "American Culture in Music Courses." *College Music Symposium* 25 (June 1985): 7–20.

Brands, Pearl Brown. "Music Written About Abraham Lincoln." *Etude* 56 (Feb. 1938): 77–78.

Brands, Pearl Brown. "Music Popular at the Time of Lincoln." *Etude* 52 (Apr. 1934), 113–14.

Bremer, William, W. "Along the American Way: The New Deal's Work Relief Programs for the Unemployed." *Journal of American History* 62 (Dec. 1975): 636–52.

Broder, Nathan. "American Music and American Orchestras." *Musical Quarterly* 28 (1942): 488–93.

"Buying American Music." *Literary Digest* 118 (Dec. 29, 1931): 24.

Byrnes, James F. "Shall We Return Relief to the States?" *Vital Speeches* 5 (May 1, 1939): 431–434.

Calverton, V. F. "Careers for Women." *Current History* 29 (Jan. 1929): 633–38.

———. "Negro's New Belligerent Attitude." *Current History* 30 (Sept. 1929): 1081–88.

Canon, Cornelius B. "Art for Whose Sake: The Federal Music Project and the WPA." In Ray Brown, Larry Landrum, and Will Bottorff, eds. *Challenges in American Culture*. Bowling Green: Bowling Green Univ. Popular Press, 1970.

Carby, Hazel V. "'It Jus' Be's Dat Way Sometime': The Sexual Politics of Women's Blues." *Radical America* 20 (1986): 9–22.

Carter, Elliott. "Coolidge Crusade: WPA, New York Season." *Modern Music* 16 (Nov./ Dec. 1938): 33–38.

Clement, Priscilla, "The WPA in Pennsylvania, 1935–1940." *Pennsylvania Magazine of History and Biography* 95: 244–60.

Clifton, Chalmers. "Federal Music Project Takes Inventory." *Musical America* 58 (Feb. 10, 1938): 144, 179.

Coates, Albert. "The Music of New Russia." *Etude* 52 (June 1934): 335–36.

Cohn, Arthur. "Americans in the Fleisher Collection." *Modern Music* 16 (Jan./Feb. 1939): 116–19.

"Considering the Vast Panorama of Federal Music Activity." Editorial. *Musical America* 57 (May 25, 1937): 16.

Cooper, Virginia W. "Women in Popular Music: A Quantitative Analysis of Feminine Images over Time." *Sex Roles* 13 (1985): 499–505.

Copland, Aaron. "Our Generation 10 Years Later." *Modern Music* 10 (May 1932): 142–47.

———. "American Composer Gets a Break." *American Mercury* 34 (Apr. 1935): 488–92.

———. "From the 20s to the 40s and Beyond." *Modern Music* 20 (Jan.–Feb. 1943): 78–82.

———. "Making Music in a Star-Spangled Manner." *Music and Musicians* 8 (Aug. 1960): 8–9.

Cowell, Henry. "Towards Neo-Primitivism." *Modern Music* 10 (Mar. 1933): 149–53.

Coyle, David C. "The WPA: Loafers or Workers?" *Forum and Century* 101 (Mar. 1939): 170–74.

Crain, Hal D. "Los Angeles Hears WPA Opera Concert." *Musical America* 57 (June 1937): 22.

———. "Native Music Given in Los Angeles." *Musical America* 57 (June 1937): 29.

———. "Los Angeles WPA Effort Criticized." *Musical America* 57 (Aug. 1937): 23.

———. "Hollywood Hears New Native Opera." *Musical America* 58 (Oct. 1938): 10.

Cutter, Charles R. "The WPA Federal Music Project in New Mexico." *New Mexico Historical Review* 61 (July 1986): 203–16.

Daoust, Norma Lasalle. "Building the Democratic Party: Black Voting in Providence in the 1930s." *Rhode Island History* 44 (Aug. 1985): 80–88.

Davis, J. P. "Blue Eagles and Black Workers." *New Republic* 81 (Nov. 14, 1934): 7–9.

Denning, Michael. "Marxism and American Studies." *American Quarterly* 38 (Bib 1986): 356–80.

Diton, Carl Diton. "The Present Status of the Negro-American Endeavor." *Musician* 20 (Nov. 1915): 689.

———. "The Struggle of the Negro Musician." *Etude* 48 (Feb. 1930): 89–90.

Downes, Olin. "An American Composer." *Musical Quarterly* 4 (Jan. 1918): 23–36.

DuBois, W. E. B. "Negro Nation within a Nation." *Current History* 42 (June 1935): 265–70.

Dunaway, David King. "Unsung Songs of Protest: The Composers Collective of New York." *New York Folklore* 5 (Summer 1979): 1–19.

Eaklor, Vicki L. "The Illinois Symphony Orchestra, 1936–1942: Microcosm of a Cultural New Deal." In *Selected Papers in Illinois History, 1980.* Springfield: Illinois Historical Society, 1982.

"Effects of Technological Changes upon Employment in the Amusement Industry." *Monthly Labor Review* 33 (Aug. 1931): 261–67.

"Effects of Technological Changes upon Employment in the Motion Picture Theatres of Washington D.C." *Monthly Labor Review* 33 (Nov. 1931): 1–13.

Eisler, Hans. "Reflections on the Future of the Composer." *Modern Music* 12 (May 1935): 180–86.

Engel, C. "What Great Music Owes to Women." *Etude* 47 (Nov. 1929): 797–98.

Erenberg, Lewis A. "From New York to Middletown: Repeal and the Legitimization of Nightlife in the Great Depression." *American Quarterly* 38 (Winter 1986): 761–78.

Farwell, Arthur. "The Struggle Toward a National Music." *North American Review* 186 (Dec. 1907): 565–70.

———. "Society and American Music." *Atlantic Monthly* 101 (1908): 232–36.

"The Federal Music and Drama Projects." Editorial. *The Musician* (Sept. 1936): 139.

"Federal Music Project." *Current History* 49 (Sept. 1938): 42–44.

"Federal Portfolio of Music and Art." *Musician* 40 (July 1935): 12.

"Federal Survey Shows Michigan's Music Needs." *Musical America* 27 (Dec. 25, 1937): 17.

Fisher, Marjory. "Coast WPA Men Led by Mary Moore." *Musical America* 58 (May 25, 1938): 29.

———. "Project Programs in San Francisco." *Musical America* 57 (Sept. 1937): 20.

———. "Search Work Given in San Francisco." *Musical America* 57 (Oct. 10, 1937): 16.

"First Negro Symphony." *Literary Digest* 115 (Mar. 4, 1933): 20.

"For the People." *Time* 33 (June 5, 1939): 60.

Foster, George. "Federal Music Project Takes Inventory," *Musical America* 58 (Feb. 10, 1938): 144, 179.

Frazier, Corinne R. "Why Pay the Fiddler?" *Parents' Magazine* 12 (Feb. 1937): 20–21.

Frazier, E. "Miss Graduate Hunts a Job." *Saturday Evening Post* 202 (Oct. 19, 1929): 14–15.

Gabrilowitsch, Ossip. "New Deal in Music." *Musician* 39 (May 1934): 5.

Gans, Herbert J. "American Popular Culture and High Culture in a Changing Class Structure." *Prospects* 10 (1985): 17–38.

Ganson, Paul. "An Era of Grandeur: Detroit's Orchestra Hall, 1919–1939." *Detroit Historical Society Bulletin* (Jan. 1971).

Garis, R. L. "Mexican Invasion." *Saturday Evening Post* 202 (Apr. 19, 1930): 43–44.

Garraty, John A. "The New Deal, National Socialism, and the Great Depression." *American Historical Review* 78 (Oct. 1973): 904–44.

Gehrkens, K. W. "Negros in Various Fields of Music." *Etude* 53 (June 1935): 375.

Geselbracht, Raymond H. "Evolution and the New World Vision in the Music of Charles Ives." *Journal of American Studies* 8 (Aug. 1974): 211–27.

"Gettysburg Farewell." *Newsweek* 12 (July 11, 1938): 12.

Gilhagen, E. "Up the Musical Scale." *Independent Woman* 17 (Mar. 1938): 83–84.

Gill, Corrington. "WPA." *Current History and Forum* 48 (Jan. 1938): 36–42.

Gillard, J. J. "Racism Rampant in U.S." *Catholic World* 148 (Nov. 1938): 152–57.

Goines, Leonard. "Black Musicians and Composers of the Thirties." *Allegro* 73 (June 1973): 6, 22.

Goldmark, J. "New Menace in Industry." *Scribner's* 93 (Mar. 1933): 141–43.

Goodrich, Lloyd. "The Federal Government and Art." *Magazine of Art* 41 (Oct. 1948): 234–38.

Graham, S———. "Spiritual to Symphonies: A Brief Survey of Negro Music in America." *Etude* 54 (Nov. 1936): 691–92.

Hamm, Charles. "Music in American Life Today." In *Music Educators Conference*, vol. 30. Chicago: n.p., 1940.

Handman, M. S. "San Antonio." *Survey* 66 (May 1, 1931): 163–66.

Hanson, Howard. "Conditions Affecting the Development of an American Music." *Etude* 50 (Apr. 1932): 247–48.

———. "Report: American Music." In *Music Teachers National Association Volume of Proceedings, 1936.* Oberlin: n.p., 1937.

Harris, Roy. "American Music Enters a New Phase." *Scribner's* 96 (Oct. 1934): 218–21.

———."Does Music Have to Be European?" *Scribner's* 91 (Apr. 1932): 204–9.

Harrison, Helen A. "American Art and the New Deal." *Journal of American Studies* 6 (Dec. 1972): 189–96.

"Head of WPA Music Issues Compilation." *Musical America* 59 (Apr. 10, 1939): 23.

"Hearing America First." *Newsweek* 12 (July 4, 1938): 19.

"A Healthful Winnowing." Editorial. *Musical America* 59 (Apr. 10, 1939): 22.

Heifetz, J. "Music for Millions." *Ladies Home Journal* 55 (July 1938): 22.

Heinemann, Ronald. "Blue Eagle or Black Buzzard? The NRA in Virginia." *Virginia Magazine of History and Biography* 89 (1981): 90–100.

Henderson, W———. J. "Why No Great American Music." *American Mercury* 32 (July 1934): 295–301.

Hendrickson, Kenneth E. "A Case Study in the Politics of Culture: The Federal Art Project in Iowa." *Upper Midwest History* 4 (1984).

———."Politics of Culture: The Federal Music Project in Oklahoma." *Chronicles of Oklahoma* 63 (Winter 1985–86): 361–75.

Heylbut, Rose. "This is Walter Damrosch Speaking." *Etude* 55 (Nov. 1937): 705–6.

Hirschman, I. A. "The Musician and the Depression." *The Nation* 137 (Nov. 15, 1933): 565–66.

Hitchcock, H. Wiley. "Sources for the Study of American Music." *American Studies International* 14 (Winter 1975): 3–9.

Hopkins, Harry. "Employment in America." *Vital Speeches* 3 (Dec. 1936): 103–7.

Howard, John Tasker. "Better Days for Music." *Harper's* 174 (Apr. 1937): 483–91.

———. "Native Elements in American Music." *American Scholar* III: 325–35.

Hansen, Chadwick. "Social Influences on Jazz Style: Chicago 1920–1930." *American Quarterly* 20 (Winter 1960): 493–507.

Hughes, Edwin. "The Effect of WPA Programs on the Work of the Private Piano Teacher." In *Music Teachers National Association, Volume of Proceedings 1936.* Oberlin: n.p., 1937.

Huzar, Elias. "Federal Unemployment Relief Policies: The First Decade." *Journal of Politics* 2 (Aug. 1940): 321–35.

"Increase in Mexican Population in the U.S., 1920–1930." *Monthly Labor Review* 37 (July 1933): 45–48.

Jervis, Harle. "Federal Music Project Takes Inventory." *Musical America* 58 (Feb. 10, 1938): 179.

Johnson, C. S. "Incidence upon the Negro." *American Journal of Sociology* 40 (Mar. 1935): 737–45.

Jones, Alfred H. "The Search for a Usable American Past in the New Deal Era." *American Quarterly* 23 (Dec. 1971): 710–24.

Karnes, David. "The Glamorous Crowd: Hollywood Movie Premiers Between the Wars." *American Quarterly* 38 (Winter 1987): 553–72.

Keyserling, H. "What the Negro Means to America." *Atlantic* 144 (Oct. 1929): 444–47.

Langley, A. L. "How to Help American Music." *Commonweal* 14 (Oct. 28, 1931): 631–33.

Laiosa, Mark. "History of the Bronx Symphony Orchestra, 1937–1981." *Bronx County Historical Society Journal* 19 (Fall 1982): 51–55.

Laubenstein, P. F. "Race values in AfroAmerican Music." *Music Quarterly* 16 (July 1930): 378–803.

Leach, H———. G. "In Praise of Boon Doggling: Cultural Relief Activities." *Forum* 93 (June 1935): 321–22.

Lindeman, Eduard C. "Farewell to Bohemia." *Survey Graphic* (Apr. 1937): 207–8.

Levine, Lawrence W. "American Culture and the Great Depression." *Yale Review* 74 (Winter 1985).

———. "Hollywood's Washington: Film Images of National Politics During the Great Depression." *Prospects* 10 (1985): 169–96.

Loomis, John P. "Reds and Rackets in Work Relief." *Saturday Evening Post* 209 (June 5, 1937): 97–98.

MacBride, J———. "Federal Music Project." *New Republic* 89 (Nov. 11, 1936): 48.

MacDonald, J. Fred. "Hot Jazz, the Jitterbug, and Misunderstanding: A Generation Gap in Swing, 1935–1945." *Journal of Popular Music and Society* 2 (Fall 1972): 43–55.

MacLeish, Archibald. "Unemployed Arts." *Fortune* (May 1937): 109–17, 168–75.

Maier, Guy. "Federal Music Project Takes Inventory." *Musical America* 58 (Feb. 10, 1938): 179.

———. "FMP's Contribution to American Music." In *Music Educators National Conference,* vol. 29. Chicago: n.p., 1938.

Marquis, Alice Goldfarb. "Radio Grows Up." *American Heritage* 34 (1983): 4–9.

Mason, Daniel Gregory. "The Depreciation of Music." *Musical Quarterly* 15 (Jan. 1929): 6–15.

Mason, Daniel Gregory. "The Radio vs. the Virtuoso." *Musical Quarterly* 20 (Aug. 1930): 454–60.

"Mass Music and the Masses." *Etude* 56 (Aug. 1938): 491.

Mathews, Jane D. "Arts and the People: The New Deal Quest for a Cultural Democracy." *Journal of American History* 62 (Sept. 1975): 316–39.

Matter, Stewart. "Music Week Events Occupy Cleveland." *Musical America* 58 (May 25, 1938): 22.

McDonald, H———. "Problems of the American Composer." *Magazine of Art* 30 (Dec. 1937): 719.

McFarland, Frances. "Federal Music Project in New York City." *Music Educators National Conference,* vol. 27. Chicago: n.p., 1936.

McKee, O. "Music and Latin America." *National Republic* 19 (Aug. 1931): 7–9.

McNary, Charles L., "Shall We Return Relief to the States." *Vital Speeches* 5 (May 1, 1939): 432–34.

Meckna, Michael. "Copland, Sessions, and *Modern Music*: The Rise of the Composer Critic." *American Music* 3 (Summer 1985): 198–204.

Mehren, Peter. "San Diego's Opera Unit of the WPA Federal Music Project." *Journal of San Diego History* 18 (Summer 1972): 12–21.

Mendel, A. "What Is American Music?" *Nation* 134 (May 4, 1932): 524.

Merritt, Richard L. "The Emergence of American Nationalism: A Quantitative Approach." *American Quarterly* 17 (Summer 965): 319–335.

Mooney, H. F. "Popular Music Since the 1920s: The Significance of Shifting Taste." *American Quarterly* 20 (1968): 67–85.

———. "Song, Singers, and Society, 1890–1954." *American Quarterly* 6 (Fall 1954): 221–32.

Moore, Earl V. "Men, Music, and Morale: The Case for the Federal Project." *Musical America* 62 (April 25, 1942): 5, 41.

"Music and Government." *Musician* 41 (Feb. 1936): 43.

"Music and Nationalism." *Musician* 44 (Jan. 1939): 14.

"Music Clubs in Relief Plan for Jobless Musicians." *Musician* 39 (Feb. 1934): 17.

"Music Given Place in Vast Federal Art Project." *Musical America* 56 (Aug. 1935): 3–4.

"Musicians in Distress." *Literary Digest* 119 (Jan. 2, 1932): 13–14.

"Musicians' Emergency Fund Drive for $400,000." *Literary Digest* 119 (Jan. 12, 1935): 24.

"Native Music Fete Is Opened by WPA Unit." *Musical America* 56 (May 10, 1936): 34.

"Negro Music." *Commonweal* 17 (Feb. 8, 1938): 396–97.

"Negro Population of the U.S., 1900–1930." *Missionary Review* 59 (June 1936): 288–89.

"Negroes in the Professions." *Literary Digest* 117 (May 12, 1934): 41.

"Negroes Northward Exodus." *Literary Digest* 110 (Aug. 29, 1931): 4.

"New Phase of Musicians' Aid Is Planned by WPA." *Musical America* 56 (Jan. 25, 1936): 20.

"NFMC Heads Issue Call." *Musical America* 56 (Nov. 25, 1935): 4.

Niles, J. J. "White Pioneers and Black." *Musical Quarterly* 18 (Jan. 1932): 60–75.

"No One Has Starved." *Fortune* 6 (Sept. 1932): 18–29, 80–84.

"Occupations of WPA Workers." *Monthly Labor Review* 49 (Aug. 1939): 355–56.

"Operas in English." *Musician* 42 (Jan. 1937): 14.

Overmyer, Grace. "Government and the Arts." *Musical America* 59 (Feb. 10, 1939): 26, 150.

———. "The Musician Starves." *American Mercury* 32 (June 1934): 224–31.

Panzer, R. M. "Stepdaughters of Orpheus." *Independent Woman* 15 (Feb. 1936): 39–40.

Pettis, Ashley. "Musical Flashlight from Moscow." *Modern Music* 10 (Nov. 1932): 49–52.

———. "The WPA and the American Composer." *Musical Quarterly* 26 (Jan. 1940): 101–12.

Polenberg, Richard, "The Decline of the New Deal, 1937–1940." In John Braeman, et al., eds. *The New Deal: The National Level.* Columbus, Ohio: Ohio State Univ. Press, 1975.

Potter, David M. "The Historian's Use of Nationalism and Vice Versa." *American Historical Review* 67 (July 1962): 924–50.

"Regional Directors Appointed." *Musical America* 56 (Oct. 25, 1935): 3.

Rich, Thaddeus. "Federal Music Project Takes Inventory." *Musical America* 58 (Feb. 10, 1938): 179.

Rout, Leslie B. "Economics and Race in Jazz." In *Frontiers of American Culture,* Ray B. Browne et al., eds. West Lafayette, Ind.: Purdue Univ. Studies, 1968.

Ryder, Georgia. "Another Look at Some American Cantatas." *The Black Perspective in Music* 3 (May 1975): 136–37.

Savelle, Max. "Nationalism in the American Revolution," *American Historical Review* 67 (July 1962): 924–50.

Seeger, Charles Louis. "Grass Roots for American Composers." *Modern Music* 16 (Mar. 1939): 144–49.

———. "Music." In *Encyclopedia of the Social Sciences,* vol. XI. New York, 1933.

———. "Music in America." *Magazine Art* 31 (July 1938): 411–13.

———. "On Proletarian Music." *Modern Music* 11 (Mar. 1934), 121–27.

Seldes, Gilbert Vivian. "Jazz, Opera or Ballet." *Modern Music* 3 (Jan.–Feb. 1926): 10–16.

Sessions, Roger. "To Revitalize Opera." *Modern Music* XV (3) (Mar.–Apr. 1938): 145–52.

"Should Women Be Allowed to Make a Career in Music?" *New Republic* 95 (July 13, 1938): 263.

Singer, Merrill. "Now I Know What the Songs Mean: Traditional Black Music in a Contemporary Black Section." *Southern Quarterly* 23 (Spring 1985): 109–32.

"Singin' High." *Newsweek* 5 (May 4, 1935): 34–35.

Smith, Carlton Sprague. "American in 1801–1825: The Musicians and the Music." *Bulletin of New York Public Library* 68 (Oct. 1964): 483–92.

Smith, T. V. "The New Deal as a Cultural Phenomenon." In *Ideological Differences and World Order,* F. S. C. Northrup, ed. New Haven: Yale Univ. Press, 1949.

Soden, Dale E. "The New Deal Comes to Shawnee." *Chronicles of Oklahoma* 63 (Summer 1985): 116–28.

Sokoloff, Nikolai. "America's Vast New Musical Awakening." *Etude* 55 (Apr. 1937): 221–22.

———. "The Federal Music Project." In *Music Teachers National Association Volume of Proceedings, 1936.* Oberlin, 1937.

———. "Federal Music Project Takes Inventory." *Musical America* 58 (Feb. 10, 1938): 144, 179.

———. "Government Gesture an Aid to National Art." *Musical America* 59 (Feb. 10, 1939): 8, 197.

———. "What the FMP Is Doing in Education." In *Music Educators National Conference,* vol. 27. Chicago: n.p., 1936.

"Sokoloff Succeeds Cameron in Seattle." *Musical America* 58 (May 25, 1938): 4.

Solomon, Izler. "A Decade to Defeat Decadence." *Musical Courier* 151 (Feb. 1, 1955): 46–48.

"Some Saving Graces." *Musician* 40 (Oct. 1935): 18–19.

Spaeth, Sigmund. "Dixie, Harlem, and Tin Pan Alley." *Scribner's* 99 (Jan. 1936): 23–26.

"Spiritual and Race Relations." *Christian Century* 48 (Feb. 18, 1931): 230–31.

"Spirituals to Swing." *Time* 33 (Jan. 2, 1939): 23.

Still, William Grant. "The Men Behind American Music." *The Crisis* 51 (Jan. 1944): 12–15, 29.

———. "The Negro Musician in America." *Music Educators Journal* 56 (Jan. 1970): 100–101, 157–61.

———. "A Negro Symphony Orchestra." *Opportunity* 17 (Sept. 1939): 267–86.

———. "Our American Musical Resources." *Showcase* 41 (1961): 7–9.

———. "Serious Music: New Field for the Negro." *Variety* 197 (Jan. 5, 1955): 227.

Studebaker, J. W. "A Federal Note." In *Music Teachers National Association Volume of Proceedings, 1936.* Oberlin: n.p., 1937.

Stutsman, Grace May. "Boston Hears Its WPA State Players," *Musical America* 57 (Dec. 25, 1937): 12.

Susman, Warren. "The Thirties." In *The Development of an American Culture,* Stanley Coben and Lormar Ratner, eds. Englewood Cliffs, N.J.: Prentice Hall, 1970.

Thompson, Randall. "The Second Year at Yaddo." *Modern Music* 11 (Nov. 1933): 175–81.

Tischler, Barbara L. "One Hundred Percent Americanism and Music in Boston During World War One." *American Music* 4 (Summer 1986): 164–76.

Thomson, Virgil. "America's Musical Maturity." *Yale Review* 51 (1961): 66.

"Total and Negro Population by State and Per Cent of Negro Population in Each State in 1930." *The Missionary Review of the World* 59 (June 1936), 288–89.

Toye, Francis. "A Case for Musical Nationalism." *Musical Quarterly* 4 (1918): 12–22.

"Trends in Employment of Women, 1928–1936." *Monthly Labor Review* 47 (Oct. 1937): 1274–76.

"Unemployment Among Negroes." *World Tomorrow* 14 (May 1931): 135–36.

"Unemployment Among Women." *Monthly Labor Review* 38 (Apr. 1934): 790–95.

"U.S. Conductors." *Time* 31 (May 23, 1938): 58–60.

Vacha, J. E. "Posterity Was Just around the Corner: The Influence of the Depression on the Development of the American Musical Theater in the 1930s." *South Atlantic Quarterly* 67 (Aug. 1968): 573–90.

———. "When Wagner Was Verboten: The Campaign Against German Music in World War One" *New York History* 64 (Apr. 1983): 171–89.

Villard, Oswald G. "Crumbling Color Line." *Harper's* 159 (July 1929): 156–67.

Waldmeir, Joseph J. "The Cowboy, the Knight and Popular Taste." *Southern Folklore Quarterly* 22 (Sept. 1958): 113–20.

Wandersee, Winifred D. "A New Deal for Women: Government Programs 1933–1940." In *The Roosevelt New Deal: A Program Assessment Fifty Years After.* Wilbur J. Cohen, ed. Austin: LBJ Library, 1986.

Ware, Susan. "Women and the New Deal." In *Fifty Years Later: The New Deal Reevaluated.* Harvard Sitkoff, ed. Philadelphia: Temple Univ. Press, 1985.

Warren, Frederic. "Needed: A New Deal for Singers." *Musician* 39 (Mar. 1934): 17.

Warren-Findley, Jannelle J. "Culture and the New Deal." *American Studies* 17 (Spring 1976): 81–82.

———. "Passports to Change: The Resettlement Administration's Folk Song Sheet Program, 1936–1937." *Prospects* 10 (1985): 197–242.

Wells, Katherine Gladney. "Symphony and Song: The First Hundred Years of the St. Louis Symphony." *Gateway Heritage* 1 (Spring 1981): 18–23.

Weed, H. H. "New Deal That Women Want." *Current History* 41 (Nov. 1934): 179–83.

"What the Depression Did for Music." *Etude* 53 (Sept. 1935): 550.

Whatley, Larry. "The WPA in Mississippi." *Journal of Mississippi History* 30 (Feb. 1968): 35–50.

"When Women Blow Horns." *Literary Digest* 11 (Apr. 2, 1932): 19–20.

Whisenhunt, Donald W. "The Bard in the Depression: Texas Style." *Journal of Popular Culture* 2 (Winter 1968): 370–286.

White, Clarence Cameron. "The Musical Genius of the American Negro." *Etude* 42 (May 1924): 305–6.

———. "The Musical Genius of the American Negro." *Southern Workman* 62 (Mar. 1933): 108–18.

———. "Negro Composers." *Negro Music Journal* 1 (Mar. 1903): 131–32.

"Why Woman Fail." *Outlook* 158 (Aug. 12, 1931): 460–62.

"Wide WPA Activity in New York City." *Musical America* 56 (Nov. 10, 1935): 34.

Wilmoth, Carol. "Heavenly Harmony: the WPA Symphony Orchestra, 1937–1942." *Chronicles of Oklahoma* 65 (Summer 1986): 35–51.

Winslow, M. I. "Mexican Labor in the U.S." *Commonweal* 10 (Sept. 11, 1929): 476–77.

Wilson, Grace V. "The Rainbow." *Music Educators Journal* 22 (Sept. 1935): 19–20.

Wollen, Peter. "Cinema/Americanism? The Robot." In *Modernity and Mass Culture,* James Naremore and Peter Brantlinger, eds. Bloomington: Indiana Univ. Press, 1991.

"Woman's Orchestra Makes Debut." *Commonweal* 21 (Mar. 1, 1935): 512.

"Women and the WPA." *The Woman Worker* 18 (Sept. 1938): 8.

"Women in Orchestras." *Etude* 56 (July 1938), 429–30.

"Women Workers and the NRA." *Christian Century* 51 (Jan. 10, 1934): 43.

Woodward, Ellen. "This New Federal Relief." *Independent Woman* 13 (Apr. 1934): 104.

"WPA Enlists Advice of Noted Musicians." *Musical America* 56 (Nov. 10, 1935): 6.

"WPA Head Explains Rift in Hartford." *Musical America* 59 (Sept. 1938): 30.

"WPA Maestro." *Time* 33 (March 27, 1939): 54.

"WPA Melody for Twenty Millions." *Literary Digest* 122 (Sept. 19, 1936): 22.

"WPA Plans a Composers' Lab in NYC." *Musical America* 56 (Oct. 10, 1935): 32.

"WPA Units Give New York Demonstration List." *Musical America* 56 (Apr. 10, 1936): 34.

Wright, Roscoe. "WPA: A Community Appraisal." *Current History and Forum* 49 (Feb. 1939): 42–44.

Wurm, Marie. "Woman's Struggle for Recognition in Music." *Etude* 54 (Nov. 1936): 687.

INDEX